Demystifying Revelation

Demystifying Revelation

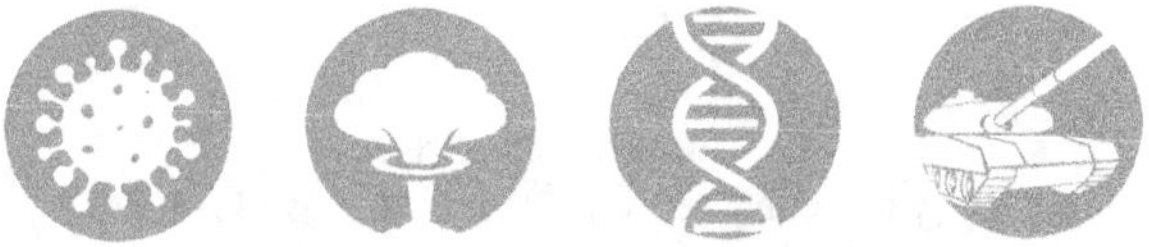

GRAHAM MISSEN

Demystifying Revelation
Published by Graham Missen
New Zealand

ISBN 978-0-473-64397-3 (Softcover)
ISBN 978-0-473-64398-0 (ePUB)
ISBN 978-0-473-64399-7 (Kindle)

Production & Typesetting:
Castle Publishing Services
www.castlepublishing.co.nz

Foreword

Demystifying Revelation, by my friend Graham Missen is his first foray into the world of writing and publishing. And what a venture it is.

It is not just a copy of his notes used for a group study. This is something much more. Turn the first page and you'll realise it is something special. To transition from group study notes to what we have here, means hours and hours of study, research, cross-referencing, checking and rechecking and verifying facts, and then there's the double-checking to make sure it is one story that has the pieces of the story all in the right place.

This book will find pride of place on the desks and bookshelves of those with a casual interest in eschatology (the study of end-time events), then the novice student of the book of Revelation, and also those focused students with an ardent and passionate interest in the Bible's prophetic plan of events as the Apostle John wrote them in the book of Revelation.

For those casually interested, for the novice student and for the ardent, passionate and focused student, it will not disappoint.

I stumbled across a major denomination's website and found these words: 'The world has changed. The Bible hasn't. We can help you understand it.' This book will be a great help with exactly that. It will help us understand the events of the end of times, which is more important now than its ever been. We are living in days which are fast approaching the days spoken of in the Bible as the last days. Sadly many read the book of Revelation, and dismiss it, gloss over it, find themselves more confused or don't bother reading it at all.

In his book, *Because the Time is Near*, John MacArthur writes,

> The late British Prime Minister Winston Churchill once described the former Soviet Union as 'a riddle wrapped in a mystery inside an enigma'. Many Christians view the Book of Revelation in much the same way. Bewildered by its mystifying symbolism and striking imagery, many believers and Church leaders avoid serious study of the book. Such shortsightedness deprives believers of the blessings the book promises to those who diligently read it (see Revelation 1:3, 22:7).

There are rich treasures to be discovered. There are life-changing, mind-expanding, spirit-lifting, hope-instilling, Christ-glorifying truths to be discovered by those who take the time to delve into and study this part of God's Divine inspiration called the Bible.

Thankfully, much of the legwork has been done. Graham has laid out for us in a readable and steadily unfolding way the important issues of the Book of Revelation. Plus, there's loads of meticulously researched details which are fascinating and illuminating.

It is very timely that this book has arrived on the scene. The world we live in can be confusing and fearful. But the message of this book points us to a loving God who is Creator, Master and is the One who is actually in control.

It's a must-read. Be warned though. Reading this book could change your life. It'll clarify your thinking, stretch your knowledge, and feed faith in your heart.

My prayer is, that the reader of this great work with a Bible alongside, will in the process of reading, study, prayer, maybe discussion with others, and quiet reflection, be drawn ever closer in communion with the One who is the subject of the Scriptures from Genesis to Revelation. As it says in the introduction to the Gideons New Testament, 'Christ is its grand subject, our good the design, and the glory of God its end.'

If this is Graham's first book, then I can't wait for the next one.

Stephen Whitwell
Tauranga, New Zealand
Author, Speaker, Connector
www.goodwords.nz

Contents

Introduction

I know the Bible is inspired because it inspires me.
- *D.L. Moody, 1837-1899, evangelist*

This book began as a study group at the Oasis Church (now called Napier Elim Church) in 2010. It was conceived as a study of the book of Revelation, and I realised some important topics are brushed over with little comment. Two examples are the Rapture and the Millennial Kingdom. A study and book about the future of humanity needs to cover these topics in more depth.

Why bother writing yet another book trying to sort out what the Bible teaches about the future?

There is a lot of confusion about Revelation. I'm looking at many of the conflicting theories or ideas and trying to make sense of them. Or at least ask some questions that may help someone clarify their thinking or get a discussion going.

The book of Revelation has a lot of modern technology embedded in it, and this is hidden in the language of the first century. Genetic engineering, robotics, and automation were unknown even 50 years ago, and we can find hints of them (sometimes descriptions of their effects) in Revelation.

Many books on Revelation are written by Bible scholars with a good knowledge of Greek, and little or no knowledge of modern engineering or technology. Most were written before the start of the 21st century when these technologies accelerated and began having a big impact.

Muslim eschatology has a lot of similarities to Christian eschatology. Reading them alongside Biblical eschatology gives some interesting insights.

I have borrowed some thoughts from ex-Muslims to give an alternative theory on some topics, especially about a future world leader. This viewpoint is seldom mentioned or acknowledged by the majority of Bible scholars.

I tried to write a book that is easy to read without too much technical or spiritual lingo. In other words, write as a layman as I am not an expert in any particular area. I have tried to cover the important topics in a credible manner.

Paul wrote to his understudy Timothy about what conditions would be like in the '*last days*'. In 2 Timothy 3:1-5, we have a description of our current society. We are living in the last days. The bulk of Bible prediction about what will happen in the future must be very close. We need to know what is predicted for the future.

Eschatology is the name Bible teachers and scholars give for the study of end times. The word comes from the Greek *eschatos* meaning 'last' and *-logy* meaning 'the study of'. It first appeared in English around 1844.[1]

The topic of eschatology is controversial, fascinating, and confusing. It is controversial because of the many different theories and interpretations available. (One good example of controversy is the Rapture. There are at least four theories I look at.)

It is fascinating because of the many insights into how the world will finish (spoiler alert: definitely not by climate change).

It's fascinating because we now start to see glimpses of where technology will be involved in some of the events predicted, or we can see things trending toward what Revelation predicts. It is confusing because of the many gaps that still exist in our knowledge.

1. en.wikipedia.org/wiki/Eschatology

Many people believe mankind is nearing their last years on planet earth. Many non-Christian people believe that for environmental reasons (climate change, resource depletion, over population, etc).

The Mayan calendar was reported to predict the end of the world as we know it to end in 2012 and a new type of world order to start. Before that, the year 2000 was supposed to usher in a wide range of catastrophes or technologies, depending on who you listened to.

Many Christians believe that Jesus Christ will return to reign over the world and put right all the wrongs. Their beliefs are often vague. This vagueness is often reinforced by church leaders or pastors not teaching the subject.

This book is based on the following tenets:

1. *The Bible is taken literally*. What is written is what will happen. No allegories. There is a lot of symbolism in the Bible, especially Revelation. I will try to explain this as we go.

2. *The church is not a substitute for Israel* (this follows from the previous point). God chose the nation of Israel, and He calls individuals to form a church. Israel and the church have different origins, different purposes, and different destinies.

   Israel was chosen from the time of Abraham while the church was built from Acts 2. The Bible teaches Israel will be the world leading nation during the millennial reign of Jesus Christ; the church is not mentioned during this time.

   The church is supposed to spiritually influence the world, not be a political force. Israel is pictured as a wife (often unfaithful), the church is pictured as a virgin bride.

   The only time Israel and the church are mentioned

together is in the description of the New Jerusalem, in the last two chapters of Revelation.

3. *This book will take the theory of pre-Tribulation Rapture as its main viewpoint.* Other theories or scenarios are covered. You are free to choose which scenario you think best fits the information presented. Please do your own research.

4. *This book is based on the Biblical book of Revelation.* Relevant topics from other parts of the Bible will be covered as needed. In fact, Revelation refers to almost all books in the Old Testament.

You will sometimes see short bits of text in boxes. These contain things that are interesting but not relevant to the main topic. They are too big to use as a footnote, and I did not want numerous appendices at the end of the book (I think I failed that aim).

There are a lot of events predicted in the Bible that are not mentioned in Revelation, or they are glossed over. These are covered in the Appendices. I have put other things in the Appendices that are related but too big to include in the main text.

I mainly used the NIV version of the Bible when writing this, but occasionally used the NKJV. Some versions may differ in their interpretation of the original language, and therefore some of the expressions they use.[2] But they are all similar and say much the same thing, whatever version you use.

You may notice I generally use *prediction* rather than *prophecy* when talking about future events. This is deliberate. We are told in Revelation that '*the testimony of Jesus is the spirit of prophecy*'

2. For example, KJV talks about Jesus ruling '*with a rod of iron*'. NIV talks about '*an iron sceptre*'.

(Revelation 19:10). This is why Paul encourages us to desire the gift of prophecy above all the other gifts (1 Corinthians 14:1, 5).

To my mind, prophecy is bringing God's message to people (1 Corinthians 14:3). Therefore, every church sermon should be prophecy, every encouragement should be prophecy, and every discussion about scripture should be prophecy. You can have a prophetic message without any predictions.

As you read this book, you will see a lot of questions. I don't have all the answers. Some of them do not have any answers, while many will have multiple possible answers. This is deliberate to get you thinking about the topic.

If you belong to a Bible study group, small group, life group (or whatever your church calls it), these may make good discussion questions. I welcome your feedback on the questions raised. You may have some thoughts or information that could begin a new line of enquiry.

Of course, the Bible is the result of the Holy Spirit inspiring the original writers (2 Peter 1:20-21). Because God is beyond our understanding, we should expect His book to us to have areas beyond our understanding.

We can expect to have unanswered questions. If we had all the answers, we would know everything God knows about what is written in the Bible.

I hope you learn something new from this book. I hope you find something to disagree on. Investigate the disagreement. Let me know about it. It may be something new for at least one of us.

> There is a principle which is a bar against all information, which is proof against all argument, and which cannot fail to keep man in everlasting ignorance. That principle is condemnation before investigation. - *Herbert Spencer, 1820-1903, writer*

Chapter 1

John's Vision of Jesus Christ

Christianity, if false, is of no importance,
and if true, of infinite importance.
The only thing it cannot be is moderately important.
- *C.S. Lewis, 1898-1963, author*

The first thing to understand about the book of Revelation is the structure. The book can be divided into three parts:

Chapter 1 is a description of the glorified Jesus Christ.
Chapters 2 and 3 are letters from Jesus to seven churches.
Chapters 4 to 22 are the chapters that look forward to the future.

There are other structural patterns we will cover later.

John was told to '*write what you have seen, what is now, and what will take place later*' (verse 19). That fits the three parts of the whole structure.

The second thing to understand about Revelation is that it is primarily about Jesus Christ. It starts with a vision of the glorified Jesus, it has seven letters Jesus dictated to seven churches, moves on to people worshipping Jesus, describes the future judgements Jesus releases, and predicts Jesus returning to rule the earth, and finally a new creation.

John's Introduction

This book is a revelation from God to Jesus Christ (verse 1). Jesus had earlier revealed some things to His disciples in Matthew chapter 24. In verse 36 Jesus made an interesting statement – not even He knew when these things would happen. Only God the Father knew when these would happen.[1]

I struggle with this. If Jesus is part of the Trinity, then Jesus should be omniscient like God is. But Jesus admits that He is not omniscient.

The Greek word for 'revelation' is *apokalypsis*,[2] hence the name sometimes given to this book. The Greek word means to uncover, to expose, to remove a veil or covering, to bring into the light. Given how much destruction and mayhem is described later, it is not surprising apocalyptic literature and films portray a world in chaos.

God revealed this revelation to Jesus so it could be passed on to His servants. Who are Jesus' servants?

God sent His angel to give the revelation to John. Which angel? One messenger angel is named in the Bible; Gabriel (Daniel 8:16, 9:21; Luke 1:19, 26). Other angels used as messengers are not named. This angel is not named. But John still recognised this angel and the message as the authentic word from God and the involvement of Jesus Christ.

And here is one particularly important reason to read the book of Revelation. This is the only book in the Bible promising a special blessing to everyone who reads it and takes it to heart (Revelation 1:3) and keeps or obeys it.

The blessing is repeated in Revelation 22:7. There are many

---

1. See also John 5:19-20; 7:16.
2. *Vine's Dictionary*, p 532.

verses encouraging reading scripture in general, but this book says, 'Read me, I'm special.'

Why is Revelation special? One reason is its relevance to us. Chapters 2 and 3 have messages or letters for every type of church. Everyone who is a believer will be in a church fitting one of these descriptions. Your church and my church fits one of these descriptions.

Revelation includes aspects from almost every other book in the Bible. Revelation contains 404 verses with over 800 allusions to the Old Testament.[3] We need a good understanding of the Old Testament for much of Revelation to make sense.

Revelation gives us an insight into the future, and particularly the end of the world. Humans are future oriented. We like to know what will happen in the future, how things will work out, how successful we will be at our jobs, how will this relationship work, etc. This book appeals to our future orientation.

The ability to write about future events is unique to the scriptures of both Jews and Christians. About 30 percent of the Bible is prediction or prophecy.[4] (As mentioned earlier, I prefer to use *prediction* because it seems a more accurate term; *prophecy* is defined in the Bible as bringing God's message – 1 Corinthians 14:1-3, 24-25, Revelation 19:10).

No other religion has scriptures with so much writing devoted to future events. And the track record of predictions in the Bible proves God's ability at prediction is amazingly accurate.[5]

3. For a list of these, see *Cosmic Codes*, pp 407-413.
4. *A Woman Rides the Beast*, pp 19-21.
5. See, for example, *Learn the Bible in 24 Hours*, p 149-161. This covers only the prophecies concerning the first coming of Jesus. See also Daniel 11:1-35 which was fulfilled between 530 BC and 134 BC. A good commentary showing a verse by verse fulfilment is in *The Bible Knowledge Commentary: Old Testament*, pp 1367-1370.

How is this possible? God's sense of time is not the same as our sense of time. God exists outside time. 2 Peter 3:8 tells us that '*a day with the Lord is like a thousand years, and a thousand years as a day.*'

Also read Isaiah 46:9-11. Two points from this passage; God knows all activities from the beginning to the end, and what is planned by God will happen.

There are some similarities between the books of Joshua and Revelation. These are shown in Appendix 7.

The Author

John introduces himself as the author of this book in verse 4. He was a disciple of Jesus, one of the three closest disciples (Matthew 17:1). His father was Zebedee. John had a brother called James (Matthew 4:21).

He and his brothers were fishermen. Like Peter, John's character was initially volatile. Jesus called him and his brother '*sons of thunder*' (Mark 3:17). They wanted Jesus to call fire down from heaven on people they disagreed with (Luke 9:54).

John reprimands a man casting out demons in Jesus' name because he wasn't in the group of disciples (Mark 9:38; Luke 9:49). John and James were involved in trying to be put in positions of glory upon Jesus' return (Matthew 20:20-22).

Despite all this, John was a loyal follower of Jesus. He was selected by Jesus to look after Mary after Jesus' death (John 19:25-27).

He was arrested for talking about the resurrection (Acts 4:1-3), and again because of a Jewish revolt about the early church (Acts 5:17-18). He is named by Paul as one of the '*pillars of the church*' (Galatians 2:9).

He wrote the gospel, three letters (epistles), and Revelation.

The gospel of John concentrates more on Jesus' teaching than the other gospels do. This indicates John may have been the thinker of the group.

John is associated with Ephesus in early church history. Two early writers say John died in Ephesus around the end of the first century.

But at the beginning of Revelation, John says he was on the island of Patmos, in the Aegean Sea. He was apparently a prisoner at that time, but he was allowed to return to Ephesus after Emperor Domitian died in 96 AD.[6]

Matthew names some of the women at the cross as Mary Magdalene, Mary the mother of James and Joseph, and the mother of Zebedee's children (Matthew 27:56). James and Joseph were two of Jesus' brothers (Mark 6:3), so was this Mary the mother of Jesus?

Mark names the two Marys and adds Salome (Mark 15:40). This could indicate that Salome may be the name of John's mother.

John names four women at the cross: Mary Magdalene, Mary the wife of Cleopas, Mary the mother of Jesus, and her sister (John 19:25). Cleopas was a follower of Jesus (Luke 24:18). If Salome was the sister of Mary, the mother of Jesus, this would make John a cousin of Jesus.

But we cannot be sure of this because Matthew records that many women were at the crucifixion. Salome may have been a woman known to Mark personally or to some of the early believers.

6. *The Bible Knowledge Commentary: New Testament*, pp 929-930.

John addresses his book to '*the seven churches in the province of Asia*' (verse 4). This was a Roman province covering eastern Turkey and parts of Syria and Lebanon. There were many more than seven churches in Asia, but only seven are mentioned. Colossae was close to Laodicea, so why was it excluded? Why these specific seven churches? The simple answer is because John is commanded to write to these seven specific churches in verse 11. But we discuss this later.

John wishes '*grace and peace*' to his readers (including us) from Jesus Christ. But he gives several descriptions instead of naming Christ, like Paul does in many of his letters:

1. '*Him who is, and who was, and is to come*' (verses 4 and 8). '*Who is*' refers to the eternal nature of Jesus. Jesus acknowledged His eternal character by saying He is the '*I am*' (John 8:58 and Exodus 3:14). '*Who was*' refers to the human Jesus who walked with John and was crucified. '*Who is to come*' refers to the glorified Jesus who promised to return again (Acts 1:11).

2. '*The seven spirits before His throne*' (verse 4) should be translated '*the seven-fold spirit*'. This refers to Isaiah 11:1-2. Verse 1 refers specifically to Jesus.

   (1) The Spirit of YHWH will rest upon him; (2) the Spirit of wisdom; (3) the Spirit of understanding; (4) the Spirit of counsel; (5) the Spirit of power (might); (6) the Spirit of knowledge; and (7) the Spirit of the fear of the Lord.

3. '*And from Jesus Christ*' (verse 5). '*Faithful witness*' refers to Isaiah 55:4. '*Firstborn from the dead*' refers to the resurrection (Colossians 1:18). '*Ruler of the kings of all the earth*' refers

to Psalm 47:2, 99:1, and Daniel 4:34. Psalm 2 gives a vivid description of the *'ruler of the kings of the earth'*.

John glorifies Jesus Christ in verse 5. He loves us. His blood and sacrifice free us from our sin. He makes us kings and priests to serve God (verse 6). This will become relevant when we get to Revelation chapter 4.

Being kings and priests is unique to Christianity. Israel had a kingly tribe (Judah) and a priestly tribe (Levi). Therefore, no Jew could legally be both a king and priest. This shows that believers (the church) cannot be a replacement for Israel. The only other person to have both roles was Melchizedek (Genesis 14:18).

The descriptions in verse 7 refer to Jesus using Old Testament allusions. Daniel 7:13 mentions coming with the clouds. *'Every eye will see him'*; Daniel 7:14 mentions worship by people from all languages (see Matthew 24:30). *'Even those who pierced him'* is taken from Zechariah 12:10. Jesus was pierced in His hands, feet, and side on the cross.

Verse 8 introduces the title, *'Alpha and Omega'*. This title appears only in Revelation (3 times). But YHWH refers to himself as *'the first and last'* in Isaiah 44:6 and 48:12. This is a reference to Christ because of His involvement in creation (Isaiah 48:13, Hebrews 1:10, and Colossians 1:15-16).

John now introduces himself as a number of things in verse 9.

First, he calls himself a *'brother'*. This was a common term for fellow believers in the early church. Paul used it a lot, as in Romans 15:30, 1 Corinthians 1:10, 3:1, 10:1, 2 Corinthians 8:1, Galatians 6:1, etc.

John's letters do not have any indication they are written by John. He does not identify himself as the author in any of them. Using this term indicates the author does not want to be considered as special. This is in character with John. How does he identify himself in his gospel? Contrast this with the introductions to the letters from Paul, James, Peter, and Jude. Contrast how John describes himself in verse 1.

Second, he calls himself a '*companion in the suffering*'. If Revelation was written around 90-100 AD, the church had gone through two lots of persecution. First by Nero in AD 54-68, then by Domitian in AD 95-96.

There were cases of local persecution caused largely by rival religions, such as Jews or Greeks. For example, Acts 4:1-22; 5:17-41; 8:1-3; 12:1-10; 13:49-50; 17:5-9; 19:23-41 and 23:12-15.

Next, John says he is a '*companion in the kingdom*'. The apostles taught all believers are part of the kingdom of God. Acts 8:12, 14:22, 28:31; Romans 14:17; 1 Corinthians 6:9-10; Colossians 1:13; 2 Timothy 4:18 and 2 Peter 1:10-11.

Finally, John says he is a '*companion in patient endurance*'. We are encouraged to endure to the end of our life. 2 Timothy 2:3, 10, 12; Hebrews 12:7; 2 Corinthians 6:4-5 and James 1:12. Endurance for what? Life? Ridicule? Persecution? Remember the parable of the sower and the seed falling in rocky soil (Matthew 13:20-21).

Why was John imprisoned? John himself says it was because of his faith. The early church writers say John was exiled on the island of Patmos in AD 95 and 96 by the emperor Domitian, but they do not give a reason for his imprisonment. After Domitian died, John returned to Ephesus after being released by the emperor Nerva.[7] So John was suffering a form of imprisonment at the time this book was written. How old would he have been at this stage?

---

7. *The Bible Knowledge Commentary: New Testament*, p 930.

What John Saw

John now describes how this revelation happened. He tells us in verse 10 that '*On the Lord's Day he was in the Spirit*'. What is meant by the expression '*the Lord's Day*'?

Some churches call Sunday 'the Lord's day'. But the Bible always refers to Sunday as 'the first day of the week'. Early church writers sometimes refer to Sunday as 'the Lord's day'.

But the Bible and church history clearly show the early Christians met on Saturday (the Sabbath) since Christianity was derived from Judaism. Maybe John had this vision on a Saturday or Sunday, the day that the early Christians would have met for worship.

Roman writers refer to the first day of the month as Emperor's Day or sometimes Lord's Day. Did John have this vision on the first day of a month?

The word 'day' is capitalised. Does this signify a specific day? The '*Day of the Lord*' is a common expression in Old Testament prophecies, referring to a time when the Messiah will judge the world.[8] This will not be a nice time to be on earth (Joel 2:1-2).

Was John taken forward in a trance to that time to witness things as they will happen? (If this is the case, this is the first recorded example of time travel.)

What is meant by '*in the Spirit*'? Most people think this is a trance-like state induced when people are under the power of the Holy Spirit.

Daniel had a similar experience in Daniel 10:4-9 where he could not move and lay on the ground. Paul did the same when confronted by God in Acts 9:3-4. The guards at Jesus' tomb were affected in Matthew 28:4. Paul had another experience where he visited heaven (2 Corinthians 12:2-4).

8. *Armageddon and Beyond*, pp 27-28.

John heard a loud voice like a trumpet. God speaks with a voice like a trumpet at times of especially important announcements to mankind. God caused a trumpet sound at Mount Sinai before giving the Ten Commandments to Moses (Exodus 9:16, 19).

The trumpets will sound again when God appears to reign (Matthew 24:30-31). Believers will be taken to heaven with a trumpet call (1 Thessalonians 4:16). Seven trumpets later in Revelation are the part of judgements on the earth.

John is commanded to write what he sees and send it to seven specifically named churches (verse 11).

The number seven always denotes completeness in the Bible:

- The creation of the earth was completed in seven days (Genesis 2:2).
- There are seven holy days or feasts in the Jewish regulations (Leviticus 23). The Feast of Unleavened Bread lasts for seven days (Leviticus 23:6).
- Purification from skin disease involved seven washings and took seven days to complete the formalities (Leviticus 14:7-9).
- The land was not allowed to be ploughed every seventh year (Leviticus 25:1-7).
- Seven days were used to conquer Jericho (Joshua 6:12-15).
- Naaman had to wash in the River Jordan seven times to be healed from leprosy (2 Kings 5:14).
- Nebuchadnezzar was punished for seven years because of his pride (Daniel 4:25).

You could find many more examples if you want to.

Why these churches? Why not include more geographically or politically important places like Jerusalem, Rome, Alexandria, or Antioch? There were churches in these cities.

First, they are all in close proximity to Ephesus where John was well known. Maybe John used to visit these seven churches while based at Ephesus. But there are other reasons.

These seven churches in their variety are representative of the church in total. Every church faces all the issues talked about in Revelation chapters 2 and 3 to varying degrees. Although each church was addressed individually, the application was relevant to all churches. The issues they face are reflected in all churches throughout history.

There are lessons for all church leaders to learn from these letters, even 1900 years later.

Each letter in the next two chapters says, '*he who has an ear, let him hear what the Spirit says to the churches.*' Note the plural word, 'churches'. This implies every church can learn from the others.

A more controversial answer is that these churches are also prophetic in that they spell out the history of the church in advance. If they were in any other order, that would not be true. We will look at this idea at the end of Revelation chapter 3.

When John turned to see who was talking, he saw seven golden lampstands (verse 12). Gold is always a symbol of God's divine nature. The symbolism of the lampstands is explained in verse 20.

Among the lampstands is a person '*like a son of man*' (verse 13). Not a man, but similar. Daniel was the only Old Testament person to use this title, and he used this expression to describe Christ in a vision (Daniel 7:13).

Jesus used this title for himself (Matthew 17:9, Mark 2:10, 8:31, 9:9, etc). This person is Jesus Christ as He appears in heaven. The title '*Son of Man*' first appears in the ancient book of Enoch.[9]

His clothing is similar to that worn by a priest. Why? Because Jesus Christ is our high priest (Hebrews 8:1-2).

---

9. *Birthright*, p 130-135.

He is dressed in a robe reaching down to His feet. The priests are always pictured as wearing robes down to the feet, but the actual measurement is not given in the Bible (Exodus 28 and 39).

There is a golden sash around His chest (Daniel 10:5). The high priest wore a sash (Exodus 28:4 and 39:29).

'*His head and hair were white like wool, white as snow*' (verse 14). White is symbolic of purity and righteousness. God's thoughts are pure and righteous (Job 4:17, Habakkuk 1:13).

'*His eyes were like blazing fire.*' Eyes are symbolic of knowledge, while fire is symbolic of punishment. Combined, they are symbols of judging the actions of people (2 Chronicles 16:9; Hebrews 4:13).

'*His feet were like bronze glowing in a furnace*' (verse 15). Bronze or brass are symbols of judgement in the Bible. Sacrifices were made on the bronze altar (Exodus 38:1-8).

The bronze snake was a picture of sin being healed (Numbers 21:6-9, John 3:14-15). Feet are a symbol of judgement. Putting your feet on someone indicated you had conquered them (Joshua 10:24; 2 Samuel 22:39:1 Kings 5:3: Psalm 8:6, 110:1). '*His voice was like the sound of rushing waters*' (Ezekiel 43:1; Daniel 10:6).

'*In his right hand he held seven stars*' (verse 16). This is explained in verse 20. '*Out of his mouth came a double-edged sword*', symbolic of the penetrating power of truth (Psalm 149:6; Hebrews 4:12). '*His face shone like the sun shining in all its brilliance.*'

Nothing clouded or took away from the majesty of God (Daniel 10:6). Jesus' face shone when he took his three close disciples up a mountain to meet Moses and Elijah (Matthew 17:2).

What does this description tell us about Jesus Christ?

John's response in verse 17 to seeing Jesus was the same as Daniel (Daniel 10:7-9). How do you think you would respond to seeing Jesus like that?

Jesus' response to John is to tell him to '*do not be afraid.*' Jesus introduces Himself by two new titles and two statements of fact.

'*I am the First and the Last*'. This title comes from Isaiah where it has a number of meanings:

- Chapter 41:4 where it refers to God as the ruler of the nations.
- Chapter 44:6 where it refers to the Messiah who protects Israel.
- Chapter 48:12-13 where it refers to the creator of the earth and heavens.

'*I am the Living One*' (verse 18). Israel at times knew their God was a living God as opposed to lifeless idols from the nations around them. The Living God is mentioned twice in the Psalms (Psalm 42:2, 84:2).

The Assyrians insulted the Living God in Isaiah 37:17. Jeremiah had to remind a godless Israel their God was the Living God (Jeremiah 10:10, 23:36). Darius, the Persian ruler in Babylon, used this title when Daniel was put in the lion's den (Daniel 6:19-20, 26-27).

'*I was dead, and behold I am alive for ever and ever.*' There is only one person who has been historically proved to have died and live again for ever. The Greek says, 'I became dead'. Jesus volunteered to die. It was a choice that He made, and not the result of a natural process (Luke 23:46). Could Jesus die naturally? (Genesis 3:19, Romans 5:12, 6:23)

'*I hold the keys of death and Hades.*' Keys are a symbol of ownership and authority. Isaiah 22:22 talks about the key to the House of David, and the authority that the key holder has. Jesus tells Peter the church will be given the keys of the Kingdom of Heaven (Matthew 16:19).

Jesus Christ has authority over death and Hades. Jesus has authority over where a person's soul goes when they die. Hades is the region where our spirit and soul go when we die.

We are conscious in Hades. There are forms of reward or punishment in Hades. We will be resurrected from Hades to heaven when Jesus returns.

Hell is not Hades. Hell is the place of punishment for Satan and his demons (2 Peter 2:4). The Greek word for hell is *Gehenna*.[10] Ultimately Jesus will dispose of Hades (Revelation 20:14).

Jesus gives John a commission in verse 19. '*Write what you have seen, what is now, and what will take place later*'. This is the division of Revelation. Chapter 1 is what John saw. Chapters 2 and 3 is what is now: the messages to the seven churches that existed when John wrote this.

Churches still exist today, and their messages apply to us. What will take place later is the rest of the book of Revelation.

Jesus explains things John obviously did not understand (verse 20): the seven stars and the seven gold lampstands. The seven stars are explained as the angels of the seven churches, and the seven lampstands are the seven churches. Angels are both messengers and protectors.

Does God allocate angels to churches? Angels are allocated to nations to help guide them and help them fulfil their destiny (Daniel 10:13, 20-21).

It seems logical that God will appoint angels for churches. Does each individual church have an angel? Or is the angel for all churches in a town or city?

Lampstands emit light when they are working. Churches are supposed to be the light of God to a world of darkness.

Jesus taught this to His disciples at the Sermon on the Mount (Matthew 5:14-16). The church should stand out as a beacon of light and righteousness to a world of darkness.

The world around us should be looking to the church for

---

10. *Vine's Dictionary*, p 300.

answers to their darkness – mental, intellectual, emotional and spiritual. That is our challenge.

What are we doing to fulfil this mandate?

Chapter 2

Letters to the Seven Churches

The Church is not a gallery for
the exhibition of eminent Christians,
but a school for the education of imperfect ones.
- *Henry Ward Beecher, 1813-1857, American clergyman*

Jesus gave John seven messages to be passed on to seven specified churches. There are areas of congratulations where things are going well. There are specific and different problems that God wanted each church to fix.

These seven churches are representative of every church today. Each church has at least one area where God has a message for us, either congratulations, encouragement to continue, or a problem to fix.

Each message has a similar design. Every detail is significant, even the name of the church. Each church is given a different title for Jesus Christ, and these were all given in chapter 1. There is an encouragement, a description of the problem, and the means to fix the problem.

Ephesus: Revelation 2:1-7

Ephesus was a major seaport, and had a temple to Artemis (completed around 550 BC) which was one of the seven wonders of the ancient world. Ephesus was started in the 10th century BC, and it flourished when it came under the Roman Republic in 129 BC when the population peaked at close to 150,000.[1]

It was the major city in the province of Asia until an earthquake destroyed much of it in 614 AD. Paul remained in Ephesus for several years (Acts 19).

Ephesus means 'my darling' or 'the desired one'. Jesus sees the church as a virgin bride being prepared for her wedding (Ephesians 5:25-27).

Jesus introduces Himself as '*he who holds the seven stars and walks among the seven golden lampstands.*' Why do you think Jesus gave this title? Do we need to see Christ as leader of the churches? This should encourage us because He is actively involved in the church. Or at least He wants to be (we will see later that the church at Laodicea had locked Jesus out).

The church at Ephesus was a large church. In Acts 20 when Paul was going back to Jerusalem, he by-passed Ephesus because of the large crowd that would meet him. He went to Miletus on the other side of the peninsula and asked the elders to come to him. In his farewell speech Paul warned them to be on the alert for false doctrine and false teaching. They apparently took notice because here (about 30 years later) Jesus compliments them on their diligence.

In verses 2 to 3 this church was recognised by Jesus as working hard, being patient, not tolerating evil, testing people's claims, and striking at their work. This was a church that was doing well and maintaining their standards.

But Jesus did have one concern in verse 4. They were so busy doing the work of the Kingdom that they didn't have time for the King. They had lost their devotion to Jesus Christ. Jesus' remedy

---

1. en.wikipedia.org/wiki/Ephesus

was to remember how they initially worshipped Him and return to doing that again. Failure would result in their lampstand being removed – their effectiveness as a church would stop. That is the warning for us. Are we worshipping God as we should? Are we so busy working that we neglect our relationship?

There was one thing in their favour (verse 6). They hated the 'Nicolaitans'. There are three ways of dealing with this word:

1. This is an untranslated word. *Nicao* means 'to rule over' and *laitans* means 'the common people' or the laity. Nicolaitans means to rule over the common people.[2]

   Why was God upset about a manager running the church? Jesus set the example for church leadership by washing his disciples' feet (John 13:12-17). His idea of leadership was to serve the common people by teaching them and helping them. Each local church is supposed to be led by a group of elders, not by a single person (1 Timothy 3:1-7; Titus 1:5-9). Maybe some people were becoming dictators over the people around them?

   The idea of the clergy ruling over the laity was introduced as churches grew and became more organised (especially during the Middle Ages[3]), and it is the most widely practised church leadership style today. It exists in my own church where we have pastors who largely run the church or its meetings. The church leadership has to be careful they do not become dictators, but remain as enablers to allow the church members to develop their gifts and abilities.

2. The second view is the Nicolaitans were teaching that

---

2. *Learn the Bible in 24 Hours*, p 277.
3. *A Woman Rides the Beast*, p 46.

certain sexual practices were allowable. The early church writers report that this was common around the time Revelation was written. Paul had already confronted the church at Corinth about one person who had an immoral relationship (1 Corinthians 5:1-13). There are numerous warnings throughout the New Testament about immorality.

3. Nicolaus was a deacon of the early church (Acts 6:5). He was a gentile convert from Antioch. But he is not mentioned again in the Bible. Could he have begun teaching that certain pagan practices or rituals were acceptable to the church? Was he compromising by saying that sacrifices in the pagan temples were acceptable?

Every message for the churches has the phrase '*He who has an ear, let him hear what the Spirit says to the churches*' (verse 7). The message was not only for the church it was addressed to, but to all churches throughout time. It is therefore relevant to the church that you and I call our spiritual home.

It is also relevant to us as individuals. We each have ears; organisations do not. There is something for us to take notice and apply in every message to every church. Each of us has to decide what part of this message, and the following messages, apply to me as an individual. What am I doing good, and what needs changing?

The final part of the message for Ephesus is a promise to those who overcome. They have the right to eat from the tree of life that is in paradise.

The tree of life is an interesting object. It was originally planted in the middle of the Garden of Eden (Genesis 2:9). With it was the tree of knowledge of good and evil. Adam and Eve were permitted to eat from the tree of life, but there is no record of them doing this.

They were told not to eat from the other tree. After Adam and

Eve sinned, mankind was banned from the Garden of Eden and they could not eat from the tree of life (Genesis 3:22-24).

Mankind eats it again in the New Jerusalem (Revelation 22:1-2, 14). What is its purpose?

Smyrna: Revelation 2:8-11

Smyrna was another large and wealthy city, and a seaport with two harbours. Myrrh was a chief export in ancient times.[4] Smyrna still exists, although the modern name is Izmir. It was rebuilt after an earthquake in 17 AD (the same earthquake affected Sardis and Philadelphia).

Smyrna means 'myrrh', which is an aromatic embalming ointment. It is therefore associated with death. The Magi brought a gift of myrrh to the infant Jesus (Matthew 2:1-2, 11). Why would they take a gift signifying death to someone who was a King of the Jews? Because it shows that Jesus was born to die.

Jesus' title here is '*the First and Last who died and came to life again.*' Again, a theme of death comes through. This message is to a suffering church, and Jesus chose an identity that gives them hope.

Jesus knows their afflictions, their poverty, and the slander being said against them (verse 9). He knew these because he experienced exactly the same things when he was alive (Hebrews 4:15). This church was being attacked on multiple fronts.

They had many trials – physical attacks combined with social and spiritual attacks. They thought they were spiritually poor, but Jesus tells them they are actually spiritually rich. The Greek (*ptochos*) signifies extreme poverty.[5]

---

4. en.wikipedia.org/wiki/Smyrna
5. *Vine's Dictionary*, p 476.

The slander is interesting. People were claiming to be Jews. There are two ways of looking at this.

First, the Jews were active in persecuting the church. This continues the pattern started in Acts and continued through the first two or three centuries. Maybe some of the persecution was coming from disaffected church members?

Second, believers claiming to be Jews may have been leading other believers away from Christ. This was the issue behind the book of Galatians where some people wanted believers to get circumcised and to obey the Law of Moses.

Paul argues in Galatians that this is not necessary.

There is another more recent way for Christians to think they are Jews. Many people think that after the crucifixion God abandoned the Jews and turned to the Gentiles to fulfil the promises and prophecies that had been given to the Jews.

In other words, believers make up a 'spiritual Israel'. That is wrong. God has not abandoned Israel, but He will again raise Israel to a place of honour (Romans 11:1-2a, 11-12, 25-32). This is covered in more detail in Appendix 11.

Jesus' exhortation contains some bad news. Some of the church would be imprisoned for their beliefs, and they will suffer persecution for ten days. This can be interpreted to mean the persecution will last for only a short time.

History shows that the persecution of the early church happened in ten distinct periods:[6]

1. Nero AD 54-68
2. Domitian AD 95-96
3. Trajan AD 104-117
4. Marcus Aurelius AD 161-180

---

6. *Learn the Bible in 24 Hours*, p 279.

5. Septimum Severus AD 200-211
6. Maximus AD 235-237
7. Decius AD 249-251
8. Valerian AD 257-260
9. Aurelian AD 270-275
10. Diocletian AD 303-313

Jesus encourages them to be faithful unto death, and he will reward them with a crown of life (James 1:12). Jesus does not promise to rescue them from death, but He tells them to finish the race faithfully. The crown of life is a reward for endurance.

Most of the church throughout most of the last 2000 years has been persecuted. Ironically, much of the persecution has been from other people calling themselves Christians.[7]

We in the western world cannot guarantee we will not be persecuted in the future just because we have not had persecution in our recent history. We need to remember that when persecution does come, God expects us to persevere through it.

Finally (verse 11), anyone who overcomes will not be hurt by the second death. The second death is the final death for wicked people when they are finally judged and sentenced to the Lake of Fire (Revelation 20:6, 14-15).

To quote Chuck Missler from his podcasts and videos, 'he that is born once dies twice; he that is born twice dies once.'

Notice that Jesus did not have anything bad to say about this church. There are no warnings about things that need improvement. Only an encouragement to persevere through their difficulties.

7. See, for example, *A Woman Rides the Beast* which describes the wars of the Roman Catholic Church against the Huguenots, Albigenses, Waldenses, and victims of the Inquisition. But Protestants also fought wars against Catholics.

Pergamum: Revelation 2:12-17

Pergamum was a wealthy city, but it was wicked. It had once been a major city under the Persians and Greek empires, but its importance decreased under Roman rule.

There were numerous temples to various Greek deities. It had a famous university with a library of around 200,000 volumes (second to Alexandria at the time).[8]

The name of this city gives a clue to the message. Pergamum means 'mixed marriage'. It hints of perversion. Paul strongly warns us against being involved in mixed relationships (2 Corinthians 6:14-15). This applies to both marriage and business partnerships.

Jesus introduces himself as having the double-edged sword in verse 12. This symbolises the ability of God's word to cut through to the bone of whatever is wrong and to cut off anything that should not be there (Hebrews 4:12).

Jesus knows they live in a town where Satan lives in verse 13. Why would it be called this?

The Greeks built a number of temples in Pergamum, but there was one called 'Satan's Throne'. This was excavated in 1879 and relocated to Germany. It was reconstructed in the Pergamum Museum in Berlin in the 19th century and is still there today.

The Nazi architect, Albert Speer, used the monument as a template for the arena for Hitler's Nuremberg Rally Complex speeches leading up to World War 2.[9]

It was the inspiration for the design of the stage where Barack Obama accepted the Democratic nomination for President of the United States in 2008.

Despite that, the church has not renounced its faith. There had

8. en.wikipedia.org/wiki/Pergamon
9. *God's War on Terror*, p 427.

been a time of persecution and Antipas had been martyred. Jesus was pleased with their faithfulness.

Eastern Orthodox tradition says Antipas was a leader of the church and had reportedly been ordained by the Apostle John. He had a reputation for delivering demons from people and healed so many people the local medical people lost money. He was accused of anti-Roman activity and was executed in 92 AD.[10]

There were concerns in verses 14-15. Some people in the church held to the teaching of Balaam, and some held to the teaching of the Nicolaitans. Both these teachings were a perversion of God's truth, hence the title at the start of the message. These people were living perverted lives and trying to entice other believers to join them.

Balaam was a prophet for hire (Numbers 22). Balaam was hired by the king of Moab to figure out a way to conquer Israel. Balaam would not curse Israel as ordered, but instead he blessed Israel. He told the king of Moab that God would support Israel as long as they were faithful to God.

The way to conquer Israel was to lead them into being unfaithful to God, primarily through sexual immorality. Balaam's strategy was what the church at Pergamos was doing – getting the church to be unfaithful to God by marrying into the world.

We covered the Nicolaitans earlier in the message to Ephesus. They may have been teaching sexual perversion, which makes sense in the context of this church.

Jesus' exhortation in verse 16 was to repent from allowing perversion in the church to continue. Otherwise, Jesus himself would come to fight against the church with his truth. His word will judge all sin and compromise.

There are two promises to the overcomer (verse 17). First, Jesus

---

10. en.wikipedia.org/wiki/Antipas_of_Pergamum

will give some of the hidden manna. Manna was the means of sustenance through the wilderness (Exodus 16:4, 31; Joshua 5:12).

Some of the original manna was hidden in the ark of the covenant as a memorial to how God provides (Exodus 16:34). The hidden manna is likely to be spiritual sustenance from the Holy Spirit. Jesus himself said, '*I am the bread of life*' (John 6:33, 35).

Second, Jesus will give a white stone with a new, unique name written on it. This probably refers to the breastplate worn by the High Priest, and it is also related to the two stones used by the High Priest in deciding what God wanted.

The breastplate consisted of a woven piece of material with three rows of stones with four stones in each row. The names of the twelve tribes were engraved on the stones. This was worn when the High Priest went into the Holy Place (daily) so the tribes of Israel were represented before God (Exodus 28:15-21, 29).

The Urim and Thummim were two stones used in making decisions about the will of God. There is no clear explanation in the Bible on how they were used (Exodus 28:30, Numbers 27:21). Was one stone white and the other black to distinguish them?

White is symbolic of purity (obviously a problem at Pergamum). Stones are long-lasting and do not decay. Believers are new creations (2 Corinthians 5:17), so we get a new name.

Thyatira: Revelation 2:18-29

Thyatira has had many names throughout history, but the name means either 'daughter' or 'continued sacrifice'. At one time it was called Semiramis, who was said to be the consort of Nimrod, the first world dictator.[11]

---

11. Semiramis was a queen consort during the late Assyrian Empire. See www.ancient.ey/Semiramis.

It was much smaller than Pergamum, but it was in an area known for its crops. During the Roman era, it was famous for its cloth dying facilities and was a centre for the purple cloth trade. It was also a defensive outpost for Pergamum.[12]

The current name for the city is Akhisar.[13] Paul's first missionary convert was Lydia who dealt in purple cloth and lived in Thyatira (Acts 16:11-40).

The descriptions of Jesus in verse 18 are indicative of knowledge and judgement. God see the reasons for what we do and the motivations involved. Hence the '*eyes of fire and feet like bronze*'.

First (verse 19), Jesus acknowledges the good things the church was doing. The church was doing a lot, and more than when the church was first started. Contrast this with the church at Ephesus which did less over time. But there is an issue. They have allowed deception to get in.

Who is Jezebel (verse 20)? Jezebel was bad news. She was a Phoenician princess who was married to Ahab the king of Israel, probably to seal a profitable trade alliance.

Jezebel introduced both the worship of Baal and goddess worship into the northern kingdom of Israel to a greater extent than it had existed before and made it the main religion at the time (1 Kings 16:31-33).

She was morally corrupt in many dealings (1 Kings 21). Her position was as a secondary political leader, but she worked her way into the position of the main spiritual leader of Israel and had a political influence greater than her position warranted.

Spiritual Jezebels do the same thing in a church. They mislead people who are unsure of spiritual truth and lead them astray

12. 'Letters from Jesus', *Personal Update*, February 2015, p 17-24, Koinonia House.
13. en.wikipedia.org/wiki/Thyatira

(spiritual fornication). They allow sexual impurity to continue, and compromise on other spiritual issues. A Jezebel will allow the mission of the church to be side-tracked.

The problem is that people are often deceived because Jezebels always operate from a position of power or influence within a church. Many people in the church may be unaware that there is a problem.

Even the church leaders may be unaware they are gradually being usurped by a Jezebel.

God always gives people time to repent (verse 21), but there is a limit. God's grace does not last forever (Genesis 6:3, Hebrews 9:27). The Old Testament Jezebel was unwilling to repent and was subsequently killed (2 Kings 9:30-37).

The later Jezebel will suffer the consequences along with the people who follow her teachings and practices.

The punishment is in two stages (verse 22). First is suffering, then death if there is no repentance.

What is the suffering? It could be physical. The main sexually transmitted disease is syphilis. Symptoms include fever, sore throat, headaches, and sometimes inflammation of joints and liver. Later stages include disfiguring growths and ulcers.[14] Other STDs also have painful symptoms.

It could be economic, spiritual or social suffering, for example, being ostracised, or discriminated against. It could be a dramatic change in finances. Whatever the form of suffering, it is designed to be a lesson to all the churches.

If the suffering does not bring repentance, the final punishment is death. Death is God's ultimate way to limit the growth or influence of sin. God's punishments are designed so other people see what happens and they will turn from their sin.

---

14. en.wikipedia.org/wiki/Syphilis

The church was charged with tolerating Jezebel (verse 20). Jesus does not say they joined in her activities. They did not raise a protest about what she was doing. This is similar to Israel when blatantly wrong and illegal actions were done, such as with Naboth's vineyard (1 Kings 21).

This raises an interesting question. Is the church tolerating Jezebel today by not speaking out about issues such as abortion, LGBTQ issues, and other moral issues? Does the lack of a public statement allow people in churches to think these activities are biblically allowable? Does any church teach what the Bible says about these issues?

In the last few years, New Zealand has legalised prostitution, liberalised abortion, decriminalised and legally recognised homosexuality, introduced civil unions to replace marriage, supported LGBTQ social groups, and legalised euthanasia.

The only church I recall publicly raising issues was the Destiny Church in Auckland. I do not recall any other church leader getting airtime on TV or radio and publicly speaking out about these issues.

The church in New Zealand has been silent on all these issues, although the Bible has defined positions on all these issues. Is this a call to New Zealand church leaders to be more vocal? Or is the church already politically irrelevant?

To the church members who have not been deceived by Jezebel, God promises they will rule over nations (verses 26-27). This will be during the millennial reign of Jesus Christ (1 Corinthians 6:2-3; 2 Timothy 2:12; Revelation 20:4, 6). Verse 27 is a quote from Psalm 2:8-9. As with all the messages, there is a time for overcoming and endurance.

What is meant by the 'morning star' (verse 28)? The only other mention of a morning star is Revelation 22:16 where it is another title given to Jesus Christ. The morning star here may refer to stars that appear shortly before the sun rises. It could mean God will give an encouraging sign that their time of overcoming will soon be ended.

The common statement in verse 29 about hearing the message is now at the end, and not shortly before the end as in the previous messages. Why?

Sardis: Revelation 3:1-6

Sardis means 'remnant'. This concept is all through the Bible. What is a remnant? It is a small group of people who have remained true to God. Examples are Noah and his family, exiles returning from Babylon, church people.

Sardis was on a trade route and was a wealthy city. Seven hundred years before this letter was written, Sardis was one of the greatest cities in the world. It probably dates back to before 2000 BC. It was at once the capital of the Lydian Empire (around 1200 BC).

Sardis was situated on a hill 300 metres above a broad valley at the foot of Mt Tmolus. It appeared to be impregnable, but the steep cliff suffered continual erosion.

This left occasional cracks that could be exploited. Because of their false confidence, whenever the city was captured, it was like a thief in the night.[15]

The title in verse 1 is '*He who holds the sevenfold Spirit of God and the seven stars.*' This probably means that the churches are in God's hands.

The good point for this church is actually a rebuke. God knows their deeds. They have a reputation for being alive. The reality

15. 'Letters from Jesus', *Personal Update*, February 2015, p 17-24, Koinonia House.

is they are a dead church. Jesus said the same thing about the Pharisees (Matthew 23:27-28).

How do we know whether a church is dead or alive? How do I determine the state of my church? Obviously being busy does not count with God. He uses a deeper criteria.

Christ encourages this church to wake up (verse 2) and see their true condition. Then they are to strengthen what remains and is about to die. Concentrate on the bits that are still working.

God doesn't say to resurrect the dead parts. This implies some things a church is doing may not be what God wants that church to do. Their activities were not complete in God's sight.

As part of the rejuvenation, they are told to remember what they had received and heard (verse 3). Go back to the basics of Christian teaching and obey it. What does this mean? Worship? Teaching? Helping the poor? Evangelism? Pure living? Anything else?

The danger is that if this church does not wake up, they will be caught by Jesus' return. There are many Biblical warnings about being ready for Jesus' return (Matthew 24:36-44, 25:13. 2 Peter 3:3-10, 1 Thessalonians 5:1-4).

Despite the church being almost dead, there were some people in it who were still spiritually alive (verse 5). The soiled clothes are symbolic of sinful behaviour, white clothes are symbolic of pure living. Christ promises that anyone who overcomes will be dressed in white and their names never removed from the book of life.

The Book of Life is referred to only in Revelation. It contains the names of everyone who will enter into the New Jerusalem (Revelation 20:11-15). How do you get your name in the Book of Life? By asking Jesus Christ for forgiveness, and by following Christ's teaching and behaviour. Can our name be removed from this book? Yes, by rejecting Jesus Christ.

Philadelphia: Revelation 3:7-13

Philadelphia means 'brotherly love'. It was founded in 189 BC by King Eumenes II, who named the city from his love for his brother who succeeded him as King Attalus II. This was an agricultural city, but it was prone to earthquakes. It had been destroyed by an earthquake in AD 17 (along with Smyrna and Sardis) and had been rebuilt.[16]

What is the relevance of Jesus' title in verse 7? God is holy and true, therefore He is the ideal person to judge the church. The key of David is mentioned in Isaiah 22:22.

Whoever has this key is able to permanently open or shut doors. This sounds similar to Matthew 16:19 when Jesus talks about the keys of the Kingdom of Heaven. Are they the same keys? And what do they open and shut?

Again, Christ says that He knows their deeds (verse 8). He has put an open door in front of the church that no one can shut (Isaiah 22:22). What is this door? An open door is usually symbolic of an opportunity, whereas a shut door means nothing is happening. See Acts 16:6-10.

Christ knows this church is weak, but they are faithful to God's teaching and have not denied God at all. Because of this, even Jews will acknowledge God is present in this church. Notice the reference in verse 9 to the synagogue of Satan. We had this earlier in the letter to Smyrna.

Verse 10 is an important verse. It divides people into two groups. The first group is those who have obeyed God's commands and have endured patiently. The second group is obviously those who have not. The first group will be preserved *from* the trial coming upon the whole world. The second group will have to go *through* the trial.

16. en.wikipedia.org/wiki/Alasehir

Revelation has two groups in the rest of the book: those who are in heaven with God, and those left on the earth. God's followers won't be protected *through* the trial – they won't be on earth to go through it. The Greek words say the church will be protected *from* (*ek terein*) the trial, not protected *through* (*dia terein*) the trial.[17]

Throughout these letters most churches have two distinct groups of people in them. One group is those who stay true to God, obey His commands, and obviously please God. The second group are those who attend the church, but they are not fully committed to God. They are Christian in name only.

Many of Jesus' parables about the Kingdom of Heaven echo a similar trend; the parable of the sower where seed fell on different types of soil; weeds grow with the crop; birds nesting in the mustard seed tree; different types of fish in the fishing net (Matthew 13).

Again in verse 11, Christ confirms He is coming soon, and encourages them to hold on to what they have. The reward for persevering is a crown.

They are made a pillar in God's temple – they will have a permanent place with God. Christ will write his name on them – give them an identity (similar to the white stone promised to Pergamum). These people are promised entry into the New Jerusalem described in Revelation 21-22.

Laodicea: Revelation 3:14-22

Laodicea was another wealthy city whose main industry was woollen goods. It was a centre for finance and banking. It had been destroyed by an earthquake in around 60 AD and had been rebuilt itself without help from the Roman Empire.[18]

17. *Bible Knowledge Commentary: New Testament*, p 939.
18. en.wikipedia.org/wiki/Laodicean_Church

Laodicea means 'the rule of the people'. That is the motto for democracy. Many churches today are trying to be 'user-friendly'; but at the same time do they run the risk of being 'God-unfriendly'?

Jesus' title in verse 14 emphasises the truth, '*the Amen, the faithful and true witness*'. This is because of his message for this church. This is one of two churches that does not have any good points.

Spiritually, this church was neither alive nor dead (verses 15-17). It was in a zombie state. Like their water supply. It was piped from Hierapolis, a few kilometres to the north. By the time the water reached Laodicea it was lukewarm, and neither refreshing nor useful for washing. They were materially rich, but it is not reflected in the spiritual description.

In verse 18, they were told to buy refined gold – gold that was pure. They needed a personal revelation of who God really is. Fire is a symbol of judgement. God will use trials to refine us. If you are going through a trial, remember it is God trying to make you better in some way (James 1:2-4). He is developing your endurance to make you stronger.

Laodicea was famous for its black woollen clothes. But they were told to buy white clothes to wear. They needed purity and righteousness in their lives. They were told to put salve on their eyes to cure their spiritual blindness.

A medical school was in the temple of Asclepius selling an ointment to heal common eye problems. This church was wealthy and content with its programmes, but it did not see its true condition as God saw it. God says in verse 19 that he rebukes and disciplines those he loves.

Verse 20 is commonly quoted as a verse for salvation, but it is really a rebuke to the church. Where is Christ? He is outside the door. He is not in the church at all. He wants to enter the church and fellowship with them, but he is shut out.

He wants to show his love, but he is prevented from doing so.

Where is Jesus Christ in our life? In our church? Are we too busy for time with Jesus Christ?

Again, the promise to overcomers is intimate fellowship with God, and honour in God's sight.

Summary of the Letters

These letters apply to every church to some extent. What was the common phrase in every letter? '*Let everyone listen to what the Spirit says to the churches.*'

Each letter applies to every church in some area. It is up to the leadership in every church to see how they rate and to determine what needs to be changed to get a better grade from the ultimate examiner.

Every church was surprised by their letter from Jesus. Churches who thought they were doing poorly were doing better than they thought.

Churches that thought they were doing well were doing badly. Two churches had nothing bad said about them (Smyrna and Philadelphia). Two churches had nothing good said about them (Sardis and Laodicea).

Historical Perspective

A controversial idea is that the seven churches predict the history of the church. If these letters were in any other order, this would not apply.[19]

Ephesus: Describes the apostolic church. It was diligent but had neglected their devotional life. Some of the epistles in the New

19. *Learn the Bible in 24 Hours*, p 285.

Testament show signs of some churches getting slack or the beginning of false teaching.

Smyrna: Describes the persecuted church through the middle Roman Empire. The exhortation was to 'hang in there'.

Pergamum: Describes the church that was married to politics. Emperor Constantine made Christianity the state religion of the Roman Empire, and this started the spiritual decline.

During the Middle Ages the pope was both the spiritual and political leader, and many decisions were made for political rather than spiritual motives. The popes were politically powerful but spiritually weak. The church during this period was largely characterised by political corruption and immorality.

Thyatira: Describes the Medieval church where the political grip was not as strong as earlier, but the Roman Catholic Church introduced a lot of idolatry. Although the church expanded, it introduced practises that were biblically wrong, such as confession to priests, buying salvation through indulgences, using the Inquisition to gain financial wealth, etc.

It introduced doctrines that are not biblical, such as purgatory, limbo, worship of Mary, infallibility of the pope, etc.

I find it interesting the Roman Catholic Church tried for over a thousand years to establish itself as an authority of the nations of Europe. But Jesus promised anyone who overcomes that they will be given '*authority over the nations*'.

Sardis: Describes the denominational church that started with the Reformation. Although a lot of good was done during this time, the church had nothing good said about it. Do we view history through wrongly tinted lens?

The Protestant churches that began during this period were mainly started for political reasons. Maybe the reason God said nothing good to them was because their focus was wrong.

We tend to see the Reformation as a good time because of a return to some correct doctrines. Church denominations can seem to be alive because they are busy, but are they doing the things that God wants? Is their focus in the right place?

Philadelphia: Describes the missionary church (19th and early 20th centuries). This was a time when churches flourished almost worldwide, the gospel was taken almost worldwide, and Christianity was admired for the good it did socially.

Laodicea: Describes the apostate church. It is wealthy, looks good, but corrupt underneath and lacking God's power. Is this a description of churches in general today? It seems to be a general description of modern (western?) churches as these churches are in chronological order.

William Booth, the founder of the Salvation Army, said, 'The chief danger of the twentieth century will be religion without the Holy Spirit, Christianity without Christ, forgiveness without repentance, salvation without regeneration, politics without God, and Heaven without Hell.'[20]

Congregational Relevance

The messages for the seven churches cover the full range of problems facing the whole church today, and individual congregations. The danger of losing our love for God, being afraid of suffering, false teaching, moral issues, spiritual deadness, not holding

20. www.azquotes.com/author/1671-William_Booth

fast, and being lukewarm. These are problems that have existed throughout history.

Every church needs to examine itself regularly to see where they stand before God. Which church does the reader attend look like? If God were to give us a report on our church, which message would he give?

Remember each church was deceived about their true condition. Some thought because they were doing a lot that they pleased God.

Some thought that because they were going through tough times God was not pleased.

Some thought being wealthy and having no persecution meant God was blessing them (does this sound like the 'prosperity' speakers?).

Personal Relevance

These letters apply to not only churches but can be applied to each of us individually. Remember the phrase in every letter, '*let everyone listen to what the Spirit says to the churches*'. We need to ask ourselves how we rate and what we need to do to ensure we pass the test. Look back through these messages to the church. How do they apply to me as an individual?

Ephesus: hard working, but have lost love for God.

Smyrna: suffering persecution, but a crown awaits.

Pergamum: have remained true to Christ, but risk being led astray.

Thyatira: doing all the right things but tolerating sin.

Sardis: have a reputation for being alive, but in reality is spiritually dead.

Philadelphia: doing all the right things even though having little strength. Persevering in obedience will be protected.

Laodicea: looking good, but in reality is spiritually dead.

We all need to ask God for his revelation of our true condition.

Chapter 3

Events in Heaven

How insignificant earth seems to me
when I consider heaven.
- St Ignatius of Loyola, 1491-1556, co-founder of Jesuits

John was told in chapter 1 to write down what he has seen, what is now, and what is to take place later (1:19). We now enter the part of Revelation where we cover future events.

These events can be broken into sections: those leading up to the second coming of Christ (chapters 4-18), the second coming (chapter 19), the millennial kingdom (chapter 20), and the new creation (chapters 21-22).

Revelation now changes to a Jewish book. Israel is now the centre of attention. Jewish symbols are now used. It is obvious the book is written for the Jews, and not the church from this point. The church is mentioned, but it is not referred to specifically as 'the church'. That doesn't mean we can ignore the rest of the book, because there is still a lot that we can learn and be encouraged with as we go forward.

One thing that makes the book difficult for some people is that the viewpoint changes. Some events describe the activities happening in heaven, while other events describe what is happening on earth. Some chapters start with historical events but merge into future events.

Some chapters are literal while a few use metaphors or symbols. Hopefully we can cover all these issues as we come across them.

Revelation 4

After writing the messages to the seven churches, John sees an open door in heaven. The voice he heard in chapter 1 told him to come up, and that he would see what must take place after this.

What are trumpets used for in the Bible? Either for sounding alarms, or for gathering people for important announcements or military service. Numbers chapter 10 records Moses making two silver trumpets, and the instructions for using them.

The number of trumpets used identified which group of people was summoned (verses 3-4). A different sound is made for either assembling or for alarms (verse 7). Psalms 150:3 encourages us to praise God using trumpets (most churches in New Zealand do not obey this instruction). But we are not told that Moses used the silver trumpets for music.

'*Things that must take place after this*' shows God has ordained for these things to happen. The obvious question is, 'after what?' It must be after the churches. The believing church has to be taken from the earth for the rest of Revelation to be a chronological description. We will investigate this in Appendix 2.[1]

'*Things that must take place*' shows the sovereign purpose of God. God is again telling history in advance, as he did with the Old Testament prophets. Jeremiah foretold that Israel would be captured by the Babylonians and exiled for seventy years (Jeremiah 25:8-14).

Isaiah predicted 200 years before the events that Cyrus would

1. We cover this in the Appendix because it is an event that is not covered explicitly in Revelation.

allow Jerusalem to be rebuilt (Isaiah 44:24-45:7). He even named Cyrus two hundred years before he was born and predicted he would authorise rebuilding the temple.

Daniel predicted in great detail the history of the Seleucids and Ptolemies (Daniel 11). And of course, you cannot ignore the numerous predictions about Jesus' birth, death and resurrection.[2] The rest of this book and related parts of the Old Testament will happen, and the future looks bleak for most people on earth.

Why does God predict the future throughout the Bible? No other religious scripture spends so much of its writings on foretelling future events.

I can think of two reasons. First, it shows there does exist a God who is eternal. Being eternal means God exists outside time, and He can therefore see the future as clear as He can see the past (Isaiah 46:9-11). Second, it allows us to know enough about the future to know that God works out all things for good to those who love Him (Romans 8:28), irrespective of what happens.

In verse 2, John was suddenly '*in the Spirit*' and found himself in front of a throne in heaven. What does '*in the Spirit*' mean? Was John having a dream, vision, trance or some similar experience? Or was John actually transferred to heaven?

Paul had a similar experience (2 Corinthians 12:2-4). Paul heard things he was not allowed to repeat, but John is told to report what he sees with only a few exceptions. Whatever it means, John is looking at events unfolding in heaven.

Who is sitting on thrones in heaven (Psalm 45:6, 47:8, Acts 7:56, Hebrews 8:1, 12:2)? Jesus Christ is either standing before the throne or sitting at the right hand of God. So, God is on the throne. See also verse 9. (Who lives for ever and ever?)

---

2. *Learn the Bible in 24 Hours* lists 21 predictions (and this is not a complete list) on pp 149-161.

The person sitting on the throne in verse 3 had the '*appearance of jasper and carnelian*' (the names of the gems vary). Carnelian is also translated 'ruby'. These are the first and last of the 12 gemstones worn on the high priest's breastplate (Exodus 28:17-20). Is this related to the title for God used in the letter to Smyrna (Rev 2:8)? Is it significant? The church at Smyrna was a persecuted church. Believers on earth in the rest of the Revelation will be persecuted until chapter 19.

These gems will also be used in the foundation for the New Jerusalem (Revelation 21:19-20).

A rainbow encircled the throne. What is the significance of rainbows? (Genesis 9:12-17) This is likely to be significant given the destruction that will be described in the coming chapters.

Surrounding the throne (verse 4) are twenty-four other thrones with twenty-four elders seated in them. The identity of these people is controversial. The two main ideas are these are angels, or they are church believers who are in heaven. They were dressed in white and had gold crowns. Why twenty-four? Who are these elders?

Where else does the number twenty-four occur in the Bible? Only once. King David divided the Levites into twenty-four groups to minister in the temple (1 Chronicles 24:3-18) and another twenty-four groups of musicians for the temple (1 Chronicles 25:6-31). Twenty-four is obviously associated with priestly service.

But the twenty-four elders are sitting on thrones. That means they have a kingly function. They are dressed in white, which means they have been judged and declared righteous. They wear crowns.

The Greek word is *stephanos* which is the reward in the Greek games. The crown of a ruler is *diadema*.[3] This means the elders have received various rewards. They are called elders which is a

3. *Vine's Dictionary*, p 139.

term applied only to leaders in the church (1 Timothy 3:1-7; Titus 1:3-9).

Put all this together, and the twenty-four elders are representatives of the church: believers who have turned to God between the resurrection and this event. The church (consisting of all true believers) is in heaven at this point. They have been judged, found righteous, and have been rewarded.

One final proof. In Revelation 5:9 the twenty-four elders are worshipping God. They say they have been purchased with Christ's blood, and have been made kings and priests to serve God. This applies only to the church of true believers.

Who else in the Bible is both a king and priest? Melchizedek (Genesis 14, Hebrews 7), and the Messiah (Hebrews 8).

Various noises, thunder, lightning, etc come from the throne in verse 5. The same thing happened on the day Moses went up Mount Sinai to receive the Law (Exodus 19:16-19). What is the significance of this? Could it indicate the start of a new era?

With Moses, it was the start of an era where God interacted with people through grace via a series of laws and sacrifices. It culminated with the sacrifice of Jesus at Calvary, although God's grace is now administered through belief in Jesus the saviour.

Here in Revelation, it signifies the start of a new era where God almost withdraws himself from mankind.

The Israelites saw the divine glory of God in the thunder and lightning. Un-regenerated man sees God as fearsome and something to be dreaded. They tremble when they see God in this form. Regenerated man sees God in a less threatening form (Exodus 24:9-11; Matthew 17:1-3).

The other thing before the throne is the seven lamps. In chapter 1 when John saw the seven lamps, they were on earth, but now they are in heaven. Chapter 1 told us the lamps represent the church (1:20), but here we are told they refer to the seven-fold spirit of God.

Why the difference? I don't know. What do you think? Between chapter 3 and chapter 4 the church has been taken to heaven.[4] The Holy Spirit dwells within believers, there are no believers on earth at this time. We will cover this event in Appendix 2.

Verse 6 tells us that in front of God's throne is something looking like a sea of glass. It would reflect all the brilliant colours of this heavenly scene. It is clear, and therefore it is pure. This is similar to the basin in the tabernacle which was used for washing and ritual purification (Exodus 30:17-21, 1 Kings 7:23-26). It represents the Word of God. We are washed in it on earth (Ephesians 5:26), but we stand on the Word of God in heaven.

Around the throne are four different creatures (verses 6-9). These are some sort of angel, and they are different from other angels described in the Bible, although there are some common characteristics.

Isaiah 6:1-4 describes angels called seraphs which have six wings, but no other description. They were involved in Isaiah's atonement. Are the seraphim always involved in atonement for sin? We cannot make an assumption based on one observation. We are not told their function.

Ezekiel 1:4-14 describes four creatures shaped like a man, but with four faces and four wings. The faces were a man, a lion, an ox and an eagle. They seem to be associated with God somehow.

Ezekiel 10:9-14 describes creatures called cherubim. Each cherub had four faces, wings, and were covered with eyes. Are these the same as the creatures described earlier in Ezekiel 1? When Hezekiah prayed in Isaiah 37, he described God as being enthroned between the cherubim (verse 16).

What do we know about cherubim? Cherubim were stationed

4. The church is mentioned 19 times in chapters 2 and 3. It is never mentioned again throughout the rest of Revelation.

outside the Garden of Eden to prevent mankind from eating fruit from the tree of life (Genesis 3:24). Cherubim were made for the top of the ark of covenant to guard the mercy seat where the glory of the Lord dwelt (Exodus 25:17-22, Numbers 7:89). God is seated between cherubim (Isaiah 37:15, Psalm 80:1, 99:1). Cherubim are associated with protecting access to God.

But there is a problem. These four living creatures are not cherubim. They look similar, but each creature is like a different animal instead of having a combination of faces. These creatures have six wings instead of four wings. Are they seraphim? Are they guarding God's throne? Are they leading worship? Or are they doing something else? What is the significance of the faces?

1. They could symbolise four characteristics of God. Man is the highest being created by God and could symbolise intelligence. The lion is the king of the beasts and could symbolise power. The ox is one of the strongest of domestic animals and could symbolise service. The eagle is the king of the bird world and could symbolise swiftness.

2. The gospels are sometimes symbolised using the same animal faces. Matthew presents Jesus as the Messiah, the Lion of Judah. Mark emphasises Jesus as the obedient servant of God (ox). Luke presents Jesus as the Son of Man and emphasises his humanness. John presents Jesus as being sent from God, hence the eagle.

3. In Numbers 2, the twelve tribes were divided into four groups for distribution around the tabernacle. Verse 2 says each group had a banner. Jewish writings say the items on the banners are said to be a lion for Judah, a man for Reuben, an ox for Ephraim and an eagle for Dan.

4. They could symbolise the created life: man (pinnacle of creation), domesticated animals, wild animals, birds.

What is the significance of the faces? They symbolise the character of God as represented by Jesus Christ.

The living creatures are continually worshipping God and proclaiming His eternal nature (verse 8). '*Holy, holy, holy*' may represent the trinity of God. Each person of the trinity is holy. The description of God as '*who was, and is, and is to come*' reflects the title John used at the start (Revelation 1:4).

This is the last time this title is used. Why?

In verse 9, the twenty-four elders respond by falling before God and worshipping. The living creatures seem to emphasise the eternal nature of God. The elders seem to emphasise the creative ability of God in their worship.

When did the church believers arrive in heaven? What else do they do there? This is covered in Appendixes 2 and 3.

Chapter 4

The Scroll

In the previous chapter the church of believers was taken to be with Jesus Christ in heaven. They have been judged and rewarded, and twenty-four elders representing the church surround the throne of God and worship him. This brings us to the end of Revelation chapter 4. The unbelieving people are left behind on earth, including some people who may have attended church. But the events of chapter 5 happen in heaven.

While the angels and elders are worshipping God (verse 1), John notices a scroll in God's right hand. It has writing on the outside as well as inside, and seven seals. This indicates the scroll is a title deed.[1] The requirements to redeem the deed were written on the outside.

Seals are a sign of authority or ownership. People had personal seals that were used to prove ownership or authority of a document or object. Tamar proved her case by producing Jacob's seal (Genesis 38:25-26). Jezebel used Ahab's seal to fraudulently obtain property (1 Kings 21:8). Jesus' tomb was sealed to prevent the disciples stealing his body (Matthew 27:66). We have God's seal upon us when we are children of God (2 Corinthians 1:22).

What is the title deed for?

---

1. See Jeremiah 32. Jeremiah was instructed to buy some land and seal the title deed for future use.

John sees a mighty angel in verse 2 asking, '*who is worthy to break the seals and open the scroll?*' Obviously, the requirements for the recipient are written on the outside. But no one was found who was worthy to open the scroll (verse 3). Notice the three groups of people: those in heaven, on the earth and under the earth. Who are these groups?

- Those in heaven are the raptured believers.
- Those on the earth are people still living at the time.
- Those under the earth are the dead people in Hades who have not yet been resurrected.

Every person who has been born since the creation will hear the angel's question. Every dimension is covered. The spiritual world (angels and demons) will also hear the question. They will be affected by the events following the scroll being opened.

From these descriptions, it is obvious that only a person could open the seals (verse 4). Angels are apparently not included in the list of possible participants.

I find it amazing that it seems even God is not allowed to open the scroll. But among all these people, there was no one found who fulfilled the requirements to open the title deed. This must be an important title deed because John wept and wept.

One of the elders told John that someone was able to open the scroll (verse 5). The titles identify this person as Jesus Christ. Notice the Jewish titles: *Lion of the Tribe of Judah*, and *Root of David*. These are two new titles in Revelation for Jesus Christ, although similar sayings have been used in the past. The tribe of Judah has been associated with lions since Jacob's blessings before he died (Genesis 49:8-10). Isaiah prophesied that a Root of Jesse will reign over Israel in the future (Isaiah 11:1, 10).

There is a reason Jesus can open the scroll. He has triumphed (verse 5). This must be related to the criteria for opening the seals.

Back to the question of what is the title deed for? It is obviously something that only a person can have title to. God was not opening the scroll, nor were angels. What has mankind been given the title to?

Mankind was given the earth to rule over on God's behalf (Genesis 1:28). Adam was told to subdue the earth and rule over all animal life. After mankind sinned, the authority over the earth and the animals was taken away and passed to Satan (Genesis 3:14-15).

In Matthew 4 we read about when Jesus was tempted by Satan after his baptism. Satan took Jesus to a location where he could show Jesus '*all the kingdoms of the world and their splendour*'. Satan offered this to Jesus if he would bow down and worship him (Matthew 4:8-9). Jesus did not refute Satan's ownership or authority over the world.

Man could not rule over the animals but were now in fear of many animals. The ground was cursed, and the ecology of the earth changed (Genesis 3:17-19). Paul writes that creation is one area still to be redeemed by God (Romans 8:18-22).

What sort of man can open the title deed? Only one who has not been subjected to sin and therefore not subject to the penalties listed in Genesis 3. Who is that person?

Ruth is a story about how restoration takes place. Jewish law states that anyone selling property can redeem it for his family in the future when he becomes financially prosperous. Or someone close to the family can redeem the property on behalf of the person. This person is called the '*kinsman redeemer*' (Leviticus 25:25-28).

What were the requirements to be a kinsman redeemer?

- You had to be a living person. Dead people cannot enter into legal transactions.

- You had to be related to who you wanted to redeem, i.e., be a kinsman.
- You had to be in a position (legally and financially) to act as a kinsman redeemer.

In Ruth, Boaz first had to offer the redeemer role to someone else who was more qualified than he was (Ruth 3:12-13). You had to be qualified, able, and willing. Jesus Christ fulfils these requirements. He is God in human form; He is related to mankind through Adam, His creation; He was born with Mary, His mother; and He can buy back the title deed because He was never subject to it, because He never sinned.

John sees who will open the scroll (verse 6). He sees a Lamb looking like it has been slain. '*The Lamb of God*' was a title that John the Baptist used for Jesus (John 1:29, 35-36). No one else used this title for Jesus. John the Baptist was obviously predicting the sacrifice that Jesus would give at Calvary (Isaiah 53:7).

The Lamb has been slain. Again, this is a reminder of the crucifixion. Only blood can cover the atonement for sin (Genesis 3:21, Leviticus 4, 1 Peter 1:18-19). What does Christ look like here? Does He still have the wounds from His crucifixion?

The Lamb is standing in the centre of the throne surrounded by the four living creatures and the elders. We saw in chapter 4 that God is sitting on the throne. Now Jesus Christ is standing where God is, showing that He is God. He is also receiving the worship and praise that God gets.

The description differs from previous descriptions in that it mentions horns. The number seven represents completeness. Horns represent authority (Deuteronomy 33:17, 1 Kings 22:11, Jeremiah 48:25, Daniel 7:24, Zechariah 1:18-21). They are often an idiom for a country or an area that is ruled. Animals prove their dominance by using their horns. Eyes represent perception and insight.

Jesus Christ has complete and total authority, knowledge, and wisdom. The 'seven spirits' is the Old Testament idiom for the Holy Spirit (Isaiah 11:2). The Holy Spirit implements all authority and perception. The Holy Spirit works in all parts of the earth. There is nowhere the Holy Spirit cannot impact.

Eyes are mentioned throughout the first three chapters, but this is the first time horns are mentioned. Until now, God has been controlling what mankind does with what seems to be limited intervention.

God is now going to intervene in history in complete authority like He has never done before. God is going to be an active participant.

The Lamb took the scroll from God in verse 7. He alone has the qualifications, is able, and is willing to be the kinsman redeemer. He begins opening the seals in the next chapter.

What follows is a series of heavenly worship descriptions.

The first group to worship are the four living creatures and the elders in verse 8. Who do these groups represent?

The Greek indicates that only the elders have a harp and bowls of incense. Harps are the only musical instrument mentioned in heaven. Trumpets are mentioned but always to announce something, not as music for worship. Are harps the only instrument? Or are they representative of other musical instruments?[2]

The bowls of incense are '*the prayers of the saints*'. God collects our prayers (Psalm 141:2, Revelation 8:3-4).

Incense is always associated with relationship with God. The

---

2. As a side question, what does worship in heaven sound like? Music on earth is based around a rhythm, which is a time-dependent system of beats. Because heaven is eternal, it is outside of any time constraints. So, does music in heaven have rhythm or a beat as we know music? Or does it sound totally different to the styles we know?

tabernacle had an altar of incense that was located in the Holy Place, in front of the curtain that separated it from the Most Holy Place (Exodus 30:1-10). The High Priest burnt incense on it daily. Only incense was to be offered on this altar, and not any other sort of offering. What does this tell us?

- We need a daily relationship with God.
- We can get into the presence of God only through a relationship with God.
- Our prayers are acceptable to God. He finds them similar to sweet smelling incense.
- We offer a pure incense to God, not something mixed. Indicative of a pure relationship.

Prayer does not occur in heaven. Adoration, praise and worship occur in heaven, always in the presence of God. Prayer still happens on earth, but not in heaven. The first group sang a song that reviews who and what Jesus Christ is (verse 9):

1. He alone is '*worthy to take the scroll and open its seals*'. We already know that because earlier in this chapter there was no one else who was qualified to do it.

2. The reason Christ is qualified is because '*He was slain, and He purchased mankind for God with His blood*'. This goes back to Genesis 9:4-6 where God states that blood must be shed to cover sin. Israel could have their sin atoned for only by shedding blood (Leviticus chapters 4 and 16).

   We are purchased for God by the blood of Jesus Christ (1 Peter 1:18-19). Blood was shed when Adam and Eve sinned and God made clothes of skin (Genesis 3:21), but the principle was not stated until after Noah's flood.

3. People have been purchased from '*every tribe, language, people and nation*'. This is amazing when there are still people groups in the world today that have not had contact with Christians. How did they become included in this group? (Romans 1:18-20, 2:9-11, 13-16)

4. The redeemed people are made into '*a kingdom and priests to serve God*' (verse 10). Kingdom involves authority, and it is reinforced when the verse says the redeemed will '*reign on the earth*'.

   Priests serve God before mankind. The church is spoken of as kingdom and priests in a number of places, whereas Israel has the kingdom separate from the priesthood. Kingdom is singular, not plural. God will establish only one kingdom.

Verse 10 makes the statement that the believers '*will reign on the earth*'. At this stage in Revelation, they are in heaven worshipping. But they will return to earth to reign with Jesus. This ties in with the parable Jesus spoke when he talks about rewarding his servants with more authority (Matthew 24:45-47, 25:21, 23, 28-29). We will cover this in chapter 15.

Verse 11 introduces a new group that worships the Lamb – angels. Their number is uncountable (Deuteronomy 33:2, Psalm 68:17, Daniel 7:10). Their worship is not personal like the redeemed (verse 12). Their worship is because of who Christ is. The Lamb is worthy '*to receive power, wealth, wisdom, strength, honour, glory and praise*'.

The word for 'sang' is better translated 'spoke'.[3] Singing is a more joyful way to express praise, and redeemed people have a lot

3. Verses 12 and 13 use *lego*, whereas verse 9 uses *ado*. See *Vine's Dictionary*, pp 578 and 548.

more to be thankful for than do angels. Notice the seven attributes of Christ. What does this represent?

Verse 13 introduces a third group of worshippers – animal life. Again, this praise is impersonal because animals are not redeemed from sin. It is spoken instead of sung. They worship God because of who He is.

Is this literal? Can animals, birds and fish praise God? We do not see any physical evidence for this, but just because we do not see something does not prove it cannot happen. If animals can praise God, will there be animals in heaven?

The response of those closest to the throne of God is interesting (verse 14). The four living creatures say '*Amen*', while the elders fall down again and worship. I find it interesting that at church we are encouraged to stand and worship, but in heaven it seems we will be at least on our knees or faces in worship. Is there a disconnect here? Maybe not. David danced and sang in worship (2 Samuel 6:16).

This concludes for now the emphasis on activity based in heaven. Our attention next turns to what happens upon the earth as the seven seals are opened. Before starting the next chapter, you may like to read Matthew 24. The most important question you need to ask yourself is this: will you be worshipping God in heaven, or receiving God's judgement on earth?

Chapter 5

The First Six Seals

Cheer up, Christian! Things are not left to chance:
no blind fate rules the world. God has purposes,
and those purposes are fulfilled.
God has plans, and those plans are wise,
and never can be dislocated.
- *Charles Spurgeon, 1834-1892, preacher*

The previous chapter has God giving the title deed to earth to the Lamb. The events that are now predicted will all happen on earth. These events are all about judging the earth and people who reject the Lordship of Christ.

It is difficult to establish the scale of the events being predicted in the next fourteen chapters. Sometimes the wording implies the entire world is involved.[1] But the Bible is centred on a small part of the world, namely the Middle East, from Greece in the west to Iran in the east, and from Turkey in the north to Egypt in the south.

These are predominately Muslim countries today, except for Israel. This topic of geography is covered in Appendix 5. I am

1. See Daniel 2. When Daniel is interpreting Nebuchadnezzar's dream, he described the king as of the whole world (Daniel 2:36-38). We know from history that the Babylonian Empire did not occupy the entire world. Daniel was obviously using hyperbole.

inclined to think these events are concentrated in the Middle East, but the consequences will be felt worldwide.

But first, an explanation on the structure of the next few chapters in Revelation. It can seem like a repetition of similar events until you realise there is a pattern to the book. The structure of this section of Revelation is a sequence of six events, an explanation about an unrelated event or events, then the next sequence. There are seven seals, seven trumpets, and seven bowls. The seventh seal triggers the trumpet events, and the seventh trumpet triggers the bowl events.

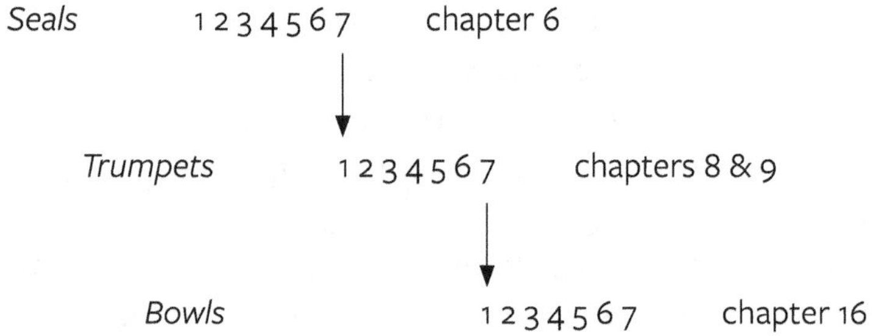

As you can see from the diagram, there are gaps where other information is given. Chapter 7 covers a group of Jewish believers, and it is slotted between the sixth and seventh seals. Chapters 10 to 15 cover a range of topics such as an overview of Satan's activities, future political and religious leaders, and economic collapse. These come between the sixth and seventh trumpets.

Matthew 24 records that the disciples asked Jesus two questions; when would the temple be destroyed, and what are the signs of the end of the age? Jesus gave a number of indicators to know when the end would be near. What are some of these signs? Deception. Wars. Famines. Earthquakes. Persecution. Evangelism. False spirituality.

The time after the church is removed is a time of God's punishment upon an unbelieving world. The seals reveal how God allows things to unfold and bring His judgement upon the earth. But remember that the seals are just the first part of a three-part process. As you progress from the seals to the trumpets then to the bowls, the intensity increases.

Significant things happen with each seal. These are roughly chronological, but there is some overlap between these events. This probably indicates they happen within a short time of each other or are consequences of other happenings.

Revelation 6

Verse 1 starts when the Lamb takes the title deed and opens the first seal. It is the Lamb (Jesus) who opens these seals. This is God's punishment. It is not the result of mankind mis-governing or over-populating the world. It is not the result of climate change. It is not the result of environmental degradation. It is not the result of the poor revolting against the rich. It is not the consequences of the globalists resetting the world finances. It is God's wrath and judgement being poured out on the earth.

One of the living creatures tells John to look at what happens. In verse 2 John sees a white horse. The rider '*was given a bow and a crown*', and he has a willingness to conquer.

Horses are the vehicle of choice for kings in the Bible. (What is the one exception? Jesus riding a donkey.) They were used for the army. Anyone riding a horse is either a king or someone in authority, and he is probably preparing for war.[2] Although the horses in

2. Saddam Hussein was often filmed riding a white horse at the head of military parades. See, for example, 'How the Coalition Won the Gulf War', a Timeline World History documentary available at www.youtube.com/watch?v=42qojj1aT8U, at 4:42.

this chapter are symbolic, they do represent actual people or situations that are used by God.

We already know white is symbolic of purity. We expect this rider to be Jesus Christ come to conquer the world.

The rider is carrying a bow but no arrows. The Greek word for bow (*toxon*)[3] indicates a military purpose. But he is not carrying arrows – offensive weapons. This is a deceptive person who acts inoffensive but whose real intentions are hidden. He will be a negotiator or a political leader. Although he initially looks peaceful, he will soon show his real intentions.

The rider is given a crown. He is given authority to rule. He is not a rightful ruler, but someone appointed to rule by some other authority. The meaning of this is uncertain. Who gives the authority? We know that ultimately all authority is given by God (Romans 13:1, 6). Maybe this person leads a coup against a current leader as part of a social uprising? Maybe Satan is involved in some way? The answer is in Revelation chapter 13.

He rides out bent on conquest. He wants to rule as much territory as possible. This seems inconsistent if he is not carrying arrows, but his intentions soon become clear. Is this Jesus Christ? It does not fit with what we know about Christ. We see Christ as the Lamb that was slain who calls people to himself, not as a ruler out for domination of as many people as possible. Christ wants people to come to Him voluntarily, not by compulsion.

The rider is not Jesus Christ. Jesus comes with many crowns (Revelation 19:12), not just one crown. Jesus comes with a sword (Revelation 19:15), not a bow. Jesus will rule with His own authority, and He will not be given authority to rule from anyone else. God is the ultimate authority, and He does not derive His authority from any other entity.

---

3. *Vine's Dictionary*, p 76.

The horse is white because this ruler is a deceptive person and will appear to be Christ. In Matthew 24 Jesus told his disciples to not be deceived at least three times (Matthew 24:4, 11, 24). Jesus warned about people claiming to be the Messiah (Matthew 24:23-26). Two options have been suggested for this rider. Option one is this rider represents false religion, with the rider imitating Christ.[4] Option two is this rider is probably the same person described in Revelation chapter 13. Or maybe both are true.

The other seals reveal other horse riders. If the rider of this horse were Jesus Christ, He would be with some nasty characters. This person is therefore a false Christ. He looks like Christ, but his actions will eventually prove he is the opposite. He becomes a ruler by political conquest, not by warfare (although wars will soon follow).

> The Russian coat of arms shows a double-headed eagle looking east and west, and it is holding an orb and a sceptre. Both these are symbols of rule. There is a smaller shield in the middle that shows a rider on a white horse. This rider does not have a crown, nor carry a bow, but he does have a spear. He is slaying a serpent or dragon. When the double-headed eagle was first used in 1472, it symbolised the union of church and state. Could this rider be a Russian?

Daniel 9 details a future ruler who will enforce or confirm a seven-year peace treaty with Israel. That single event begins the time called '*the Tribulation*'. The rider of this horse is probably the same person talked about in Daniel. Daniel tells us that the treaty

4. *Armageddon and Beyond*, p 16-18.

will be broken after three and a half years, which is consistent with this rider who deceives nations by offering a false peace. We will investigate this in more detail in Appendix 4.

The Muslims are looking forward to a predicted Messiah-like person called the Mahdi who will conquer the world for Allah. The Quran predicts the Mahdi will return on a white horse and establish worldwide worship of Allah. Could this person be a Muslim?

To summarise, the rider on this horse gives a false sense of security. He puts himself in the place of a Messiah to bring peace to the world, but he is secretly bent on conquest in one way or another.

When the second seal is opened in verse 3, another horse and rider appear. This horse is fiery red, and its rider is '*given power to take peace from the earth*'. He is given a large sword.

Red is symbolic of shed blood, and it is therefore associated with war because of the blood loss that occurs (2 Kings 3:21-23). The rider on the red horse is a military person who will engage in war. Swords are an offensive weapon.

The ruler may establish his government in peace, but it soon turns to war. We are told that '*peace is taken away from the world*'. Alliances are broken and war is declared to either re-establish the alliances or as punishment for breaking the alliances. There are many references to major wars in the Old Testament (Ezekiel 38-39, Daniel 11, Zechariah 14:1-2). We know from history and current events that Muslim countries are not peaceful.

The world is full of different types of weapons of mass destruction; nuclear, chemical and biological. Most countries spend large parts of their budgets on military equipment and personnel.[5]

5. Total military expenditure in 2019 was $US1.9 trillion. Most countries spent 2 to 3 percent of their GDP on military spending. One exception was Saudi Arabia which spent over 8 percent. worldpopulationreview.com/country-rankings/defense-spending-by-country

Many countries have compulsory military training and can quickly call up large numbers of reserve people when wanted. Military alliances are continually being made and broken.

But these verses indicate that people will have an urge to kill each other. If this is correct, nowhere will be safe. People will be killed anywhere, and not just in military action. It may be by terrorism. It may be by Jihad. It may be by the breakdown in law and order. It may be for survival as the next horseman indicates.

The third seal in verses 5 to 6 reveals a black horse with a rider holding a set of scales. One of the living creatures states the price for food commodities. '*One day's wages for half a kg of wheat and a day's wages for one and a half kg of barley*'.

Black is symbolic of death in the Bible and in Western culture (but not in Asian cultures). The rider is holding a set of scales. Scales are usually associated with judgement (Job 31:6, Psalm 62:9, Daniel 5:27). They are also associated with commerce and the weights of goods being sold (Leviticus 19:35-36, Deuteronomy 25:13-16, Proverbs 20:10, 23).

This is a picture of famine. The wheat and barley are being rationed because of their value. A day's wages will buy only enough grain to make one loaf of bread. Barley was used as animal feed but is used as human food when other sources of food are unavailable.

Oil and wine will be so expensive that none of it will be wasted. It shows the hyper-inflation that will occur. According to historians, these prices are eight times higher than normal for wheat and barley in the Roman Empire at this time. The famine won't be caused by climate change, but by political factors and war affecting the economy.

If people are randomly being killed, the workers required to grow and harvest crops may have disappeared, and there are not enough people to farm the land.

Most food shortages in the world today are caused by political factors or war disrupting production; not by the failure to grow crops. In 2008 as the financial crisis made its effects felt, food commodity prices rose.

As rice quadrupled in price, countries like Haiti could not afford to import food, and many people starved. Poor people in Asia starved among plenty of rice because they could not afford to buy it. What caused this? Political manipulations.

In the ten years that Robert Mugabe was president of Zimbabwe, he forced the white farmers off their land or killed them. The farms were given to his supporters, who did not know anything about farming. Within five years, Zimbabwe went from exporting food to importing food. Hyperinflation caused the Zimbabwe dollar to go from $1.10 to the US dollar (1980) to one million Zimbabwe dollars to $US0.02 (2008).[6] Zimbabwe now does not have an official currency, but it uses mostly the US dollar. It does not have enough hard cash, and bartering is the method of choice for transactions. In August 2018, South Africa announced they would begin seizing farms from white farmers.

More recently, Venezuela went from being one of the most prosperous countries in South America to being a political and economic cot-case within ten years.[7] The reason? A socialist government whose policies resulted in farmers being paid less than the cost of production for their produce, so they stopped farming. As the cost of food increased, public pressure forced the government to subsidise food. To pay the subsidies the government increased taxation, which meant people had less money to pay for the more expensive food.

Inflation rates for Venezuela went from 29 percent in 2013 to 10,000,000 percent in 2019.

---

6. en.wikipedia.org/wiki/Hyperinflation_in_Zimbabwe
7. en.wikipedia.org/wiki/Hyperinflation_in_Venezuela

What do people do in times of extreme famine? Once people cannot afford to buy food, they resort to anything to keep themselves alive. They begin eating things that they would not normally eat, and which are not nutritious. Leaves and bark from trees, which means the trees are destroyed.

Pets are eaten because they are available, and they are starving. Any animals are caught for food, such as mice, rats and birds (2 Kings 6:25). Finally, people resort to cannibalism, eating their own children or spouse, and anyone they can kill (2 Kings 6:28-29).

The fourth seal in verses 7 to 8 reveals a pale horse with a rider called Death. The Greek says the colour is a pale yellowish green,[8] the colour of struggling vegetation. Hades followed close behind. They were given the power to kill a quarter of the population of the earth by war, famine, plague, and wild beasts. The Greek for 'kill'[9] means to kill in any way possible.

This is obviously a time of depopulation for the earth. We saw the first rider going out to conquest, and the second rider making war. Famine will kill a lot of people. Plagues are caused by bacteria and viruses, and they have a greater impact when people are malnourished.

Wild animals will flourish because the people will be too weak from starvation to fend them off, and many will scavenge on dead bodies. Zoos may release their animals because they cannot afford to feed them because no one can afford to visit them. Amos 5 says there will be no place to hide from wild animals.

The wild beasts may include microscopic beasts – bacteria and viruses. We have been lulled into a false sense of security by recent viruses such as SARS,[10] bird flu and swine flu. These have all spread

8. *Chloros*. See *Vine's Dictionary*, pp 281, 456.
9. *Apokteino*. See *Vine's Dictionary*, p 342.
10. An acronym for Severe Acute Respiratory Syndrome.

quickly, but they have not been particularly dangerous with low fatality rates.

Legionella kills more people than flu every year, but we don't have the government doing vaccination programmes like they do for the various flu viruses. This contrasts with the worldwide panic caused by Covid-19. What is different about Covid-19?

Various plagues in the past have had huge impacts on the population at the time, and they have sometimes changed history.[11]

- Justinian Plague – 6th century – 25M people (50 percent of Europe's population, led to the decline of the Roman Empire)
- Black Death – 14th century – 200M people (50 percent of Europe's population, led to the rise of the middle class society)
- Smallpox – 16th century – 55M people (helped Spain conquer Central and South America)
- Spanish flu – 20th century – 50M people
- HIV – 1981 to present – 36M people
- Covid-19 – 6M people at May 2022 (seasonal flu 0.5M people per year)

Old diseases that were thought to be eradicated have re-surfaced and continue to cause problems globally. Biological warfare or bioterrorism are terms that have been coined since World War 2 to refer to using pathogenic bacteria or viruses to kill people. Much of this development is financed by governments through their military research budgets.[12]

---

11. www.livescience.com/worst-epidemics-and-pandemics-in-history.html.
12. www.khouse.org/articles/1995/78/

The swine flu virus from 2009 is interesting. It consists of genes from the original 1918 H1N1 virus, the avian flu virus (bird flu), and two new H3N2 virus genes from Eurasia.[13] H1N1 viruses easily infect people, where as other HN type viruses do not.

It is obviously a manufactured virus, but the reasons are unclear. Was it released to see how fast it would spread, and determine how deadly it was? Was it a pharmaceutical company or companies developing a vaccine for a disease that did not yet exist? Was it to condition gullible people into getting untested vaccinations where more deadly ingredients or mind control chemicals could be hidden?

HIV is another man-made virus made from combining bovine leukaemia virus and sheep maeda-visna virus.[14] Both viruses are lethal to their host animals, but harmless to mankind on their own. It is triggered by the herpes virus (cold virus).

It is more lethal in people from an African background because of epigenetic factors. Development of this virus was funded by the US Defence Department. Why is the military interested in viruses?

Sun Microsystems founder Bill Joy was an early pioneer of the minicomputer. He wrote an essay in the April 2000 issue of *Wired* magazine. He wrote, 'My own major concern with genetic engineering is ... that it gives the power – whether militarily, accidentally or in a deliberate terrorist act – to create a 'White Plague'.[15] Genetic engineering has become much easier and cheaper since the development of CRISPER/Cas9 technology[16] in 2005.

---

13. *Uncensored*, Issue 17: Sept-Dec 2009, p 4.
14. *Behold a Livid Horse*, part of the 'Four Horseman' video series published by Koinonia House. Reference is made to *The Strecker Memorandum* (www.youtube.com/watch?v=s0aAC2F6Tcs). Information is also available at streckermemorandum.com.
15. Quoted in *Armageddon and Beyond*, p 13.
16. www.livescience.com/58790-crispr-explained.html. This article is a

Dr Mark Siegel is a FOX medical correspondent. In a 2019 interview with Tucker Carlson, he spoke about using genetic engineering to create bioweapons. He said, '...we've entered an era when we put together novel viruses called synthetic biology... make it something your immune system hasn't seen. Make it something that spreads easily that we don't have vaccines for.'[17]

Later in the interview, he raised the scenario of the Spanish Flu epidemic of 1918 being repeated. He said, 'Somebody could take a flu virus, change it just a little bit and we have 1918 again.' This sounds very much like Covid-19. But what if someone used a lethal but slow-spreading disease like Ebola modified so that it spread easier? (Ebola was unknown until an outbreak in 1976.)

If you think this sounds unlikely, think about this:

1. Most vaccines have a chemical preservative called thimerosal.[18] It is 50 percent mercury which is a neurotoxin. It binds to the nerves in your brain and causes brain damage. Remember the mad hatter in *Alice in Wonderland*? Hatters often went mad from handling mercury throughout their working lives because it was absorbed through the skin. Could thimerosal be a partial reason for the rise in mental illness over the past 30 years?

2. Swine flu killed 20,000 to 30,000 people around the world in 2009. Normal seasonal flu typically kills around 400,000 people per year. But the government publicity at the time was all about the swine flu. Why the publicity? Was it being

---

good overview of CRISPER technology, some of its applications, and its limitations.

17. *Hybrids, Supersoldiers and the Coming Genetic Apocalypse,* Vol 2, p 60.
18. www.cdc.gov/vaccinesafety/concerns/thimerosal/index.html

monitored to measure its mortality? Or was it a trial to see how well the world reacts to a new biological threat?

3. The HIV virus was (deliberately?) aimed at third world countries by contaminating smallpox vaccines. In the early 1980's, many third-world African, Asian and south American countries were mass vaccinated for smallpox. But smallpox had been almost eliminated for a few decades, so why pick on this disease? The real problem is that almost all poor countries are now fighting the problem of AIDS epidemics. The pharmaceutical companies have found a new gold mine.

4. Anthrax was another disease that was almost eliminated until 2001. After 9/11 the US government did a couple of controlled releases of anthrax into government buildings on the pretext of anti-terrorism training. It is almost impossible to completely clean up any contaminated site. It is the commonly suggested bacterial bioweapon.[19]

5. Many bacteria have built up resistance to antibiotics and are on the verge of becoming uncontrollable. They may develop into strains that have no cure. Examples are HIV, Ebola, new strains of tuberculosis, the Zika virus, and MRSA (staphylococcus aureus). An outbreak of Ebola in 2014-2016 killed over 11,000 people. In May 2017 it was reported that up to 10 million people a year may die from bacteria that are resistant to almost all antibiotics.

   In September 2018, New Zealand health officials warned about CPE (carbapenemase-producing Enterobacteriaceae). This bacterium is resistant to almost all antibiotics.

---

19. www.ncbi.nlm.nih.gov/pmc/articles/PMC1200731/

Carbapenem is a class of antibiotics, and it is generally considered to be the drug of last resort for some infections. CPE was found in just 30 people in the six years from 2009 to 2014, 33 people in 2017, and 48 people had tested positive between January and September in 2018.

6. In late 2019 China announced they had found a variation of the SARS coronavirus (SARS-CoV-2) that supposedly originated in bats. It was linked to the Wuhan Institute of Virology that is financed by the Chinese military, and it is the world's leading coronavirus research centre (why is the military researching viruses?). This infected people, and was particularly dangerous to people with respiratory problems, which is mainly the elderly. The S-proteins on the virus (the spikey bits) are what triggers an immune response. They have been modified to resemble human proteins, so the body does not automatically reject the virus and trigger antibody production. This virus became known as Covid-19[20] and has spread throughout the world.

   Once herd immunity is achieved, this virus may become less lethal than seasonal flu. But in the meantime, many countries have damaged their economies by locking down people's movements. It is causing social, economic and political chaos. In late December 2020 it was announced that the virus had mutated (genetically engineered?) into more virulent and possibly lethal forms. The long-term consequences are unknown at this stage.

   Vaccines have been rapidly developed based on mRNA that is derived from the Covid virus. The vaccines have

20. 'CO' stands for corona, 'VI' for virus, and 'D' for disease. '19' stands for 2019, the year it was found.

not had long term (5 to 10 years) testing, so their effectiveness and safety are still being assessed. Imbalances of mRNA in people is a contributor to cancer development.[21] Yet governments around the world are urging people to get vaccinated with vaccines that have been approved only for emergency use by the United States FDA (Food and Drug Administration).

In New Zealand, the Health Act 1956 gives the Medical Officer of Health the power to quarantine people until they have had 'preventative treatment'. This could include vaccination. The same Act empowers police to use force to assist in carrying out directions from the Medical Officer of Health.

Another danger is genetic engineering, cloning, and other genetic modification techniques. CRISPR/ CAS-9 is the genetic engineering technology of choice.[22] The main area of research using CRISPR is to '...repair certain disease-causing genetic mutations.'[23]

Techniques to remove harmful DNA from one egg and replace it with normal DNA from another results in the babies having DNA from two mothers.[24] A Chinese researcher, He Jianki, edited the gene CCR5 in twin babies that were born in November 2018. This gene gives resistance to infection from the HIV virus.[25]

---

21. *The Epigenetics Revolution*, pp 201-204, 231-232.
22. www.livescience.com/58790-crispr-explained.html. This website gives a good and readable summary of the technology and some of the reported research.
23. *Hybrids Super Soldiers and the Coming Genetic Apocalypse*, p 22.
24. 'One baby, two mums', *New Scientist*, 7 June 2008, pp 38-41.
25. www.bbc.com/news/world-asia-china-50944461#:~:text=A%20scientist%20in%20China%20who,give%20them%20protection%20against%20HIV.

A lot of the research is about incorporating animal DNA into humans, and vice versa.[26] This is being researched for both military and transplant purposes.

The relatively low cost of CRISPR makes this available to anyone with some knowledge to accidently or deliberately make an organism that we may not be able to control. There have been suggestions in the popular press that Covid-19 may have been a modified virus that somehow got out of the laboratory.

Recent revelations that the US National Institute of Allergy and Infectious Diseases financed 'gain of function' research which looks at making any virus more infectious to humans.[27] DNA tests by organisations like Ancestry.com can trace your ancestry by using epigenetics.

What can stop someone engineering a virus or bacteria to infect people based on their ethnic ancestry? In other words, develop a bacteria or virus designed to target a particular ethnic group. Imagine if Hitler had developed a lethal virus to target Jews.

Transhumanism is a current research area involving the combination of genetic engineering, nanotechnology, robotics and artificial intelligence.[28] The aim is to integrate these four cutting edge technologies to control human evolution and enhance humans.[29]

---

26. *Hybrids Super Soldiers*, chapter 6.
27. www.wnd.com/2021/02/new-evidence-ties-covid-19-creation-research-funded-fauci/
28. For a concise definition of transhumanism, see *Hybrids,* vol 2, p 285-286.
29. There are numerous sources for this. A good secular video is 'The coming transhuman era: Jason Sosa at TEDxGrandRapids' available on www.youtube.com/watch?v=1Ugo2KEV2XQ. A Christian perspective is 'Transhumanism and the Human Enhancement Revolution' by Tom Horn available at www.youtube.com/watch?v=V-zKCooqvGE

Genetic engineering may be used to eliminate disease, enhance our abilities, and generally improve humans for the people who can afford to pay for the process. The ultimate aim is for people to live forever (see Revelation 9:6). No one knows where this technology will lead as it is the fastest growing technology, and the technology is outpacing the legislation.[30]

A recent paper examines the legal implications of genetic engineering. It begins by saying, 'Advancements in genetic technologies are rapidly blurring the boundary between fact and fiction. New technologies may soon make possible genetically engineered super soldiers, similar to Captain America. Legal and ethical questions concerning human enhancement technology arise. Every technology we develop carries potential for great good or harm.'[31]

Later in the article, it states, 'The risk that terrorists or non-state actors may use enhancement technology carries dangerous consequences.' The paper implies there are few legal constraints on genetic engineering.

Irrespective of how people die, the fact remains these verses predict the death of one quarter of the world population.

What is Hades? It is the place where our souls go when we die.[32] The Hebrew word is *sheol.* The Bible often calls this place '*the grave*' (Genesis 37:35, Psalm 49:15, Acts 2:27). Jesus told a story about a beggar called Lazarus and a rich man who both died and were in Hades (Luke 16:19-31). There are important things we can learn about Hades from this story another time, but we need to know

30. See *Hybrids Super Soldiers.* The last chapter is a summary of how the previous technologies combine for the transhumanist future.
31. Shah, Morial (2019) 'Genetic Warfare: Super Humans And The Law,' North Carolina Central University Science and Intellectual Property Law Review: Vol. 12: Iss. 1, Article 2. Available at: archives.law.nccu.edu/siplr/vol12/iss1/2
32. *Vine's Dictionary*, p 286.

it is a real place. It is generally pictured as under the earth. It will eventually be destroyed by God (Revelation 20:14).

The fifth seal in verses 9-11 reveals an altar somewhere. Is this in heaven, on earth, or somewhere else? Under the altar are the souls of martyrs who have been slain because of their belief in God. They ask when God is going to *'judge the earth and avenge their blood'*. Each person was given a white robe. They were told to wait until the number of martyrs was completed.

This altar must be in Hades, the place where our souls go when we die. If they were in heaven, they would be rejoicing with Christ. If they were on earth, they would not be martyrs because they would still be alive. They ask when God is going to avenge those still on the earth, so they are not included in that group.

They must therefore be one of two groups. Old Testament believers who are not yet resurrected, or people who have believed in God since the Rapture and have been killed for their beliefs. Not all the Old Testament believers had been killed for their belief. The context implies the post-Rapture believers because there are still more people to be killed.

White robes are symbolic of being declared righteous. White is the colour of purity. These people are acknowledged by God as being declared sinless.

The Greek words used are interesting. '*Slain*' is *sphazo* which means to be violently butchered.[33] '*Cried out*' is *krazo* which means screamed.[34] Together, these words imply the believers will be subject to terrible atrocities. We have knowledge of similar activities by Jihad attacks against Christians and Kurds from recent years, especially during the time when ISIS was active in Iraq and Syria.

---

33. *Vine's Dictionary*, p 581.
34. *Vine's Dictionary*, p 140. This refers to the cry or scream from fear or pain. The same word is used about Jesus' sayings on the cross.

They asked when God would avenge them, but they are told to wait. Their number is not yet complete. More people will be killed for their belief in God. We read later in Revelation about mass killing of believers on a scale never seen before. This is not going to be an easy time to believe in Jesus Christ.

The sixth seal (verses 12 to 17) reveals several signs; a great earthquake, the sun goes black, the moon turns red, stars fall to earth, the sky disappears, every mountain and island is moved. The effect of these terrifies every strata of society. From rulers to slaves try to hide because they all finally realise this is God's judgement of earth.

This seal triggers a number of physical and astronomical events. The sun going black and moon turning red could be due to atmospheric pollution caused by the earthquake and subsequent volcanic eruptions.

A similar event happened in 535 AD when the Krakatoa volcano erupted. Ash was blown high enough to block the sun for months. World temperatures dropped, the climate got drier, and droughts and famines resulted. The combination of low temperature and less sunlight meant most crops failed. This led to the eventual downfall of the Western Roman Empire.[35]

Physicists tell us that the earth's magnetic field is weakening and is overdue for a reversal of the poles.[36] When this happens, the magnetic field will be too weak to protect the earth from the impacts of solar radiation. Large solar storms could damage or destroy the electricity grids that power our economies. Increased gamma radiation will result in more cancers and genetic mutations.

Sackcloth was a dark cloth, usually made from goat's hair. As

35. Watch 'Why Was 536 AD the Worst Year in History?' (www.youtube.com/watch?v=oJBdedLx-GI).
36. www.businessinsider.com.au/weak-spot-magnetic-field-growing-could-harm-satellites-2020-8?r=US&IR=T

the name implies, it was usually made for sacks. It was used during times of mourning, and during times of despair (Genesis 37:34, 2 Samuel 3:31, 1 Kings 21:27, Nehemiah 9:1, Matthew 11:21, etc). It was a way of showing how distressed or sad you were.

Stars are often symbols of important people (Genesis 37:9-10, Daniel 8:10). Does this mean that a number of important people have their reputations irreparably damaged or die? Or is the disruption so universal that physical disturbances in the heavens cause massive asteroid showers? Asteroid impacts are known to cause damage, depending on their size. Maybe this verse has a double meaning.

What is meant by '*the sky rolling up like a scroll*'? We cannot imagine such a large three-dimensional object like the sky being rolled up. This is obviously a supernatural event. For an object to be rolled up it has to go into a different dimension, and it has to be thin in at least one dimension.

This is a time of great disruptions. Everything familiar and stable for centuries are changed with no natural explanation being available. Everything is thrown into chaos. People finally realise this is God's judgement. But they do not turn to him for forgiveness. They do not repent of their evil. Instead, they try to hide (Isaiah 2:10, 19-21).

We are not given a time frame for these events, but they must take place over a reasonable period of time. They probably take place during Daniel's 70th week (see Appendix 4), so probably occur over at least a seven-year period. They may have begun earlier. There is no indication of the length of time between the Rapture (if it happens before the Tribulation) and the start of the 70th week.

These events have parallels in Old Testament predictions.

- Isaiah 13:9-13 talks about solar events and earthquakes, and human population decreasing.

- Isaiah 29:6 predicts God will return with an earthquake and other phenomenon.
- Isaiah 34:4 talks about the stars dissolving and the sky rolling up.
- Isaiah 50:3 talks about turning the sky black like sackcloth.
- Isaiah 54:10 says the mountains will be shaken and hills removed.
- Jeremiah 4:23-24 talks about the heaven having no light and the mountains quaking.
- Ezekiel 38:19-20 says there will be an earthquake and mountains crumble.
- Joel 2:10, 30-31 describes events immediately prior to the Day of the Lord. It is interesting that these verses come after verses usually associated with the Day of Pentecost.
- Nahum 1:5 describes the earth's reaction to God – earthquakes.

Red Cross published the following information in their 2018 Disasters Report.[37] The report compares various disasters for 1998 to 2007 and 2008 to 2017. Some of the averaged data is shown:

	1998-2007	**2008-2017**
Floods	230	385
Cyclones	61	103
Earthquakes	89	86
Droughts	38	29
Food insecurity	15	39
People affected	?	2 billion

37. media.ifrc.org/ifrc/wp-content/uploads/sites/5/2018/10/B-WDR-2018-EN-LR.pdf

A similar report in 2011 gave the following report:

- In 1980 there were 120 natural disasters; in 2010 there were over 500.
- In 1980 there were 60 weather-related disasters; in 2006 there were 240.
- In 1985 there were about 174 million people affected by disasters; in 2010 there were 254 million people affected.

There are parallels between Matthew 24 and Revelation 6. They are describing the same events:

False Christ	Matthew 24:5	Revelation 6:1-2
War	Matthew 24:6-7	Revelation 6:3-4
Famine	Matthew 24:7	Revelation 6:5-6
Death	Matthew 24:7-9	Revelation 6:7-8
Martyrdom	Matthew 24:9-10,16-22	Revelation 6:9-11
Astronomy	Matthew 24:9	Revelation 6:12-14
Divine judgement	Matthew 24:32-25:26	Revelation 6:15-17

Matthew contains some items not mentioned in Revelation, such as the abomination that causes desolation. This will be covered in Appendix 6.

This chapter opened with four horsemen causing death and destruction. There is a fifth horseman in Revelation. He also rides a white horse and carries a sword. He comes to rule. We will cover this horseman when we get to Revelation 19.

Chapter 6

God's Sealed Servants

About the times of the end, a body of men
will be raised up who will turn their attention to
the prophecies and insist upon their literal interpretation
in the midst of much clamour and opposition.
- *Isaac Newton, 1642-1727, scientist*

Revelation chapter 6 gave an overview of events on earth from a human viewpoint, the rise of a major leader, war, famine, diseases, earthquakes, etc. It is no wonder Jesus said, '*men will faint from terror, apprehensive on what is coming on the world*' (Luke 21:26). But what is happening spiritually on the earth during this time?

In Revelation chapter 7, John sees '*four angels standing at the four corners of the earth holding back the four winds to prevent any blowing on the land, the sea, or any tree*'. What are the four corners of the earth? What are the four winds? Why are there four angels?

Four is the number associated with anything to do with the earth. The earth and universe were created in four days (Genesis 1:1-19).[1] The Garden of Eden had four rivers (Genesis 2:10).[2] Most

1. Days 5 and 6 were used for creating animal life. But planet earth and the universe were completed by then. Fish and birds were created on day five. Terrestrial animals, including mankind, were created on day 6.
2. The fact that rivers flow downhill indicates the Garden of Eden was on a fairly high hill or plateau.

animals have four legs (Leviticus 11:20-27). These four angels seem to be in control of earth's environment or climate. There are another four angels (demons) who are bound at the River Euphrates (Revelation 9:14).

In this case the four angels are told to hold back the wind. Is the wind symbolic or literal? Or both?

Wind is an essential part of earth's climate. Its movement produces rain and regulates the temperature. Holding back the wind can be a form of punishment as it will result in a drought and extreme temperatures. Releasing the winds can be a punishment as hurricanes and tornados are destructive. Extreme wind is symbolic of God dispersing nations because of their sin (Jeremiah 13:24, 49:36).

In contrast to the two extremes, a gentle breeze is symbolic of refreshing and revitalising (Ezekiel 37:9).

Wind is associated with acts of God. A wind helped dry up the water after Noah's flood (Genesis 8:1). A wind blew all night to allow the Israelites to cross the Red Sea (Exodus 14:21). A wind brought quails to the Israelites to feed them (Numbers 11:31). The apostles heard a sound like a violent wind when they received the Holy Spirit (Acts 2:2).

Daniel 7:2-3 says the four beasts Daniel saw came out of the sea churned up by the four winds. Maybe the four winds are now being held back because there are no more kingdoms to be raised up?

Verse 2 gives us another clue. Another angel '*descends from the east*' and tells the first four angels to not harm the earth.

The east is always the direction of God. The Garden of Eden was planted in the east (Genesis 2:8). The entrance to the tabernacle was on the east side (Exodus 27:13-15, 36:23-27). The glory of God comes from the east (Ezekiel 43:1-2). This messenger angel is coming direct from God with a command.

The messenger tells the other four angels to not harm the earth. This implies the four angels holding the wind have been given a mandate to affect the land and the seas. Are they an integral part of the judgements of God? Are they involved in the famines and subsequent plagues of chapter 6? Or are they involved in the later judgements (chapters 8 & 9)?

The four angels are told not to harm the earth '*until a seal is put on the foreheads of the servants of God*' (verse 3). These angels are holding back winds that will cause harm on the earth. This is an environmental judgement (Deuteronomy 28:15, 22-24).

This angel has a seal of the living God. What does this mean? A seal is a symbol of ownership. No one could use any object with someone's seal on it unless they had authority.

The first example of someone having a seal on them is Cain having a mark to protect him (Genesis 4:15). God is a master at protecting people from disaster. Noah and his family were saved from God's first worldwide judgement.

Israel was saved from the plagues in Egypt. It was saved from the death of their first-born by the blood of the Passover lamb. Rahab and her family were saved from the destruction of Jericho. Jerusalem was saved from destruction by the Assyrians (2 Kings 18-20).

When we accept Jesus as our Saviour and are cleansed from our sins we are sealed with the Holy Spirit (2 Corinthians 1:22, Ephesians 4:30, 2 Timothy 2:19). This ensures our eternal salvation, but it does not protect us from losing our rewards if we do not persevere.

What mark is used on these people? Revelation 14:1 tells us it is a combination of Christ's name and God's name. Is this a physical mark? Or something God can see but people cannot?

Another seal or mark is put on the heads of people subjecting themselves to the beast (Revelation 13:16-17). This one is something that can be physically detected because it is used in commerce. It is impossible for anyone to have both marks.

Who are these servants of God? They are not the church believers because they are already in heaven. Verses 4 to 8 show us they are Jews who have believed in Jesus Christ and acknowledged that He is their Messiah since the Rapture:

1. They come from tribes of Israel.
2. They know which tribe they come from.
3. They will stand with the Messiah on Mount Zion (Joel 2:32, Revelation 14:1).
4. They are celibate (Revelation 14:4).

Why are these people saved? What is their role? Why do these people need to be sealed? This is not stated in these verses. Many commentators say they will be evangelists, primarily to Jews around the world.[3] If these people are evangelists, they are very successful. We read in Revelation 6:9-11 that a large number of people had been martyred for their belief in God. We read that an uncountable number stand before God's throne in worship (Revelation 7:9). We are not told the number, but we are told they will be resurrected and will rule with the Messiah for one thousand years (Revelation 20:4).

They are given special protection against the attacks upon Jews during the Tribulation. The Tribulation on the earth will affect everyone, but most of the attacks are specifically aimed at Jews (Daniel 7:21, 8:11-12, 11:31). Jeremiah calls this period '*the time of Jacob's trouble*' (Jeremiah 30:7). These 144,000 will be protected throughout this period.[4]

---

3. For example, *Agents of the Apocalypse*, pp 66-78.
4. I originally titled this chapter 'Jehovah's Witnesses' as a play on the

Given the pressures these people will be under, it is understandable why these 144,000 people remain unmarried. Paul had a similar discussion with the church in Corinth (1 Corinthians 7:29-35).

Why are the tribes listed? Various people claim to be descended from the ten missing tribes of Israel. One idea propagated by *Tomorrow's World* on TV and in their literature is that the English-speaking people come from the tribe of Joseph.[5] But God shows us here the ten tribes are not missing at all. God knows the people who are from all the tribes. These people are recognised as being completely Jewish and able to prove their tribal affiliation. (DNA analysis?[6])

As you read through this list, you will notice two tribes are not named, but twelve tribes are there. How does this work? Who is missing?

The tribes are listed in the Bible over twenty times, and each time they are in a different order. Often one tribe is missed for a reason. For example, the Levites were exempt from military duty. Any list involving the armies will have Levi missed out (Numbers 1:45-49). How do they still get twelve names?

The tribe of Joseph is often listed under the names of his sons, Ephraim and Manasseh. Why? Because Jacob adopted Joseph's two sons into his family, and he ranked them along with his own

---

beliefs of the JW sect. But as I continued, I could not find any direct reference to them acting as witnesses. Hence the current title.

5. *The United States and Great Britain in Prophecy*, pp 26-38.
6. 'Written for a Generation to Come: A History of the World in the Molecules of Life.' A paper by Wendy S. Wippel submitted to Koinonia House in 2006. A summary is found at www.khouse.org/articles/2006/670/. I cannot find the original pdf on the website, so email me if you want a copy. Warning: it does contain a lot of technical information.

sons (Genesis 48:13-21). If you want a list with one tribe missing, you list both Ephraim and Manasseh. Joseph is listed in verse 8, and his son Manasseh is listed in verse 6. Ephraim is sealed, but his name is hidden. Is this significant? It must be, but why? None of my commentaries have any reason.

Both the tribes of Dan and Ephraim were involved in introducing idolatry into Israel (Judges 17:4-5, 18:30, 2 Kings 10:29, Hosea 4:17). Dan is omitted from this list, and it is omitted from the genealogies in 1 Chronicles (chapters 1 to 8).

We know some of the tribe do survive this period because they are given land in the millennial kingdom. Dan is the first tribe listed to receive land (Ezekiel 48:1). The tribe of Dan were involved in making the tabernacle (Exodus 31:6), but they still went into idolatry. There is a warning here for us; we can be busy doing stuff for God but still be led into sin.

Verse 9 onward looks forward to the end of the Tribulation when Christ resurrects the remaining believers.

John sees a great multitude that was uncountable '*standing before the throne and in front of the Lamb*'. They came '*from every nation, tribe, people and language*'. Where have we heard this before? Revelation 5:9. Are these the same group of people? No. The elders (representative of the church) are mentioned separately (in verse 11).

These people are wearing white robes (symbol of what?), but they are holding palm branches in their hands. This is a Jewish form of celebration (Leviticus 23:40, John 12:13). These are Jews and other people who have believed in their Messiah during the Tribulation.

They call out in worship to God in verses 10-12. All the angels around the throne join in worship. Do just the angels join the Jews in worship? Or are the four living creatures and the elders also involved? Verse 11 suggests everyone is involved.

John is next asked a question from one of the elders in verse 13. Why is this question asked? There is obviously a need to explain something we are likely to miss. What is so important? The elder asks, '*who are these people in the white robes, and where did they come from?*'

John admits he is not sure, and he is given the answer. These people have '*come out of the Great Tribulation*', the time when the world leaders try to eliminate all believers in God. The Great Tribulation is the last three and a half years of the seven-year period.

This coincides with the period of persecution (Daniel 7:25, Revelation 11:2-3, 12:6). They may have been evangelised by the 144,000 servants of God. They have recognised the Messiah as the Lamb slain for sin (Zechariah 12:10, Romans 11:25-27). They have recognised the need for blood to remove sin. And they have lived righteous lives.

These people have a special status in heaven described in verses 15-17.

- They are before the throne of God.
- They serve God day and night in his temple. There is a temple in heaven that was the template for the tabernacle and subsequent temples (Hebrews 8:2, 5, 9:23-24).
- They will be protected by God's covering. Spreading a tent is symbolic of coming under God's protection (Psalm 52:5). Entering a tent meant coming under that person's protection (Judges 4:17-18, see Genesis 19:4-8 where the same protection was provided by a house). Ruth asks for protection in a similar manner (Ruth 3:9).
- They will be fully provided for.
- They will be protected from things that cause discomfort.
- The Lamb will be their shepherd. In the past, the Jews had

rejected their shepherd (Numbers 27:15-17, Psalm 28:9, 2 Chronicles 18:16, Ezekiel 34:5-6, 8, Matthew 9:36). Jesus said that he is the good shepherd (John 10:11-16).

- They will be led to springs of living water (Jeremiah 2:13, 17:13, Zechariah 14:8, John 4:10, Revelation 21:6, 22:1-2).
- They never again experience sorrow (Isaiah 25:8, 35:10, 51:11, 65:19, Revelation 21:4).

Some people teach that God has wiped his hands of the Jews after they rejected him before Pilate. They say the Jews talked themselves out of God's plan when they brought a curse upon themselves (Matthew 27:25). They teach the church has taken Israel's place in God's plans.

This is obviously wrong. God has not written off the Jews. We read in this chapter that God will save and seal 144,000 to be his servants. Paul wrote that God is still going to save Jews and has plans for Israel (Romans 10:1-3, 21, 11:1, 5, 25-27).

God will restore Israel again as it is an example to the rest of the world (Zechariah 8:20-23, 14:10-11, 16). The Jewish nation still has a lot of hardship to go through, but God is protecting it and will bring it to its place of prominence among the nations that was its destiny.

A question for you to think about. How does God's plan for the Jews differ from God's plan for the church? What are the two groups supposed to achieve? What were the origins of the two groups? What is their final destiny? How does God relate to the two groups?

Chapter 7

The Trumpets

God's grace is not infinite.
God is infinite, and God is gracious.
We experience the grace of an infinite God,
but grace is not infinite.
God sets limits to His patience and forbearance.
He warns us over and over again
that someday the axe will fall
and His judgment will be poured out.
- *R.C. Sproul, 1939-2017, theologian*

Chapter 6 has Christ opening six of the seven seals and various things happening on the earth. The world leader is revealed during a time of peace but soon involves the world in war. Famine results, and along with plagues kills a quarter of the population. Finally, an earthquake and various signs in the sky cause worldwide panic. We will cover more of this time as we go through Revelation.

Chapter 7 covered the sealed Jews on earth during the Tribulation and their ultimate vindication.

In chapters 8 and 9, Revelation returns to events that happen on earth. To refresh our memories, who is opening the seals? The Lamb, Jesus Christ. The seals are on what? The title deed to earth.

Revelation 8

What happens when the last seal is opened in verse 1? '*Silence for about half an hour*'. No worship. No service. No proclamations. Silence. Why? I think it is because God is going to start a new judgement. What do you think was happening in heaven while Jesus was on the cross? Would the angels have continued their worship? I think they would have stopped and looked and wondered what was happening and why.

The seven angels close to God are given seven trumpets in verse 2. Seven symbolises what? Completeness. What do trumpets symbolise? God's proclamation or announcement. Trumpets in the Bible were used to announce judgements or as a sign of a king coming. In Revelation, we find the trumpets are used for both uses. They announce a judgement on the people still on earth, but they ultimately announce that the ultimate King is coming.

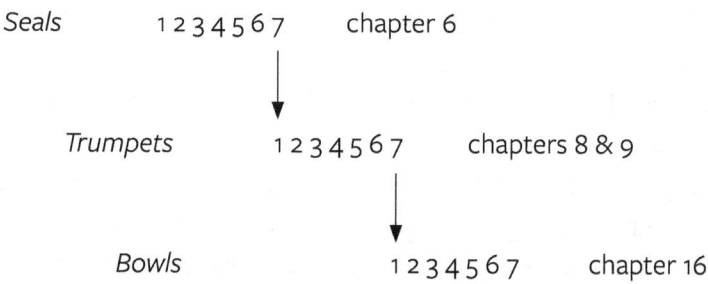

Seals 1 2 3 4 5 6 7 chapter 6
↓
Trumpets 1 2 3 4 5 6 7 chapters 8 & 9
↓
Bowls 1 2 3 4 5 6 7 chapter 16

Israel used to celebrate the Feast of Trumpets every year. This was the first of the autumn feasts, which are generally prophetic of end times.

The book of Joshua has a lot of parallels with Revelation, especially with regard to trumpets. These are summarised in Appendix 7. Both are involved in taking back ownership of land.

Verse 3. Another angel came who had a golden censer. The

censer was a metal vessel shaped like a saucepan. It was used for holding incense. The censers used in the tabernacle were bronze (Numbers 16:39). Why is this censer gold? Bronze was the metal of judgement. Gold is the metal of deity. Sin has been judged on earth, and there is no sin in heaven.

The angel came and stood at the altar in heaven. What altar is that? The tabernacle had two altars. There was a bronze altar for the burnt offering (Exodus 27:1-8). This was in the courtyard where everyone could access it, and it was used for the sacrifices made by the people. There was a gold altar of incense used for the twice-daily incense (Exodus 30:1-10). This was inside the tabernacle and in front of the curtain that separated off the Most Holy Place. Only the priests used this altar.

The altar in heaven is the altar of incense. Two reasons. One, it is gold. Two, it is used only for incense. Sin has already been judged through the blood of Jesus Christ, there is no need for an altar for sin offerings in heaven. Incense is symbolic of our prayers (Revelation 5:8).

The angel was given a lot of incense to offer with the prayers of all the believers ('*saints*') in verse 4. The smoke and the prayers all go up before God. Our prayers have already gone before God when we prayed them, but they go before God again now.

Verse 5 tells us that when the incense had all been burnt, the angel filled the censer with fire from the altar and hurled it on the earth. As a result, there were '*thunder, rumblings, lightning, and an earthquake*'. We had an earthquake in chapter 6, but without the other effects. Is this the same event or another earthquake? I think this is another one.

The first one was the result of the sixth seal, but this one is the result of the seventh seal. The previous one affected the sky, but this one starts activity on the earth. We are not given a time between these two earthquakes, except for the half-hour of silence.

The end of the seven seals signifies the start of another series of judgements in verse 6. Chapter 6 had a series of wars, famines, and general destruction. These were largely man-made. They were all the result of what man was doing on the earth, but directed by God. The effects of the upcoming seven trumpets are all God's judgement on the earth and on unrepentant man still on the earth.

The first trumpet results in '*hail and fire mixed with blood*' falling on the earth in verse 7. The result was one third of the earth's vegetation was burnt. It is not the result of global warming. It is God's judgement. Global warming is too slow, and people could attribute it to natural causes.

A sudden devastation like this can only be attributed to God. Hail is a common occurrence. Fire falling from the sky is much less common, and is mostly due to volcanic activity. Blood falling is unheard off. The combination shows this is definitely an act of God's judgement. One third of the vegetative food supply is destroyed.

This sort of thing has happened before. Sodom was destroyed by fire (Genesis 19:23-25). What was the real reason for Sodom's destruction? (See Ezekiel 16:49-50.[1]) Joshua had similar help defeating a federation of Canaanite kings (Joshua 10:9-11).

Verses 8 to 9 show that the second trumpet results in a mountain-like object going into the sea. Is this a comet or an asteroid? A third of the sea was affected. A third of all fish died and a third of all shipping was destroyed.

Nebuchadnezzar had a vision with a large rock destroying the kingdoms on the earth and establishing a new one (Daniel 2:34). That rock was obviously symbolic of Jesus Christ. This rock is

1. Many people think Sodom and Gomorrah were destroyed solely because of homosexuality. Ezekiel does not mention it in the list, although the '*detestable practices*' would include homosexuality along with many other sexual deviances. But the whole list can equally apply to our current society. Are we also in line for judgement?

probably a large comet or asteroid. Such a large object would have a massive impact. Imagine tsunamis larger than any previously recorded; possible increased volcanic activity from the shock waves; possible chemical contamination of the water.

The third trumpet in verses 10 to 11 results in a large comet-like object affecting a third of the water supplies. The name of the star or comet is Wormwood or Bitterness. Wormwood (*Artemisia absinthium*) is a perennial herb that tastes bitter, but it has stimulating qualities.[2] It is used in making vermouth (Italian white wine) and is used in some medicines. It is mentioned seven times in the Old Testament where it represents sorrow and judgement.[3] One third of the water turns bitter and many people die from drinking the water. The water supplies are contaminated.

The fourth trumpet in verse 12 results in one third of the light from the heavenly bodies being lost. There are two possible ways to interpret this. First, this could mean that the hours of sunlight are reduced by one third (days become about four hours shorter) and the night goes completely black for about four hours. Second, it could mean that only two thirds of the normal light reach the earth (which would probably have a similar effect). The rest may be blocked out. Jesus warned his disciples this would happen (Matthew 24:29). This will result in global cooling and reduced crop growth, causing more famine and starvation.

This shows God is in control of all creation. God can alter conditions on earth and in the sky. All things in creation are controlled by Him (Colossians 1:16-17).

NASA has an asteroid on their watch list that was first seen in 2004. This asteroid has been named Apophis,[4] after the Egyptian

---

2. en.wikipedia.org/wiki/Artemisia_absinthium
3. *Bible Knowledge Commentary: New Testament*, p 952.
4. en.wikipedia.org/wiki/99942_Apophis

god of chaos. The asteroid is 370 metres wide (50 percent larger than Mauao (Mt Maunganui), similar height to the Eiffel Tower), weighs 20M tonnes, and travels at 30,700 km/s.

It was originally predicted to hit earth on 13 April 2029 (Friday), but is now predicted to come within 31,000 km (one tenth of the distance to the moon). If this asteroid (or any other large asteroid) hits earth, it will trigger tsunamis, earthquakes, and volcanoes. All these combined effects will release enough material into the atmosphere to block the sun for months, causing massive environmental damage and crop failure. Millions of people will die from the immediate effects of the impact with many more dying from the secondary impacts. Could this asteroid be the means God uses to bring destruction to the earth?

John sees an eagle flying saying, '*woe to the inhabitants of the earth, because of the next three trumpets*' (verse 13). He is not mourning the losses from the first four trumpets. He is giving a warning that worse is yet to come. If the first four are relatively light, then what are the last three like? How much worse can things get for the people still on earth?

What is the significance of the eagle? The eagle symbolises swift action (Deuteronomy 28:49, Proverbs 23:5). This is an indication that the next lot of judgements will be very swift. The fact that this eagle is concerned about the next three trumpets indicates that things are going to escalate.

Revelation 9

The fifth trumpet (verse 1) sees a star '*that had fallen from the sky to the earth*'. This star is obviously an angel because it is given a key. Stars are often symbolic of angels (Revelation 1:20). This angel had already fallen, and so is a demon (Revelation 12:4). If it were one of God's angels John would have seen it descend. But it was an earth-dwelling angel. It was given the key to the shaft of the Abyss.

What is the Abyss? The first mention of the Abyss is in Luke 8:31. It is obviously a place where demons are sent for punishment. Jesus had the authority to send them there, and they recognised that fact. For some reason Jesus decided not to send them there. Why not? Can we command demons to go to the Abyss when we do deliverance?

The only other place the Abyss is mentioned in the Bible is in Revelation:

- Revelation 11:7 – the beast that comes from the Abyss will kill God's two special witnesses.
- Revelation 17:8 – the beast has apparently been destroyed but comes back to earth.
- Revelation 20:1-3 – Satan is locked in the Abyss for one thousand years.

What is the Abyss like? We are not given any information, but we are only told who comes and goes from it. It is obviously not a nice place because the demons do not want to go there (Luke 8:31).

When the door to the Abyss was opened, smoke rose from it (verse 2). This again darkened the sun and sky still further from the previous darkening. Earth becomes a gloomy place, both physically and spiritually.

Out of the smoke come locusts (verses 3-5). These are not natural locusts. These locusts were given power like scorpions – they can now harm people. These locusts are a demonic plaque that God sends to the earth to torment mankind for their continual refusal to recognise God.

- Natural locusts destroy vegetation but have no effect on animal life (other than eating the food supply of herbivores).

These locusts are told not to harm vegetation, possibly because one third of it has already been destroyed.

- They can only harm people who do not have God's seal on their foreheads (Revelation 7:3). Who has the seal? The 144,000 Jews from twelve tribes of Israel (and other people who believe in God?). Natural locusts will not harm people.
- They torture mankind for five months. Locusts do not naturally torture people.

The locust bite is described as similar to the sting of a scorpion (verses 5-6). Does the pain from the sting last five months? Or are the creatures affecting people for five months and then disappearing? It will be so painful people will want to die but not be able to. Does this mean God suspends the ability for people to die during this period? Why would He do this? Or does it mean that if you are stung, you will not die from the sting?

> One of the aims of genetic engineering and the trans-humanism movement is immortality. Maybe by the time this happens those goals have been met or partially met. That must be the worst sort of punishment – being desperate to die because of pain but not being able to.

The locusts are described in verses 7 to 11. They are obviously not natural locusts, nor are we given any indication of their size:

- They look like horses prepared for battle. They are ready to do what they were released for.
- They wore something like crowns on their heads. They had been given authority to do what they were doing.

- Their faces resembled human faces, as do many of the angels that have been described to us.
- Their hair was like women's hair. Does this refer to the length or something else? Why is this detail important?
- Their teeth were like lions' teeth. They are designed to destroy life.
- They had breastplates like breastplates of iron. They were able to defend themselves. From who or what?
- Their wings made a sound like cavalry rushing into battle. This could be due to the massive numbers of these locusts.
- They have tails and stings like scorpions, and the sting torments people for five months. Natural scorpion stings only last a few hours. A minor sting is neutralised by our immune system. A massive sting quickly results in death. A sting that lasts for five months is unnatural.
- They have a ruler over them who is the ruler of the Abyss. The name in Hebrew and Greek is given. His name is Destroyer. Who is the destroyer? Is Satan ever called this name? (Matthew 10:28, John 10:10) Is this a separate demon? Or is it Satan?

Joel 2 describes the '*Day of the Lord*', and he describes an army of horse-like creatures that causes devastation wherever they go. People will be terrified by these creatures (Joel 2:1-9). Is Joel describing the same thing?

Are these actual physical beings? Are they a genetic chimera?[5] Or is this a description of a type of demon? I think that because we are given a physical description, it indicates that these could be a physical phenomenon. But these creatures have a ruler over them, whereas most animal life does not have a ruler. I therefore suspect

5. *Hybrids, Supersoldiers and the Coming Apocalypse*, Vol 2, pp 103-104.

these are demons who are able to be physically seen. If these are physical creatures, how will the news media report their sudden appearance? And how will governments respond?

Verse 12 refers to Revelation 8:13 where the eagle says three woes. Each woe corresponds to one of the last three trumpet blasts. There was no time frame given for the first four woes. They could happen instantaneously, although this is not likely for the third trumpet. But the first woe does not involve the death of anyone. It prolongs the time under which people endure the judgement of God.

The sixth trumpet (verses 13-14) causes a voice from the corners of the golden altar giving instructions to release the four angels bound at the River Euphrates. Who are these four angels? They are demons because they have been bound as some form of punishment. Why were they bound at this river and not in the Abyss? I cannot find any reference to this in the Bible.

Verses 15 and 16 tell us these four angels were kept here for this very moment. Their sole function is to mobilise troops to kill a third of mankind. The fourth seal showed a pale horse that killed a quarter of all mankind and animal life. Combine that with these four angels and how much of mankind has been killed by God's judgements? The combined death toll is half the earth's population.

The number of troops used in this judgement was 200 million. That would be roughly equivalent to five times the size of the population of the Roman Empire at that time.[6] It is approximately ten times the size of China's military,[7] although they claimed to have an army of 200 million in 1965.[8] This is a massive movement of troops.

---

6. en.wikipedia.org/wiki/Demography_of_the_Roman_Empire
7. www.statista.com/statistics/264443/the-worlds-largest-armies-based-on-active-force-level/
8. *Time*, 21 May 1965, p 35. Quoted in *Bible Knowledge Commentary: New Testament*, p 953.

Verses 17 to 19 describe the horses and riders. Obviously, these are not the ordinary horse and rider that John was familiar with. Are these demonic beings as the locusts were? Demons are not usually described as marshalled into a military force.

This could be John's way to describe a modern war machine like a tank or armoured personnel carrier? Are the colours on the breastplates the colours of a coalition army? The mouths shoot fire, smoke and sulphur. Is this a description of a missile or shell being fired? The tails were like snakes having a head to inflict injury. Is this a gun turret being described?

If these are some type of four-legged horse-type animal, who are the riders?

Whichever way you want to interpret this, these are dangerous things that God uses to judge mankind.

Now we know why the eagle said the next three trumpets were terrible (8:13). They are unlike anything experienced on earth before. These are new phenomena. They seem to be plagues of demons. If this is true, there is no physical cure any government or international body can devise.

Verses 20 to 21 show how resistant mankind is without the Holy Spirit working in people's lives. Mankind will continue on with their sinful lifestyles. They will not recognise the problems they were experiencing as God's punishments. The term translated '*magic acts*' is the Greek word *pharmakia*,[9] from which we get our word pharmacy. The Greek word is associated with witchcraft and sorcery. Does this refer to the drug culture expanding in our generation? Or does it foretell today's merging of the occult with drug taking, as exampled by the 'sex, drugs, and rock and roll' mantra?

Are we any different today? Do we recognise the increase in natural disasters may be God trying to call people back to Him?

9. *Vine's Dictionary*, p 587. The Greek word for magic is *magia*.

Do people recognise that when they act against Israel some form of natural disaster occurs? See Genesis 12:3.

- Bill Koeing has compiled a list of natural disasters that affected USA while they were trying to pressure Israel to deal with the Palestinians.[10] The list was only for the period October 1991 to August 2005. The financial cost was at least $US30 billion, with many disasters not having a monetary cost listed. Has the USA learned the lesson?
- When Jerusalem announced that their capital is Jerusalem in 2018, most of the world spoke out against what God had previously ordained. Our Prime Minister, Jacinda Adern, publicly called for the Jews to reverse their decision. The summer of 2018 was wetter and colder than normal, and many people's summer holidays were ruined. Did New Zealand repent?

10. www.1timothy4-13.com/files/prophecy/disasters.html

Chapter 8

The Little Scroll and the Two Witnesses

Revelation 10

We have had six of the seven trumpet blasts. Each blast was a judgement upon the earth. We now have a break between the sixth and the seventh trumpet where some events are described. We had the same between the sixth and seventh seal. The seventh trumpet is sounded half-way through chapter 11.

John sees another mighty angel descend from heaven in verse 1. This angel has similarities to previous descriptions of God. Both Revelation 1:12-16 and Daniel 10:5-6 have similar elements. All three have legs like fiery pillars. Daniel described his person as having a face like lightning and eyes like flaming torches.

Revelation 1:14 describes God as having a head white as snow and eyes like blazing fire. This angel had '*a rainbow above his head*' (is it a full circle rainbow?), and '*a face like the sun*'. Is this God, or Jesus Christ? Or is it an angel involved in judgement of some kind?

The angel was '*holding a little scroll in his right hand*' in verse 2. The scroll was open for everyone to read. What is the significance of this? Most writers think this scroll is a smaller version of the one in chapter 5 with the seven seals. Another opinion is that it contains the angel's mission that it had been given.[1]

---

1. *Bible Knowledge Commentary: New Testament*, p 954.

The angel '*planted his right foot on the sea and his left foot on the land*'. Planted means that it is firmly established. Nothing will move it. The sea is symbolic of mankind (Isaiah 57:20, Luke 21:25, Jude 13). They are restless and often get enraged. But what is the land symbolic of? And why is the right or left foot mentioned? It must be important, but why?

Verse 3 tells us that the angel sounded like seven thunders. When the first seal was broken, the living creature has a '*voice like thunder*'. Is there significance about seven thunders, or does this simply indicate the volume?

John was going to write what the voice said, but he was told not to record it (verse 4). Maybe the seven is significant. Maybe God wants what is spoken to be a complete surprise. Or maybe what the voices said do not add anything to what is being recorded.

Daniel was twice told to seal up his words until the time of the end (Daniel 8:25, 12:4). Daniel tried to get more understanding, but he was told the words were sealed (Daniel 12:8-9).

There is an indication in Daniel that people reading his writings when the things are happening will understand and be able to gain further insights (Daniel 12:10). Maybe the same thing will happen with Revelation.

We are trying to understand it and tie it in with other parts of the Bible. We try to tie it in with the current political situation as we suspect we are getting closer to the final fulfilment.

Our understanding is incomplete. The political situation could quickly change. We may be missing important things that people living during these times will recognise and understand. Revelation is a Jewish book, written by a Jew, using Jewish symbols, and referring to the Jewish scriptures. We do not fully understand all the hints and nuances in this book. But a Jewish person reading this book during these times may be able to understand much more.

The angels raised his right hand in verses 5 to 6. He swore

by whom? By '*the eternal God, the God of the earth and the God of creation*'. The angel announces that the mystery of God will be accomplished in the days of the seventh trumpet. This had already been announced to God's servants, the prophets.

What are the '*mysteries of God*' mentioned in verse 7? They are things that God has kept hidden from the Old Testament prophets but has since been revealed. Paul talked about various mysteries.

1. The mystery of Israel rejecting God, but God still having a plan to return and be their God (Romans 11:25, Ephesians 3:6). The prophets taught that the Messiah will reign over Israel in the future, but the events leading to that were hidden.

2. Related to this is the mystery that God will go to the Gentiles (Colossians 1:25-27). The Jewish prophets thought God was exclusively for Israel, but that He tolerated Gentiles.

3. The mystery of the Messiah as our saviour (Romans 16:25, Ephesians 1:9, 3:3). The prophets did not mention their Messiah dying for the sins of the world; their Messiah was a Jewish deliverer. Various types or actions portrayed salvation, but many of these things were seen in hindsight (Genesis 22, the tabernacle, Ruth, Isaiah 53, etc).

4. The Rapture and instantaneous changing from earthly to heavenly realms (1 Corinthians 15:51-52). The resurrection is hinted at in the Old Testament, but the New Testament gives much more detail.

5. The church as a group of believers (Ephesians 3:9-10, 5:32). The Old Testament prophets did not foresee believers in

> God based on the sacrifice of Jesus Christ. There are no prophecies concerning the church, although there are some types of the church in the Old Testament.

What mystery is being referred to here? I believe it will be the exact details around the Day of the Lord. This is often mentioned as a day when the Messiah comes to judge the earth and establish His kingdom. Where does it fit among all the judgements we have been reading about? How does the future ruler and various anti-religion campaigns fit with the Day of the Lord? Various wars and destruction of cities are predicted, but what is the sequence for these? Or is the mystery something else?

The angel announces that '*there will be no more delay*'. The time for repentance is quickly closing, and God will very soon do his final judgement.

In verses 8 to 11 John is told to take the scroll from the hand of the angel. He is instructed to eat it. He is warned that it will taste sweet, but it will be bitter in his stomach. Sure enough, that happened. What does this mean?

Good news may be good to hear, but the implications may not be so good. For example, the good news may be that a war has ceased, but the bad news may be the defeated country is forced to pay reparations to the conquerors and cause an economic collapse.

This is what ultimately allowed Adolf Hitler to come to power in Germany in the late 1920s and eventually led to the Second World War. Similarly, the good news was the Allies won World War 2, but Britain's economy was so damaged they had rationing for most things for almost a decade afterwards.

What is John's good news? That God is going to rule over the earth? What will be the bitter reaction? That more judgements are yet to come? That more people are going to suffer because of their rejection of God?

David described God's ordinances as sweeter than honey (Psalm 19:9-10). Other people in the Bible had been commanded to eat scrolls (Jeremiah 15:16, Ezekiel 2:8-3:3). What does it signify? Does it represent the person absorbing God's word for them?

Whatever the good news may be, John is told that he must prophesy again about many peoples, nations, languages and kings (verse 11). Again, every possible people group is included. No one is exempt. Some of these prophecies will be sweet, particularly to believers because they will end in the new heaven (Revelation 21:1-8). Some of these prophecies will be bitter, particularly to unbelievers or non-believers because they finish in the Lake of Fire (Revelation 20:11-15).

Revelation 11

At the start of chapter 11 John is told to measure the temple of God, the altar, and count the worshippers (verses 1-2). John is told to not measure anything outside the temple. We know this is the temple in Jerusalem because the following verses talk about things to happen on earth. In particular, Jerusalem will be over-run ('*trampled*' probably means it is trashed) with Gentiles for forty-two months. Where have we heard of this time period before?

Daniel 7:25 talks about the three and a half years when the saints will be persecuted by a future ruler. In Daniel 9:27 we are told about the abomination that causes desolation happening at the start of the three and a half years. These verses are covered in more detail in Appendix 4.

Christ returns to rapture all believers in Jesus Christ (the church). Sometime after this a seven-year covenant is signed with Israel (an international agreement for peace in the Middle East?). The ruler is revealed before this time, and he begins his rule over ten nations. In the middle of the seven-year agreement, he

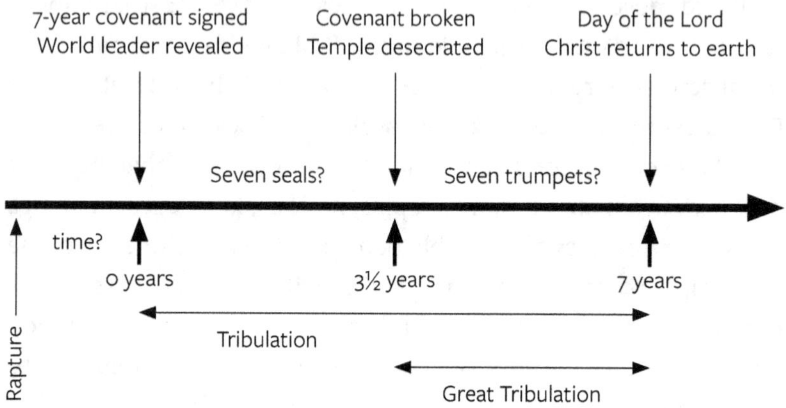

desecrates the temple and causes a revolt by predominately the Jews. This results in the start of a series of wars and persecution of all religious beliefs. The second half is called '*the Great Tribulation*' by Jesus in Matthew 24:21.

God now tells John that there will be two special witnesses during one of the forty-two month periods (verse 3). God's love for people never ceases, even during times of judgement (2 Peter 3:9). He raises up people who will spread his message of love and repentance.

These two witnesses are in addition to the 144,000 we read about earlier. Verse 3 tells us that they will prophesy – give God's messages for that group of people. They will be clothed in sackcloth – the clothing of mourning and sadness. They will be immune from harm and be given special power or ability from God. They have this protection for 1,260 days (42 months of 30 days).

Why two witnesses? The Torah required that a minimum of two witnesses is required to convict someone in a court of law. No one could be sentenced to death on the testimony of a single witness (Numbers 35:30, Deuteronomy 17:6, 19:15). The testimony of a single witness can be corrupted, incomplete, or subjective. But two witnesses who agree confirm the truth of the matter and make it credible.

> Two witnesses are often used in the Bible. Two angels testified to the resurrection of Jesus, and two angels testified to his ascension. God often sent people in pairs for specific tasks. Examples are Moses and Aaron, Joshua and Caleb, Paul and Silas, Timothy and Titus. The disciples were sent out in pairs. Two men talked with Jesus on the road to Emmaus.

What is meant by the two olive trees and two lampstands (verse 4)? It could refer to Zechariah 4 where Zechariah had a vision in which he saw two olive trees and one menorah. When he asked for an explanation, Zechariah was told the two olive trees are the two who are appointed to serve the Lord of all the earth (Zechariah 4:14). In Zechariah's time, these two people were Zerubbabel, the governor, and Joshua, the high priest.[2] Maybe the high priest at that time is one of the witnesses?

Olive trees could be symbolic of Israel (Romans 11:17-24). They could be symbolic of life (Genesis 8:11). Olive oil was used for light and food. Lampstands are symbolic of churches (Revelation 1:20), but Jesus also referred to individual lampstands (Matthew 5:14-16). By combining these two symbols, the two witnesses will bring spiritual light to the world during a time of spiritual darkness, and they will be a spiritual witness to the world.

What will these witnesses say? We get a hint from their clothing. Sackcloth is clothing associated with mourning or repentance.

2. *Agents of the Apocalypse*, p 92.

They will point Israel back to the Messiah that they rejected. They will testify about human wickedness.

They will explain the character of the judgements already encountered and those still to come. They will counter the aspirations of the ruler to be God. And they will claim Jerusalem is sinful on a par with Sodom and Egypt in the Old Testament.

Verses 5 and 6 says these two men will have unique spiritual powers. They will be given power to protect themselves. Fire from their mouth will consume anyone who tries to harm them. They can control the weather (prevent rain), turn water into blood, and strike the earth with plagues.

Are these powers implemented at the time the trumpets are being blown? Or will these be local demonstrations leading up to the multi-national effects from the trumpets being blown?

These two men are not going to be messed with. They will have the world's attention because of their powers. Imagine the impact if they declared no rain for New Zealand for three months. Or six months. They would certainly get New Zealand's attention.

These two men will demonstrate more divine power than Jesus did when he was doing his miracles. The difference is that Jesus was dealing predominantly with individuals, whereas these two men will be dealing with at least a national audience, and possibly an international audience.

There are various opinions about who these two people are.[3] Some writers think these two witnesses are Moses and Elijah.

- The judgements of the witnesses are like those used by Moses and Elijah. Elijah proclaimed a three and a half year drought, and he twice called fire down from heaven. Moses

3. *Bible Knowledge Commentary: New Testament*, p 955-956. *Agents of the Apocalypse*, pp 92-94.

turned water into blood and was instrumental in several plagues.

- Elijah is predicted to appear again before the '*great and dreadful Day of the Lord*' comes (Malachi 4:5-6). But Jesus indicated that this prediction was fulfilled by John the Baptist (Matthew 11:14, 17:10-12). However, when John was asked if he was Elijah, he stated that he was not (John 1:21).
- Both Moses and Elijah were involved in the transfiguration (Matthew 17:3).
- Both had their ministries interrupted for various reasons (Numbers 20:12, 1 Kings 19:16). But does that mean they have to return to fulfil their ministry?
- Israel expected both Moses and Elijah to return (Deuteronomy 18:15, Malachi 4:5-6, John 1:19-22).

One possible problem is that Moses has already died (Deuteronomy 34:5, Jude 9). Why is this a problem? See Hebrews 9:27.

Another suggestion is Enoch and Elijah since neither of them has died. One problem – the two witnesses are Jewish, but Enoch was not a Jew.

But the fact is these men are not named. They will almost certainly be two people alive at the time who are given a special anointing by God for this task. Is there any reason these men could not be from the 144,000 sealed servants?[4]

These two men have a limited time for their work. Verse 3 tells us they will be active for 1,260 days. Verse 7 tells us that during this time, they fulfil their testimony. They do not die prematurely

4. There is one reason I think they are not part of the 144,000 people. In Revelation 14:1 we read that all the 144,000 people are all with Jesus on Mount Zion. They are not missing two people.

like Elijah and Moses did. But when that time is up, the beast who comes from the Abyss will attack them, overpower them, and kill them.

Who is this beast? Revelation 13 talks about two beasts which are symbolic of specific people. One comes out of the sea and one comes out of the earth. The Abyss is pictured as being in the centre of the earth because it is bottomless. This beast here could be the same person as the beast coming out of the earth. Whoever he is, he is inspired by Satan because of his origin. He is the same person as the ruler on the white horse we saw when the first seal was broken.

Their bodies will lie in the street of the great city (verses 8-9). They won't be in a hurry to bury these men because the people want to gloat about their demise. Jewish law and tradition were to bury the people on the day of their death (Deuteronomy 21:22-23). Typical Muslim treatment of executed people is to leave the bodies on display for up to four days.

What city does this happen in? It is figuratively called Sodom and Egypt. Sodom is predominantly known for its sexual sin (Genesis 19:4-5), but it was destroyed because of its lack of social care for the less fortunate people in society and their debauchery (Ezekiel 16:49-50). Egypt was known for its physical and spiritual bondage (Exodus 1:11-14, 7:16), and for persecution of the Jewish nation.

The final phrase tells us the city is Jerusalem. At this time it is a city sinking in sin.

The last phrase tells us that Jesus is their Lord. This is an unusual expression for a Jew. These men know that Jesus was more than the Messiah. They knew He had been crucified for them. Jesus is the Messiah, and He is a Saviour. When He becomes both, He becomes the Lord of our lives. We live for Him, not for sin.

For three and a half days people around the world will gaze on their bodies (verses 9-10). How? Via global television and internet. We are the first generation with the technology to fulfil this prediction. That was impossible when the author was born. They will celebrate because these two men had tormented them with God's judgements. This is the only time in Revelation that we read about the people on earth rejoicing. Notice how they blame these men rather than themselves and their sin.

But after three and a half days they will be resurrected, '*stand on their feet, and cause terror in those who see them*' (verses 11-12). I wonder if this will be televised? Will they give one final message? The men will be called up to heaven, and they will '*go to heaven in a cloud while their enemies look on*'. Apparently, this event will be televised. The Greek word for '*look upon*' is *theoreo*, which means a transfixed stare.[5]

Believers at the Rapture are snatched away very quickly, '*in a flash, in the twinkling of an eye*' (1 Corinthians 15:52). These witnesses go slowly so the world can see them go. Will the police try to shoot them to prevent them ascending?

Given that Muslims revere Jerusalem, and in particular the Temple Mount,[6] will the bodies be resurrected from the Temple Mount? That would cause consternation to many Muslims because their avowed enemies are given a treatment not given to Muhammad. He was buried at Medina, and he was not resurrected. For these two witnesses to be resurrected would show they are more pious than Muhammad was.

At that hour an earthquake will hit Jerusalem (verse 13). Details of casualties are given so the event can be confirmed as a fulfilled prediction in the future. One tenth of the city will be collapsed and seven thousand people killed.[7]

---

5. *Agents of the Apocalypse*, p 102.
6. *The Truth about Muhammad*, p 83-87.
7. The 2020 population of Jerusalem is around 900,000 (worldpopulationreview.com/world-cities/jerusalem-population).

Muslims believe Muhammad rode an animal to heaven from Jerusalem. In 620 AD, Muhammad had a vision in which he miraculously travelled from Mecca to Jerusalem, then ascended into heaven from the Temple Mount and met the other prophets. The animal was a white horse-like animal with wings, called a Buraq. This incident is known in Islam as 'The Night Journey'.

The survivors will be terrified, but in this instance they will give glory to God in heaven. The resurrection of the witnesses and the earthquake finally cause people to recognise the power of God. Are the survivors part of the 144,000 people from the tribes that have God's seal? Elsewhere when God's judgements are given the people refuse to acknowledge God.

Two woes are past (verse 14). The third woe and the seventh trumpet are still to come. What were the two woes?

The first one was the hordes of locusts that sting people (Revelation 9:12).

The second woe was the earthquake that coincides with the resurrection of the two witnesses. I wonder how the timing of this event works with the army of 200 million. But more judgement is to come when the seventh trumpet is blown.

The seventh angel sounds his trumpet in verse 15. From here to the end of the chapter, all the action is in heaven. The previous trumpets all involved judgements on the earth. But we now see some reaction in heaven to the seventh trumpet.

There are loud voices proclaiming the transfer of the title to the earth. Who do the voices belong to? '*The kingdom of the world has become the kingdom of our Lord and His Christ.*' How did this happen? Sinful mankind is still on the earth. Revelation 9:20-21 tells us the people have not repented. The only people praising God are the survivors of the earthquake that destroys part of Jerusalem (Revelation 11:13).

Is this a prophetic statement? Maybe. Jesus Christ has not yet come to the earth to take possession and begin His rule. This is a statement that it will happen soon. The earth is in a bad state. There is environmental damage, there are demons causing havoc, there is worldwide war, and the people do not recognise God's judgements. But is it possible that Christ can reign without being physically on the earth?

We see that Jesus returns to the earth in Revelation 19:11. At that time, Christ will judge mankind and begin His rule over the nations (Revelation 19:15). This section looks forward to that event. The book of Revelation is not fully chronological.

The voices proclaim Christ will reign for ever and ever. This is also prophetic. Revelation 20 tells us that Christ will reign for 1,000 years (Revelation 20:6), then Satan is released for a final rebellion before he is finally punished. But after this Christ will reign for ever and ever in the new creation (Revelation 21).

Do you remember who the twenty-four elders are (verse 16)? Representatives of the church believers (chapter 4). They fall on their faces and worship God.

As a side issue, do we worship God properly? These church elders fall on their faces every time they worship God (Revelation 4:10, 7:11, 11:16, 19:4). Other people recorded as worshipping God face down are Abraham's servant (Genesis 24:26, 48 – first mention of worshipping face down), the Israelites in Egypt (Exodus 4:31, 12:27), Hezekiah when the temple is rededicated (2 Chronicles 29:28-29), Ezra (Nehemiah 8:6).

We tend to stand or sit during worship. Maybe we don't have a full understanding of Jesus Christ and what He has done for us, and so we don't worship Him like other people did. Maybe we need a personal revelation about Jesus Christ so that we can worship Him as He deserves to be worshipped.

The twenty-four elders worship God because He has begun to reign (verse 17). But notice how they describe God. '*The One who is and who was.*' How does John describe God in 1:4? What is missing in chapter 11? Why?

God has begun to reign. Reigning does not involve just physical presence on earth. There are spiritual powers behind the earthly rulers. Daniel was shown this in several visions.

- Daniel 7:26. The world ruler has his power taken away by a court. Where is this court? It is not on earth, because this person rules the earth. It is in heaven because verse 27 tells us the sovereignty, power and greatness are handed over to the saints of the Most High.

- Daniel 10:13. The prince of the Persian kingdom had resisted the angel bringing Daniel a message for 21 days. The prince is obviously a spiritual power because the angel is a spiritual being. Another spiritual being, Michael, came to help. Michael is called one of the chief princes. This passage also tells us these spiritual authorities have a hierarchy structure. If Michael is a chief prince, there must be lesser princes.

- Daniel 10:20. Daniel was talking to an angel who knew that another authority was coming, called the '*prince of Greece*'.

Paul had a similar understanding of political power (Romans 13:1). All authority is established by God (Isaiah 40:23-24). We find this hard to live with when we look at leaders like Robert Mugabe, Idi Amin, Adolf Hitler, Joseph Stalin and so on. These leaders have all killed or allowed multiple thousands of people to die.

Stalin is credited with over 20 million deaths,[8] while Hitler is said to be responsible for the death of over 6 million Jews,[9] plus other people groups. How can God allow this to happen? But we read that Stalin's authority was given by God, as was Hitler. What is going on here?

Does this show how cruel people can be to each other? Is this God's way to get people to pray for their country? Does it show how bad situations can get without God? Is this one of the ultimate results of sin?

In verse 18, the elders say, '*the nations were angry, and your wrath has come*'. Who or what are the nations angry about? They are angry at God. Daniel 8:23-25 talks about the future world leader. Verse 25 is the important bit. Who does the ruler take his stand against? The Prince of princes. Christ himself. This ruler has the guts to take on God in a military battle (how do you do that?). Guess who will win.

Psalm 2 talks about this time. Verse 2 has the kings of the earth gathering together against the Anointed One. Verse 4 says that God laughs and scoffs at them. Verse 5 says God rebukes them in his anger and terrifies them in his wrath. But that still does not stop the arrogant rulers trying to mount a military battle with God. Verses 7 to 9 tell us what God plans for the nations.

God will give the nations to His Son, Jesus Christ, to rule. Many people take verse 8 out of context and say that we should ask God for the nations. This verse is a quote from God telling Christ to ask for his inheritance. At some point in the future, Christ will ask for the nations and God will give them to him.

---

8. www.nytimes.com/1989/02/04/world/major-soviet-paper-says-20-million-died-as-victims-of-stalin
9. encyclopedia.ushmm.org/content/en/article/documenting-numbers-of-victims-of-the-holocaust-and-nazi-persecution

God's wrath has come (verse 18). We have seen his wrath in the first six trumpets. We will see more of God's wrath in Revelation 15 and 16. Psalm 2:12 says God's wrath can flare up in a moment.

I believe the seven bowls of God's wrath in Revelation 15 and 16 will take place over a short time period. Up to now there have been various time frames given. Scorpion stings last for five months. The two witnesses can affect the earth for up to three and a half years. But now the time has come for God's wrath.

We sometimes forget that God is a God of wrath. We like to think of God as a God of love, peace, mercy, grace, and forgiveness. We tend to forget that God is also a God of judgement, holiness, and righteousness. We forget that God is a God to be feared because of the punishments that he can dish out. The Bible tells us to fear God more than we are told to love God.

We need to get the balance right. Too much fear brings legalism where we make rules for ourselves so that we do not incur God's anger. This was the mistake the Pharisees made. Too much love brings in liberalism where anything goes because 'God loves me and will forgive me'. This is wrong. We need to remember God loves us as a person, but He hates our sin.

'*The time has come for judging the dead*' (verse 18). The final judgement of the dead is recorded in Revelation 20:11-13. All the righteous dead have been resurrected previously or will be soon.

- The church believers are already in heaven in chapter 4:4.

- People who believed God during the Tribulation are resurrected in Revelation 20:4. This is at the end of the Great Tribulation when Christ returns to the earth. Verse 5 tells us there will be another resurrection after the 1,000-year reign.

- The Old Testament believers will be resurrected when

Christ returns to the earth. Job 19:25-27 places his resurrection at the time Christ stands upon the earth. Isaiah 26:19-21 relates the awakening of dead bodies with when Christ comes to judge the world. Although many people believe they were resurrected when Jesus was resurrected.

We need to teach in our churches God will one day judge everybody. It is a subject largely missing from our Sunday teaching programmes. Hebrews 5:11-6:3 is a reprimand to the people it was written to. It says that the writer must go over some basic teaching again because they do not know or understand it. Among the topics listed in 6:1-2 are the subjects of resurrection and eternal judgement. Most churches have done some teaching on the resurrection of Christians or believers, but how many teach the resurrection and judgement of non-believers? Teaching this on Sundays will help achieve two things.

1. It will warn any unbelievers who come to church that there is a judgement waiting for them.
2. It should motivate us believers to do more evangelising among our workmates and people we meet.

'The time has come ... for rewarding your servants the prophets, and for your saints and those who reverence your name, both great and small.' All of God's judgements are a reward. Either a good reward for believing in God in whatever manner is appropriate to the era, or a bad reward for sin. The church believers have already been rewarded. Now it is the turn of the non-church believers to be rewarded. We are not told what those rewards will be. One of the rewards will be eternity with God.

'The time has come ... for destroying those who destroy the earth'. Who is this referring to? The coming world ruler and his helpers

were instrumental in destroying the earth. They caused widespread war, famine, and economic ruin. It could refer to Satan and his demons. They are the origin of sin in Genesis 3. They continue to encourage sin and cause both people and the environment to be destroyed.

In verse 19, God's temple in heaven is opened for John to see inside for the first time. Paul tells us in Hebrews 8:5 the Israelite priests served in a temple that was a copy and a shadow of the one in heaven. We have had this temple mentioned before in Revelation 7:15. The believers from the Tribulation serve God in His temple day and night.

John sees the ark of God's covenant inside the temple. The ark of covenant in the old temple was where God met with Israel (Exodus 25:21-22). This was the first item made for the tabernacle, showing how important relationship is to God. God wants relationship before anything else.

The ark was used as a reminder of God's covenant with Israel. It originally contained three objects: the stone tablets with the law of God, Aaron's staff, and a jar of manna (Deuteronomy 10:5, Numbers 17:10, Exodus 16:32-33, Hebrews 9:4). Why these three objects?[10] By the time it was taken into Solomon's temple, it contained only the stone tablets (1 Kings 8:9, 2 Chronicles 5:10).

Which covenant does the ark in heaven represent? There are several possibilities.

1. The covenant made in the Garden of Eden (Genesis 3:14-19). This is the first covenant made by God. It is a tripartite covenant, made between God, man, and Satan.
2. The covenant made with Noah (Genesis 9:1-16).

---

10. Do the tablets show God's requirements, Aaron's rod shows God's leadership, and the manna shows God's provision?

3. The covenant made with Abraham (Genesis 12:1-3, 15:13-16, 18-21, 17:3-14).

It cannot be any covenant later than this because the one Moses made was modelled on the one already in heaven (Hebrews 8:5). Personally, I believe it represents the first covenant God made to provide a means of dealing with sin.

Associated with seeing into the temple are cosmic changes. Lightning, rumblings, thunder, an earthquake, and a hailstorm. Thunder, lightning and earthquakes were associated with Moses at Mount Sinai (Exodus 19:16, 18).

These are similar to what happened when the seventh seal was opened (Revelation 8:5), except there is now a hailstorm. These are the same as the seventh bowl (Revelation 16:17-21). Are these parts of the same event? I think they simply indicate the start of a new era and method by which God interacts with mankind.

What can we learn from this? The time is coming when God will act in final judgement. Which judgement will you be at? The first one (1 Corinthians 3:13-15, 2 Corinthians 5:10), or the last one (Revelation 20:11-15)?

Chapter 9

The Red Dragon

The next three chapters in Revelation are a break from what is happening in heaven, and a return to what is happening on earth. These three chapters are the most important to grasp in terms of the events to happen during this period. Chapter 12 gives an overview of both the history of Israel, and Satan's attempts to derail God's plans. Chapter 13 gives an overview of two important and influential people during the Tribulation. We have already met one of these people, but we will cover him in much more detail. Chapter 14 is a bit of a 'wrap up' chapter that tidies up some loose ends.

Revelation 12

In verse 1 we are introduced to a woman who appeared in heaven with the sun, moon and twelve stars. Who is this woman? Two theories are the church or Israel. Which one?

Many commentators claim this is the church.[1] They claim the sun represents God, the moon represents the Israel from whom the church was originally given the light of the scriptures, and the twelve stars represent the twelve apostles. There is a problem with this picture. The church is represented in scripture as a pure virgin bride (2 Corinthians 11:2, Ephesians 5:25-27, Matthew 25 – parables

1. For example, *Armageddon and Beyond*, p 26.

of virgin brides). But verse 2 tells us this woman is pregnant. This woman therefore cannot be the church.

The symbolism of the sun, moon and twelve stars has appeared before in scripture. Where? Genesis 37:9-11. How did Jacob interpret this symbolism? He recognised it as symbolising his family. This woman is a symbol of Israel, the descendants of Jacob.[2] This is consistent with the Old Testament descriptions of Israel as a wife of God. Israel is often portrayed as a '*woman in travail*',[3] as in Isaiah 26:17-18, 66:7-8, Micah 4:10, 5:3. Isaiah 60:1-3 talks about the sun as Israel's future glory.

The woman was pregnant and about to give birth. To whom? The answer is in verse 5. Who? This goes back to Genesis 3:15 when God punishes Satan for deceiving Eve. The Hebrew says there will be hostility between the woman's seed and Satan's seed. There is a contradiction here. The seed is in the male, not the female. This verse is a prediction of the virgin birth of the Messiah.

Everywhere else in scripture, offspring are referred to as the seed of the man (Genesis 15:5, 21:12, 22:18, 2 Samuel 4:8, 1 Chronicles 17:11 and so on). The woman is figuratively giving birth to the Messiah. This is confirmed by this passage where it says, '*she gave birth to a ... male child who will rule all the nations with an iron sceptre (rod).*' Jesus Christ is the only person to rule with an iron rod (Psalm 2:9, Revelation 19:15).

It is interesting that as the lineage of the Messiah has been defined by God, the attacks directed toward Israel have intensified. After Eden, demonic angels tried to breed with women to dilute the pure seed (Genesis 6:1-3).

Noah's flood was because of sin and inter-breeding in the world. God selected Abraham, and his descendants come under attack.

---

2. *Bible Knowledge Commentary, New Testament*, p 957.
3. *Agents of the Apocalypse*, pp 115-116.

Esau tried to kill Jacob (Genesis 27:41). While Israel is in Egypt, the land promised to Abraham is filled with sin and idolatry. The Egyptians try to kill off the Israelite males (Exodus 1:15-17).

The Israelites are attacked by various groups as they go through the wilderness. The Gibeonites try to deceive Israel (Joshua 9). When God promises the Messiah will come from David, in-fighting threatened to wipe out David's family line. Various descendants are under attack and are hidden as children.

The royal line is taken into captivity by Nebuchadnezzar. Jesus himself was a target during his life (Matthew 2:17, Luke 4:29, 13:31, John 8:59, 10:31). Satan's final attack will be an intense persecution of Israel during the Great Tribulation.

An enormous red dragon appears in verse 3 with '*seven heads, ten horns, and seven crowns*'. Does this sound familiar? Daniel 7:7 talks about a beast with ten horns, but three are displaced leaving a final seven horns. Red is symbolic of what? War and bloodshed. We know there is a war coming up. This dragon is defined in verse 9. It is the devil, Satan.

What is the meaning of seven heads, ten horns and seven crowns? The most common consensus is that the emerged final empire will consist of initially ten nations, but three merge and are rearranged into seven nations with seven leaders (Daniel 7:24, Revelation 17:12). Satan will be the spiritual power behind the rulers of this part of the world.

A recent idea is that the ten horns are ten '*kings*' who are the leaders of ten major corporations. Notice that in Revelation 17:12 that they do not have kingdoms. How can you be a king without a kingdom? But the kings could be the rulers of commercial enterprises that are international, and often have a financial turnover that exceeds many of the countries that they trade in.

They may have expertise in technology that the future ruler(s) will be interested in, such as data collection and analysis, surveillance, satellite technology, artificial intelligence, digital currency, etc.[4]

For example, the DHS in the USA is already using data companies to spy on its citizens.[5] Examples could include Google, Facebook, Twitter, and other companies with a similar large customer base that can be mined for personal data.

There is an alternative interpretation of this. There have been six major kingdoms or empires throughout history that controlled Israel, with one more predicted to come in the future. The six historical ones are Egypt, Assyria, Babylon, Persia, Greece, and either Rome or Parthia.[6] The future one will be the emerged final empire. Why ten horns? One idea is because the Greek empire was split into four after the death of Alexander the Great, giving a total of ten geographical regions.

Another idea is the world will be divided among ten major groupings. Or they could be ten nations surrounding Israel.

The serpent's tail '*swept a third of the stars out of heaven and flung them to the earth*' in verse 4. The stars are symbolic of angels (Job 38:7, Isaiah 14:13, Jude 13, Revelation 1:20). At some point in the past Satan led a rebellion against God that involved a third of the angels. They were thrown out of heaven and flung to the earth (Isaiah 14:12-20). Satan had pride in his heart and wanted to be like God, but he has been demoted to the earth.

Ezekiel 28:12-19 has more details. This passage is obviously not talking about the physical king of Tyre; he was not in the Garden of Eden, he was not an angel, he was neither sinless nor blameless. This is talking about Satan, the power behind the king of Tyre.

---

4. See a discussion of this topic at www.youtube.com/watch?v=eKxkoXwv884. This is based on an article in *The Prophecy Watcher*, Nov 2020, pp 4-10, 16-17.
5. www.wnd.com/2021/03/feds-contractors-compile-lists-dissidents
6. See Appendix 5 for a discussion on this topic.

Satan was originally made perfect and full of wisdom. He was a guardian cherub, one of those around the throne of God. He was blameless until pride caused his expulsion. Pride was followed by violence and dishonesty. His ultimate end is to become of no importance to anyone.

When Satan was cast to the earth, he apparently took one third of the angels with him. When did this event happen? Two theories are common.

One theory is between Genesis 1:1 and 1:2. The word '*was*' in verse 2 is *hayah* which means 'to become' or 'to come to pass'.[7] The verse can read '*the earth became formless*'. This idea says there is an undetermined amount of time between verse 1 and verse 2, and verse 3 is the start of a re-created earth.

The earth became formless when Satan was cast down to the original earth because he destroyed it.[8] There is no other scripture to back up this idea, but it is hinted at in the book of Enoch.

The second theory is sometime between the creation and the temptation. The same word *hayah* is used in Genesis 3:1. An alternate reading could be '*the serpent became more cunning than any wild animal.*' This could tie in Ezekiel 20:13 where Satan was in Eden, but it is not necessary for that. We know Satan was there in the serpent.

The dragon '*stood in front of the woman to devour the child the moment it was born*' (verse 4b). Who is the woman? Israel. Who is the child? Jesus. King Herod had all babies born in Bethlehem at the time killed (Matthew 2:16). His successor tried to kill Jesus (Luke 13:31). The Jews tried to kill Jesus at least three times (Luke 4:28-30, John 8:59, 10:31).

Verse 5 reveals the identity of the child. Compare the job

7. *Vine's Dictionary of Old and New Testament Words*, p 13.
8. *Birthright*, pp 45-50.

description of the son with Psalm 2:9, Genesis 49:10, Psalm 45:6, 47:8, 110:5-6, Isaiah 2:4, 42:1, Jeremiah 10:6-7, Ezekiel 20:33, Zechariah 9:9-10, Revelation 2:27, 19:15. The child is the Messiah who will reign on the earth. He has already come to earth, but the Jews did not recognise Him as their Messiah. He ascended back into heaven (Acts 1:10) where He is seated on His throne (Hebrews 1:3, 13, 8:1). This single verse contains three significant events in the Messiah's life:[9]

1. His incarnation: '*She bore a male child.*'
2. His ascension: '*Her child was snatched up to God and his throne.*'
3. His second coming: '*He will rule all nations with an iron sceptre.*'

Some commentators think this is a reference to the Rapture. The church is the body of Christ and is taken up into heaven where they gather around the throne of God. The same word is used here as for describing the Rapture (*harpazo*). But the rapture of the church would not be sufficient to describe a man-child being delivered from Satan.[10]

Also, the church is described as a pure virgin (2 Corinthians 11:2, see also Ephesians 5:25-27), not a pregnant woman.

The reference to 1,260 days in verse 6 puts this at the start of the Great Tribulation. There is a gap of around 2,000 years between verses 5 and 6. This is the period that we are presently in. Verse 5 has already happened, but verse 6 is still future.

Israel will flee into the desert for protection during the Great Tribulation. Where to specifically? South-western Jordan across the Dead Sea. Daniel 11:41 lists the areas which will be exempt from the future ruler's armies.

---

9. *Agents of the Apocalypse*, p 116.
10. *Bible Knowledge Commentary: New Testament*, p 958.

Notice the '*place is prepared for her by God*', and she is taken care of. If God can care for and feed around one million people in the wilderness for forty years, then He can easily care for other groups of people for three and a half years. Which raises an interesting question; will these people be eating manna again?

Another spiritual war erupts in verse 7. Michael is the angel in charge of Israel (Daniel 10:13, 21, 12:1). Satan will launch a war in heaven before being again defeated and ejected. He will begin a great war on Israel. Hitler's holocaust destroyed one third of all Jews in the world at the time. The coming war against Israel will destroy two thirds of all Jews (Zechariah 13:8).

There have been two on-going wars throughout history. The first is between angels led by Satan against the angels led by God. The second is between people led by Satan against people led by God. There is a war between Michael and Satan (see Daniel 10 and note what Michael is doing).

Satan and his angels are kicked out of heaven in verse 8. Many people are surprised to learn that Satan has not yet been kicked out of heaven. But in fact, Satan still has access to heaven (Job 1:6-7, 2:1, Zechariah 3:1, Luke 22:31, Ephesians 6:12) where he accuses us before God. The good news for us is that Jesus Christ has paid the penalty for our sin so there is no basis for Satan to claim we deserve punishment.

We have Jesus acting as our advocate before God (1 Timothy 2:5, Hebrews 7:25, 9:24). But Satan can claim that we are not following Christ when we do things that go contrary to what Christ desires.

Verse 9 names the dragon, and his activity is identified. He '*leads the whole world astray*' (Isaiah 14:12, 16-17). Notice he is called '*that ancient serpent*' identifying him as the person who deceived Eve (Genesis 3:1-7, 13). Deception has been happening ever since that time. But his immediate fate is that he and his angels are hurled down to the earth (Luke 10:18, John 12:31). A more permanent fate awaits them later.

It is interesting that Satan's path is always downwards. He was expelled from heaven to earth (verse 9), will be imprisoned in a bottomless pit (Revelation 20:2-3), and ultimately finish in the lake of fire (Revelation 20:10).[11]

A loud voice is heard in verses 10-11 declaring several things about Satan. Who is this voice? We are not told, but I suspect it is an important angel.

- The authority of Christ is now being established and the kingdom of God has arrived.

- Satan is called '*the accuser of our brothers*', and we read that he accuses us before God day and night. He has now been dispossessed of a place in heaven. Question – after God demoted Satan, why did he continue to have access to God? Let me know if you have any suggestions.

- Who has overcome Satan who by the blood of the Lamb? How does this happen? (Hebrews 9:13-14, James 4:7, 1 Peter 5:8-9) I think the context implies the believers are the overcomers.

- They overcame '*by the blood of the Lamb and by the word of their testimony.*' By accepting the death and resurrection of Jesus as the penalty for their sin, and by acknowledging what Jesus has done (Romans 10:9-13).

- Martyrdom is another way of resisting the devil. Everywhere the blood of believers has been shed results soon afterwards

11. *Agents of the Apocalypse*, p 117.

in Christ being victorious. There is an unseen power working through sacrifice, especially the sacrifice of blood (2 Kings 3:26-27). Are you prepared to sacrifice your life for Christ?

Heaven and its inhabitants will rejoice because of this event (verse 12). But the earth and the sea are warned to be afraid because this is now the dwelling place for Satan. He is filled with fury because he knows his time is short. How short? Who does he take his fury out on?

After being expelled from heaven, Satan pursues the woman, or Israel in verse 13. This is predicted in Daniel 7:25, 8:24 where the future ruler fights and oppresses the '*holy people*'.

Why does Satan hate Israel so intensely? First, because Christ comes from this nation. Second, if Satan can destroy Israel, this would deny its people a home when the Messiah returns to establish his kingdom. Third, if Satan can eradicate the Jews, this would cause God's reputation to be ruined. God has promised numerous future blessings to them, and it would show that God was incapable of fulfilling them.

But Israel is given supernatural help in escaping from Israel to the hiding place in the desert in verse 14. Jesus warned about the need to flee in a hurry (Matthew 24:15-20). Are the two wings of a great eagle representing modern aircraft?

Physically, it is not a great distance from Jerusalem to western Jordan (about 120 km). The Old Testament uses the idiom of eagle's wings as fast-moving (Exodus 19:4, Deuteronomy 32:11-12). The metaphor of eagle's wings indicates the speed at which Israelites flee. The verses quoted describe God's grace as he delivered them from Egypt.[12] Again here, we have God's grace as he delivers Israelites from destruction.

12. *Agents of the Apocalypse*, p 127.

Where do they flee to? Into Jordan. Into the area that used to belong to their former enemies; the Edomites, Moabites and Ammonites (Daniel 11:41). Edom denied the Israelites permission to pass through their country when they were travelling through the wilderness (Numbers 20:14-21). Now Edom will hide the same nation.

It is interesting Jordan is the only Arab country with an agreement with Israel and actively keeps it (as at April 2022). How long is Israel cared for? Where have we heard this before? (Daniel 7:25) During this time, those in hiding are safe from the serpent's reach.

Notice a change in wording. Satan is now called a serpent instead of a dragon. Why? Is it because the serpent was the animal of deceit in the Garden of Eden? Or is it because he is now confined to earth? Chinese tradition says dragons could fly, and the Welsh flag shows a dragon with wings.

In verse 15, the serpent is now seen to spew water from his mouth and cause a flood to try to dislodge Israel. Is this a literal flood, or is it symbolic? Water is a symbol of the cleansing power of the scriptures, especially when it is associated with Christ.

A flood coming from the mouth of the serpent could be symbolic of false words, lies or propaganda designed to displace the hiding Israelites.

This idea ties in with the changing of wording from dragon to serpent. It fits with the description of the future ruler who is described as a chronic liar and deceiver.

It could be a flood of armies hunting down the Israelites to exterminate them. Two thirds of the Jews will be killed during this time (Zechariah 13:8). What happens to the 144,000 from chapter 7 during this time? (Revelation 14:1)

It could be a literal flood caused by Satan because the rulers of Jordan are thwarting him from getting at the Israelites. A physical flood would cause the people to come out of hiding and be hunted easier. But the topography of Israel or western Jordan does not lend itself to a physical flood.[13]

Whichever way you interpret the flood, it is ineffective (verse 16). The flood is absorbed by the earth. If the flood is a flood of lies and propaganda, the rest of the world ignores it and does nothing to help find the Israelites. If it is a flood of armies, the hilly terrain allows the people to remain hidden. The precedent was when Saul was hunting for David (1 Samuel 23:14, 26, 24:3).

If it is a natural flood, then the earth could open and absorb the water. After all, if God can make water come out of a rock (Exodus 17:5-6, Numbers 20:10-11), He can make water go into the earth (Numbers 16:31-32).

Because the dragon (not the serpent) could not reach the hiding Israelites, it makes war against the rest of the Jews and other believers in verse 17. Notice the two groups targeted. The '*rest of her offspring*' are the Jews scattered around the world. But there is the spiritual offspring – those '*who obey God's commandments and who hold to the testimony of Jesus*'. The two groups targeted are Jews and believers – anyone who will not worship the future beast (Revelation 13:8, 15).

Some versions have a verse 18, but it is really the beginning of chapter 13.

Chapter 12 is a summary of the entire history of God redeeming His chosen people. It is a summary of Satan's war against God. It started some time before the creation and will continue until the final judgement at some time in the future.

What can we learn from this chapter?

1. God is perfectly able to protect His people against the most satanic attack, including us. The history of the Jews is proof

13. *Bible Knowledge Commentary: New Testament*, p 960.

that God has preserved them throughout a history of various rulers trying to wipe the Jews off the face of the earth.

2. God is still sovereign over Satan, despite our apparent weakness to resist temptation. Job is a perfect example. God allows Satan to test Job, but limits what Satan can do in each test. How often do we thank God for that protection? (See 1 Corinthians 10:13.)

Chapter 10

The Beast From the Sea

In times of universal deceit,
telling the truth will be a
revolutionary act.
- George Orwell, 1903-1950, author

Chapters 12, 13 and 14 take a break from what is happening in heaven and describe what will happen on the earth. These three chapters are the most important to grasp in terms of the events to happen during this period.

Chapter 12 gave us an overview of the history of Israel, and the struggle that Israel has with Satan. Satan's plan has always been to disrupt what God is doing through people, and Israel is one of the means why which God has accomplished things in the past. The Bible predicts that God will use Israel again in the future.

Chapter 13 gives us an overview of two important people during the Tribulation period. These two people work in conjunction with each other, and both are absolutely controlled by Satan. We have already met one of these people, but this chapter will describe him in much more detail. This chapter continues from the previous one. The difference is the emphasis is on two people that Satan uses rather than Satan himself.

Revelation 13:1-10

Verse 1 could be considered as the last verse of chapter 12. After trying to destroy Israel and failing, the dragon makes war against people who obey God's commands.

Satan stands on the seashore. What does the sea symbolise? (Daniel 7:2) Humanity, especially the Gentile nations. Mankind is always restless because of sin. Likewise, the sea is always moving, and it is regularly stormy. People without Jesus Christ cannot find rest. Sin is the source of temptations we all experience, and without Christ in our lives, we are inclined to yield to those temptations.

Out of the sea came a beast with '*ten horns, seven heads and ten crowns*'. The Greek word for beast is *therion*, which means a beast of prey or a wild animal. This contrasts with *zoa* which means living creatures or domesticated animals.[1]

'*On each head was a blasphemous name*'. Where have we seen this picture before? (Daniel 7:7-8, 24) But in chapter 12 we have the dragon with seven heads, ten horns, and seven crowns (verse 3). What is the meaning behind the ten horns and seven heads (re-read the last chapter if you have forgotten)? The fact that this person comes out of the sea indicates that he is a Gentile.

Daniel 7:25 tells us the beast will speak against God. Daniel 11:36 tells us that he will speak against every god. Revelation tells us that he will have blasphemous names. What does this mean? A name that indicates that he thinks he is God? Or a name that denigrates God? Or are they names that blaspheme all gods worshipped throughout the world?

John now gives a description of the beast in verse 2. '*It resembled a leopard*' – a fast-moving and stealthy predator. It '*had feet like a bear*' – claws that grab its prey and doesn't let it escape. It has

1. *Vine's Dictionary*, p 53.

'the mouth of a lion' – devours everything it gets. These animals are all mentioned in Daniel 7:4-6. This beast is a composite of the first three great world empires. What are they? (Babylon (lion), Persia (bear), Greece (leopard).) This may indicate the person that the beast represents comes from this part of the world, the Middle East.

There is another possibility, based on recent progress in genetic engineering. This person could be a hybrid human-animal.[2] It is well documented in scientific journals that many organisations are trying to combine various animal characteristics into the human genome. For example, cat's eye DNA into human eyes so soldiers can see in the dark, lizard tail regeneration genes into people so they can heal quicker.[3]

How much animal DNA can be incorporated into humans before God considers them to be non-human? Is that why this person is called a *'beast'*? If they are non-human, can they be spiritually saved or have their sin forgiven? (This question becomes relevant as more mRNA vaccines are developed.)

Who does this person get his power from? Verse 2 tells us it is from Satan. Paul calls this person *'the lawless one'* (2 Thessalonians 2:9). Notice that Satan delegates to him three things: power, throne, and great authority.

Power gets this man his position. A throne signifies a position of rulership. This person will be effectively the ruler of the world, either directly or as a by-product of his influence from the Middle East. Satan also gives him great authority – authority and influence greater than his position should justify.

In verse 3, one of the heads seemed to have a fatal wound but it

---

2. *Hybrids, Supersoldiers and the Coming Genetic Apocalypse*, Vol 2, pp 100-103.
3. Ibid, pp 250-265.

healed. Does this head represent the ruler we are discussing? Or is it one of his underlings? I think the context implies it is the ruler himself that is injured.

Satan cannot resurrect people. Only God has the power to give life. Only God has been credited with any resurrections recorded in the Bible (1 Kings 17:22, 2 Kings 4:32-35, 13:21, Mark 5:41-42, Luke 7:14-15, John 11:43-44). But Satan obviously has the power to heal.

Some people think the deadly wound prediction has already been fulfilled. One claim is that the beast is the Roman Catholic Church, and the deadly wound occurred when Pope Pius VI was taken prisoner by Napoleon's General Berthier and later died as a prisoner in France. The revival came when Mussolini gave the Vatican State back in 1929, and it has gained greater power and influence since.[4] If this is true, what was the beast with the ten horns and seven heads?

A related claim is the Roman Empire died when it collapsed, and it will get revived in the future. Another claim is the beast is someone from history, such as Judas Iscariot, Nero, Hitler, Stalin, Kissinger, etc.[5] But as far as I know, none of these candidates have survived a fatal head wound.

The whole world will be astonished, and it seems that this apparently miraculous healing causes the world to follow him. What does this mean? Verse 14 says the wound was caused by a sword, and that it happened to the beast himself. Is this an actual sword, or does it symbolise a wound caused by a weapon that John was unfamiliar with? For example, a terrorist attack or an assassination attempt? A failed car bomb?

Zechariah 11 has a description of a worthless shepherd. This person is a leader who oppresses the land and does not care for

---

4. *2017: 500 Years After Luther*, p 9.
5. Quoted in *The Bible Knowledge Commentary: New Testament*, p 960.

the people under his authority (11:15-16). We have a physical description of this person in verse 17. A sword strikes this person on '*his right arm and his right eye*'. As a result, he is blind in his right eye and his right arm is useless. Is Zechariah describing the same person as the beast?

Maybe the sword is John's way of describing an assassination attempt on the beast. Or does his power diminish because most people are right-handed? Arms and eyes are symbolic of strength and intelligence.

It is interesting the sword is still the weapon used by Arabs to punish religious crimes. The only punishment in the Koran for changing religion or blaspheming Allah is beheading. How many hostages have the Arab countries beheaded over the last few years? We saw numerous beheadings from ISIS when they first established themselves in Iraq in 2014.

It is possible that if this person sets himself above all Gods, someone with a strong Jihad instinct will try to assassinate this person with a sword and almost succeed. Maybe the attack is captured on TV and the world watches as this man recovers from what should have been fatal injuries.

Muslims believe in the return of the Mahdi, their version of the Messiah coming to rule the world in peace.[6] The Ottoman Empire ruled most of the Middle East from the fall of the Eastern leg of the Roman Empire in the 1400s. This empire was ruled by the Caliph.

The Ottoman Empire came to an end on 3 March 1924 when the Caliphate was abolished by the first president of the Turkish Republic, Mustafa Kemal Ataturk. The Republic of Iran and ISIS are both trying to re-establish the Caliphate, although from different origins. Is this person the next Caliph ruling a resurgent Islam republic or coalition?

6. *God's War on Terror*, p 53-56.

Verse 4 is interesting. Satan is worshipped because '*he has given authority to the beast*'. Satan has always desired worship (Isaiah 14:13-14), and at last he gets his wish. But why do people worship Satan? Daniel 7:25 tells us the ruler sets up a religion based upon Satan worship. He speaks against God, and he oppresses everyone who is a believer in God. He also tries to change the set times and laws.

This probably means the religious festivals and religious laws, but it could also apply to the secular calendar which is still based on the seven-day week established by God (Genesis 1). This will affect every religion, not only Christianity. All religions will become subservient to him. He even sets himself up in the temple as though he is God (2 Thessalonians 2:4). See also Daniel 8:23-25, 9:27 and 11:37.

Satan is worshipped because '*he has given authority to the beast*'. Obviously, the beast publicly acknowledges Satan as the source of his authority, so the people know this. This causes them to worship Satan. But the people also worship the beast. Not only is this man the political leader, but also a religious leader of the world. He gives the impression of being all-powerful with the population praising him in language similar to the ways God is worshipped (Psalm 35:10, 71:19, 89:6, 8, 113:5, Isaiah 46:9, Jeremiah 10:6-7, Micah 7:18).

Satan sets up a counterfeit religion with himself at the head (imitating the Father) and the beast as the king (imitating Christ). When is this likely to occur? (Does Daniel 9:27 indicate it will be when he goes into the holiest part of the temple?) The beast is a counterfeit Christ.[7]

---

7. *Agents of the Apocalypse*, p 143.

Christ	Beast (Antichrist)
Son of God (John 1:34)	Son of perdition (2 Thessalonians 2:3)
Holy One (Mark 1:24)	Lawless one (2 Thessalonians 2:8)
Came down from heaven (John 3:13)	Came up from the bottomless pit (Revelation 11:7)
Energised by the Holy Spirit (Luke 4:14)	Energised by Satan (Revelation 13:4)
Does the Father's will (John 6:38)	Does his own will (Daniel 11:36)
Cleansed the Temple (John 2:14-16)	Defiles the Temple (Matthew 24)
Man of sorrows (Isaiah 53:3)	Man of sin (2 Thessalonians 2:3)
Humbled himself (Philippians 2:8)	Exalts himself (Daniel 11:37)
Called 'the Lamb' (John 1:36)	Called 'the Beast' (Revelation 11:7)
Received up to heaven (Luke 24:51)	Sent to the lake of Fire (Revelation 19:20)

Verse 5 tells us that he speaks proud words and blasphemies. We have already seen this from many passages in Daniel. Pride and blasphemy are the two hallmarks of his personality.

His authority lasts for forty-two months. Does that sound familiar? Daniel 9:27 tells us this person reigns for half of a seven-year period. Satan is given free rein on the earth for three and a half years, but his time is still under God's control.

The beast slanders God, heaven, and the angels (verse 6). Most people today will only blaspheme against God and Christ but go no further. This person is so demonic that he also blasphemes against heaven and the angels. But does the phrase '*those who live in heaven*' mean more than this? Could it also mean believers who have been resurrected earlier?

Verse 7 says he tries to wipe out any form of God worship from the earth and conquers the believers. This contrasts with Matthew 16:18 where Jesus says that the gates of Hades will not overcome the church. The church is obviously not in this scenario. This war is largely against Judaism and its followers, but also against any believers in Christ. The 144,000 sealed people we read about in chapter 7 will be kept safe because we read they meet Christ when he returns to Mount Zion (Revelation 14:1). We also know from chapter 12 that the Jews who flee to south-west Jordan will also be kept safe.

The beast is given authority over every person on earth. He is in effect the ultimate world dictator. He has authority over all people, something that the United Nations has not succeeded in doing. Daniel 7:23 tells us the beast's kingdom will devour the whole earth, trampling down and crushing everyone.

Mankind has always recognised the need for leadership, but they have rejected God as a leader many times. First, was in the Garden of Eden where both Adam and Eve disobeyed God (Genesis 2:17, 3:6). Second, when the people disregarded Noah's warnings (2 Peter 2:5). Third, the Israelites turned away from God by rebelling numerous times (Numbers 11:1, 14:1, 21:4-5, Judges 3:7, 12, 4:1, 6:1, 8:33, 10:6, 13:1, 1 Samuel 2:12, 8:7, 1 Kings 11:3-6, 12:28-30, etc). The Jews rejected their Messiah Jesus and had Him crucified. Finally, mankind has been in constant rebellion against God (Romans 1:18-23).

We are again told in verse 8 all the inhabitants of the earth will worship this person. Finally, man's goal of a universal religion will be accomplished. The Pope is currently trying to reconcile a number of religions.[8] He has initiated discussions with both the Anglican church and the various Orthodox churches to try to establish a single Christian church worldwide. He has also apologised to the Arabs for some of the atrocities committed during the Crusades, and he has discussed forming a united religion with Islam.[9,10]

The World Council of Churches has a single, universal Christian faith as one of its goals. These efforts may be partly successful, and they are probably helping to prepare the world for the final unification step.

The final religion will be worship of Satan and the beast.

There is a qualifier to the people engaged in this worship. There is a small group who will not worship them. People whose names are written in the Book of Life do not worship this man. The Book of Life is used again in Revelation 20:13, 15. People whose name is not written in the book are eternally punished. This book belongs to the Lamb that was slain. Who is that? And when was the Lamb slain?

Time has a different relationship with God than it does with us. We know that Jesus was crucified on the Passover of April 32 AD. But this verse tells us that Christ, the Lamb, was slain before the creation of the world. Ephesians 1:4 tells us God chose us before the creation of the world. God exists outside of time, so He sees the Lamb as slain before the creation.

No matter how long or short a time since you became a believer

---

8. en.wikipedia.org/wiki/Catholic_Church_and_ecumenism and A *Woman Rides the Beast*, pp 5-11.
9. en.wikipedia.org/wiki/Pope_Francis:_ecumenism_and_interreligious_dialogue
10. www.usip.org/publications/2019/02/pope-francis-cradle-islam-what-might-it-bring

in Christ, God had chosen you before the world was created. What an amazing fact.

Verses 9 and 10 sound similar to the ending of the messages to the seven churches in chapters 2 and 3. But this message is given to individuals instead of a church. Where is the church at this time? What is the message for this time? Two warnings can be taken from verses 9 and 10.

The first warning is that the final universal religion will not deliver what it promises. All religions promise that if you live by its standards, you will receive a good life on earth, spiritual fulfilment, and some sort of reward in the afterlife. This religion will result in spiritual captivity when you follow it. It will ultimately result in captivity in hell for its followers.

The second warning is for the believers at that time. Executions will be common, and few people will escape. The believers at that time will need patient endurance and faithfulness to survive. We will see other reasons in the next chapter.

What else does the Bible say about this world leader?

1. The leader is likely to emerge from what was previously the Seleucid part of the Greek Empire. Daniel 11:1-35 gives the history of the wars between the Seleucids and the Ptolemies. Verses 36-40 concentrate on Antiochus Epiphanes who desecrated the temple. Daniel continues from this person to the world ruler. So, the future world leader may come out of the region around Iraq, Iran, Jordan or that area.

2. Micah 5:5-6 talks about the Assyrian who will come into Israel and tread in their palaces. The Assyrian is also mentioned in Isaiah 10:5-25, 14:25, and 30:31. The Assyrian empire preceded the Babylonian empire by several centuries. It covered the region we know today as Syria and Iraq.

Micah 5:6 mentions Nimrod. He was the first world dictator who ruled from Babylon (Genesis 10:8-10). The future leader will be similar to a return of Nimrod. If you believe in taking the Bible literally, Babylon will be rebuilt (more on that later) and may well be the leader's capital.

3. He is accepted by the world as a false Christ. The Greek word is *Antichristo*, which means 'instead of Christ'. He is a pseudo-Christ, but he is also against Christ. He is initially accepted by Israel as their Messiah until he desecrates the temple, and they realise their mistake. He is apparently also accepted by the Muslim world who are expecting the Twelfth Imam at any time. The name of 'Antichrist' is given to this person in many books.

4. A quick summary of various verses gives the following description of this person:
   - An intellectual genius (Daniel 7:20, 8:23, Ezekiel 28:3).
   - A persuasive orator (Daniel 7:20, Revelation 13:5).
   - A shrewd political manipulator (Daniel 11:21).
   - A successful commercial genius (Daniel 8:25, 11:38, 43, Ezekiel 28:4-5).
   - A forceful military leader (Daniel 8:24, Revelation 6:2, 13:4, Isaiah 14:16).
   - A powerful organiser (Revelation13:1-2, 17:17).
   - A unifying religious guru (2 Thessalonians 2:4, Revelation 13:3, 14-15).
   - A master of deceit (Daniel 8:25, Matthew 24:24).

What can we learn from this chapter?

We need a personal relationship with Jesus Christ to avoid being deceived by pseudo-Christs. We need to know the real Christ, not the imitation Christ. Jesus warned us three times in Matthew 24 about being deceived. We must know the real God who gives salvation. This is the only way to prevent us being deceived by the fake who sets himself up as God.

We also need to be aware that Satan can and does mimic many of the activities that God does. This chapter shows us that Satan can apparently heal what appears to be a fatal wound. Speaking in 'tongues' is a common phenomenon among pagan religions. Séances and Ouija boards are used to gain information about the future. Not all miracles are from God. We need discernment to know which events are satanic and which are Godly.

Chapter 11

The Beast From the Earth

When men choose not to believe in God,
they do not thereafter believe in nothing,
they then become capable of
believing in anything.
- *G.K. Chesterton, 1874-1936, writer*

Revelation chapter 13 gives us an overview of two important people during the seven-year Tribulation period. We have already met the first person. He is the beast that comes out of the sea, and he is destined to be the world ruler. We meet the second person in the remainder of this chapter. These two people work together as we will see.

Revelation 13:11-18

John sees a second beast in verse 11. But this one comes out of the earth, whereas the previous one came out of the sea. If the sea is symbolic of the nations, what is the earth symbolic of? The commentaries have few comments to make about this.

- Some suggest it could mean this person is a Jew, but they cannot find any supporting scripture to back up this claim.

The best suggestion is that the sea represents Gentile nations, therefore this person must be a Jew. But we have no clues as to this person's nationality or origins.[11]

- Another suggestion is that this person comes out of an organisation that is already in existence. Because of the religious nature of this beast, could he be an existing church leader at that time? The Roman Catholic Church is often suggested as a possibility,[12] largely because they are leading the inter-faith dialogue. But it could be any leading cleric from any religion, including Islam.

The fact the Bible describes this person also as a beast gives us a clue that he is not going to be a nice person.

He has '*two horns like a lamb, but he speaks like a dragon*'. You could not pick two animals so diametrically opposed to each other. As a lamb, this person will appear meek to imitate Jesus. As a dragon, he will be demonic. Jesus warned about false prophets '*who come to you in sheep's clothing*' (Matthew 7:15).

What are horns symbolic of? Authority. Lamb's horns are much smaller than horns on goats, bulls, deer, etc. This person appears to have less authority than the first beast, but as we will find out he will work together with the first beast.[13]

What does '*speaking like a dragon*' mean? The only dragon in the Bible is Satan. This person speaks Satanic messages. Revelation 16:13, 19:20 and 20:10 all refer to this person as the '*false prophet*'. This person speaks messages claiming to be from God, but they are actually from Satan. In other words, he is deceptive. That is

11. *Bible Knowledge Commentary: New Testament*, p 962.
12. *Exo-Vaticana*, pp 535-536 and *A Woman Rides the Beast*, pp 44-46.
13. *Agents of the Apocalypse*, p 169.

probably why he works well with the first beast – they are both infamous for being deceptive.

We see in verse 12 that the false prophet and the ruler work together. He exercises all the authority of the first beast. He exercises political power and reinforces the rule of the Antichrist. He also makes the earth dwellers worship the ruler '*whose fatal wound has been healed*'. The one world religion mentioned in the last chapter is based on worshipping a man instead of worshipping God.

This is the greatest question that everybody must answer for themselves. Who will you worship? Jesus Christ? Or Satan?

Can you see similarities between this religion and both Christianity and Judaism?

- Both involve a working trinity: Satan, the first beast (the world leader), and the false prophet, similar to the Father, the Son or Messiah, and the Holy Spirit.
- Both involve worship of the second person in the trinity: either the ruler, or Jesus Christ the Messiah.
- Both involve a resurrection: the ruler received a fatal wound but was apparently healed by Satan; Jesus Christ the Messiah died at Calvary and was resurrected by God.
- Both involve a third party to cause people to worship: the false prophet causes people to worship the ruler, and the Holy Spirit causes people to worship Christ the Messiah.

There is another similarity between Islam and the Bible. Both teach that a final '*beast*' arises to bring a religious revival (Quran 27:82).[14]

The false prophet performs great and miraculous signs, '*even causing fire to come down from heaven to earth in full view of men*'

14. *God's War on Terror*, p 377.

(verse 13). Satan is perfectly capable of doing a range of miraculous signs. In Exodus, Pharaoh's magicians did some of the same signs that Moses did (Exodus 7:10-12, 20-22, 8:6-7) but there were limits (Exodus 8:17-19). What were the names of the magicians? (2 Timothy 3:8).

The greatest miracle this person does is call fire down from heaven. The two witnesses from chapter 11 had fire come out of their mouths (Revelation 11:5). This is a signature sign of Elijah. How many times did Elijah call fire down? (1 Kings 18:38, 2 Kings 1:9-12) Elijah's fire was always in response to a request to prove who really was the prophet of the true God. Satan here duplicates the miracle to try to prove to people that the false prophet is a godly messenger.

Is this an attempt to claim to be the fulfilment of Malachi 4:5 where Elijah is predicted to arise before the coming of the Messiah? But Jesus claimed this prediction was fulfilled by John the Baptist (Matthew 17:10-13).

Because of the signs the prophet can do, he will deceive the inhabitants of the earth (verse 14). Revelation 12:9 tells us that Satan leads the world astray. Jesus warned about this in Matthew 24:24. He said, '*...false Christs and false prophets will appear and perform great signs and miracles to deceive even the elect – if that were possible.*'

This verse also tells us God's chosen people, '*the elect*', will not be deceived. They have already been sealed and are free from deception. Paul warns us that people who reject God are given over to a depraved mind (Romans 1:28). The inhabitants of the earth have rejected God earlier, and they are now deceived to worship a man instead of the creator of man.

Paul repeats this in 2 Thessalonians 2:9-12. Why do these people perish (verse 10)? Because they refused to love the truth and be saved. What is the punishment (verse 11)? God sends them a powerful delusion and they will believe the lie.

There is a warning here for us. If we reject God's truth, we will become open to all sorts of deception. We see this in the history of the Roman Catholic Church where many deceptive teachings were introduced during the Dark Ages (such as indulgences, Mary's ascension, infallibility of the Pope, purgatory, etc) and are still being taught as church doctrine.[15]

We also see this in some of the other denominational church leaders who have rejected the fundamental teachings of the Bible (creation, virgin birth, resurrection, etc). Maybe we know someone personally who was once a dedicated believer, but they are now living in sin or have decided the Bible is a work of fiction.

The false prophet sets up an image of the world leader for the people to worship (verse 14). Is this image installed in the temple? (Matthew 24:15-16, 2 Thessalonians 2:3-4, Daniel 11:31) It would certainly make sense to install it in the Jerusalem temple to convince people that the leader is the Messiah. The image must be an important part of those times because it is also mentioned in chapters 14, 15, 16, 19 and 20. It is also a direct disobedience of God's commands (Exodus 20:4).

Why does John repeatedly identify the ruler as '*who was wounded by the sword and yet lived*'? To emphasise the identity of the ruler? To make sure we know who he is referring to?

Verse 15 says the false prophet is given power to make the image speak. This causes a problem. Satan does not have the power to give or take away life. Only God, the creator, can do this. Does the image have a built-in mechanism that allows it to appear to be speaking? Or does God allow Satan to cause this image to speak?

Artificial intelligence and robotics are progressing at such a rate that current robots can almost look human and are being designed to mimic people. This image could be the most up-to-

15. *2017: 500 Years After Luther*, pp 12-27.

date version of robotics that will be seen. It may have artificial skin and facial expressions that are far in advance of what is currently being developed.

But this may be even more miraculous than that. How many people would worship a robot? But they may worship an idol that is demonically empowered to speak, especially if the speeches are awe-inspiring.

Several scriptures mention idols that cannot speak (Psalm 115:4-7, 135:15-16, Jeremiah 10:5, Habakkuk 2:18). But Satan may cause this image to speak and further deceive the earth dwellers.

A similar incident to the false prophet setting up an image of a world leader for the people to worship (verse 14) almost occurred a few years before the Jerusalem temple was destroyed in 70 AD. In 37 AD, Caligula became the emperor. He began referring to himself as a god, and had many Roman statues altered with his head replacing the original heads of various gods. In 39 AD Caligula ordered that a statue of himself be erected in the Jerusalem temple. The governor of Syria was Publius Petronius, and he knew that this act would cause a riot in Jerusalem and spread throughout the Jewish population. He delayed acting on this order for over a year.

Caligula wrote a letter to the authorities in Syria demanding the death penalty because of Petronius' lack of following orders. The ship carrying the letter was caught in a storm and took three months to sail from Rome to Caesarea. Caligula was murdered, and the news of his murder arrived 27 days before the execution order. The execution could not occur because the person ordering it was dead, and so Petronius was spared.

The false prophet is also given the power to kill everyone who refuses to worship the image. This is a repeat of history. Nebuchadnezzar did the same thing in Daniel 3:1-6, but some people refused to bow down to his image. Similarly, there will be a small group of people who will not bow down to this image (Revelation 15:2). There is always a group of people who do not get deceived by idols or false religious leaders. Elijah thought he was alone in Israel, but there were seven thousand others who had not bowed to Baal (1 Kings 18:3-4, 19:10, 18).

Revelation 6:9 and 7:9-17 shows that many people will be martyred during this time because they refuse to worship the beast or his image. How do we know these people are from this period? Verse 14 tells us they have come out of great tribulation, which is the last three and a half years of Daniel's 70th week.

Everyone receives a mark of some kind on either their right hand or forehead to show allegiance to the Antichrist[16] (verse 16). People from all levels of society will receive this mark. The Greek word for mark is *charagma*.[17]

Historically the mark was associated with the emperor and was necessary for transactions.[18] The Greek word for 'receive' derives from *lambano*, and it means to 'choose' or 'receive voluntarily'[19]. This means that we are not given the mark hidden in a vaccine, or in some underhanded method. It is something that is volunteered for. People make a deliberate choice to receive this mark and to worship the beast.

---

16. Islam believes that wearing the Shahadatan on the forehead or arm helps outweigh your bad deeds on the judgement day. See *God's War on Terror*, p 377.
17. *Vines Dictionary*, p 393. It denotes a stamp or am impress. The word for a tattooed mark or a burnt brand is *stigma*.
18. *Agents of the Apocalypse*, p 177.
19. *Vines Dictionary*, p 510.

Why on the right hand and forehead? The world leader is identified as being blind in the right eye and having a useless right arm. Are these points used to show allegiance to the ruler? They are also easily accessible points on the body to put marks for identification. The Quran teaches that the 'beast of the earth' will mark all Muslims on the forehead to distinguish them from non-Muslims (Quran 27:82).

Moses commanded the Israelites to write the law and *bind them for a sign upon your hand, and they shall be as frontlets between your eyes.* (Deuteronomy 6:7-9). This was to symbolise that God's law was to guide their thinking and their actions. This action by the ruler is a counterfeit admission that he wants to control people's thinking and actions. We see a similar trend in the 'cancel culture' happening now.

The marks also serve the economic purposes of the ruler (verse 17). This person is both the religious and economic leader. No one can buy or sell without the mark. If a transponder is used, a cashless society is introduced. Every transaction can be traced to the individual via their chip. No more theft or fraud. No black market. This is another way of forcing allegiance. Become part of the new religion, or effectively have no part in society.

Religion and economics are linked. Satan was involved in economic activity before he challenged God (Ezekiel 28:16, 18). What sort of trade occurs in heaven? Jesus warned that we cannot serve both God and money (Matthew 6:24). Love and service of one mutually excludes the other. We can use money for God's kingdom or to do good on earth, but love of money excludes love for God (1 Timothy 6:10). Church leaders are especially told to be cautious about their attitude toward money (1 Peter 5:2). Judas is the ultimate example of someone who exchanged money for Christ (Matthew 26:14-16).

I personally find the combination of the two beasts interesting.

The first beast sets up a new religion, but he is a political and economic leader. The second beast sets up the economic system, yet he is a religious leader. It again shows the link between economics and religion. Here we see the final linkage being completely fulfilled with one world government, one world economy, and one world religion based around one man. Our economic system depends on the prevailing religion in our society.

- Communism and socialism are economically similar, and both deny the existence of God. Communism absolutely denies God, while socialism says that any concept of God is irrelevant. You do not have a free will; the state will tell you what to think and do (sounds like New Zealand during the Covid 'emergency'). Socialism tends to become the predominate economy in countries that are apathetic toward God or deny God.

- Buddhism and Hinduism are two examples of eastern religions where most of the population are in poverty while the ruling elite are extremely wealthy. Women are usually chattels of the family. It does not matter what you think, your fate is determined by karma.

- Only Judaism and Christianity have a capitalist system whereby wealth can be accumulated by anyone, but more importantly where human life is valued. Free will is the ability to deliberately choose to behave contrary to God or the government, or to behave in accordance with the requirements of God.

Also notice how the economies of the Western world have deteriorated as their population has turned away from God. New

Zealand was at its most prosperous during the late 1950s and early 1960s. It was also the time when church attendance was highest and social morals were the most Biblically based.

The economy has deteriorated as anti-Bible legislation has been passed permitting abortions, homosexuality, prostitution, civil unions, etc. Increasing unemployment, housing issues, and growing foreign debt all show a deteriorating economy. See Haggai 1:5-7 for a warning about turning away from God. What are the implications for New Zealand given recent social trends?

What is the mark that people receive? There are many theories about this. Some people have suggested a unique identifying number or bar code that will follow you throughout your life. Others have suggested it is the number tattooed onto your skin. They suggest the sores on people's bodies in Revelation 9:4-6 are caused by a reaction to the chemicals in the tattoo or marking. People without this mark are immune from this suffering. Another suggestion is that a microchip is injected under the skin to allow cashless trading.

The Bible tells us it is the name of the beast or his number. It may be an insignia that the world leader uses to identify himself or his organisation, analogous to a company logo.

Verse 18 has caused a lot of discussion and some hysteria. But look at the warning at the start of the verse. We are asked to exercise caution about how we interpret this. But we are expected to use this verse to identify the person when he arises. So, what does the number 666 mean or signify?

Even most non-Christians have heard about the mark and think that 666[20] is a number associated with the devil. The heavy

---

20. Some very early documents have 616. The early church writer Irenaeus wrote this was a scribal error. See *God's War on Terror*, pp 368-369.

rock group *Iron Maiden* released an album in 1982 titled 'The Number of the Beast' which featured a song by the same name. It was thought to be a Satanic praise song by many people, but the lyrics are a warning against getting involved in Satanism.[21]

Many people have attempted to work out who is the ruler by putting numbers with letters of the alphabet and work out whose names add to 666. This process is called 'gematria', and it is closely associated with a form of Jewish mysticism called Kabala.[22]

Recent suggestions have included almost any political leader from Asia or the western world. Henry Kissinger was a popular target during the 1960's and 70's because of his worldwide influence as the US Secretary of State. The Pope is another common suggestion. Most modern leaders have been suggested at some stage (pick any politician you don't like and make the numbers fit the name). Many other historical figures have been suggested over the centuries.

There are two problems with this process. First, only two alphabets in the world have numbers that correspond to each letter: Greek and Hebrew. Latin has a few letters with attached numbers, but not the whole alphabet. (If you add those numbers, they total 666. 'M' for 1,000 was a much later addition.)

Any attempt to use the English alphabet depends on which number you attach to each letter. Should we use only the Greek equivalent letters because Revelation was originally written in Greek? Do we need to translate the name into the Greek equivalent to be consistent?

The second problem is that 2 Thessalonians 2:7-8 indicates that he will not be revealed until the restraining factor (the believing church and/or the Holy Spirit) is taken away from the earth. If that

21. en.wikipedia.org/wiki/The_Number_of_the_Beast_(song)
22. *God's War on Terror*, p 367.

is true we will be only guessing his identity at the best. The Bible clearly says his actions will be the revealing key, not any maths associated with his name.

So how do we make sense of 666? There are three ways to look at this.

The first way is from a symbolic view. We know that seven is the number of completion or perfection, and that six is the number associated with man and his activities. Man was created on day six (Genesis 1:26-27) and he is supposed to work six days each week (Exodus 20:9-10). The giants or Nephilim had six fingers (2 Samuel 21:20, 1 Chronicles 20:6). King Solomon's throne had six steps (1 Kings 10:19-20). Nebuchadnezzar's statue was sixty cubits high and six cubits wide (Daniel 3:1).

Does the 666 indicate a trinity based on man's achievement that falls short of God's perfect trinity? This is the usual interpretation.[23]

The second way is an extension of the above. Mankind are composed of three components. We are a spirit with a soul inside a body. The number associated with each component is six. Hence 666 can indicate the total composition of mankind.

The third way is to look at the textual hints. Whenever a number is given everywhere else in scripture, it is spelt out in words and is not written as a number. Why should this be any different?

If John was writing what he saw, he may not have written Greek at all. He may have been writing another language or drawing a sketch at this point, but later people copying his writing wrote what they thought were the closest Greek numbers (chi xi sigma). If we turn each Greek letter 90 degrees to the left it gives marks similar to Arabic:[24]

23. *Bible Knowledge Commentary: New Testament*, p 963.
24. *God's War on Terror*, p 369.

Greek writing: Χξϛ Arabic writing: لله ا ⚔

If this is the case, it spells 'Allah', and the letter chi becomes the two crossed swords which is a common symbol in the Muslim world. This implies the religion forced on everybody will be a form of Islam.

The important thing is not so much what the mark or what 666 means, but what we need to take from these verses. We need to be aware that the first and second beasts are both working against God. They are both against anything that is godly. We are warned about getting involved in anything associated with Satan.

One final comment. Many Christians think the world will get continually better through preaching and social work until Christ finally reigns in people's hearts, if not physically on earth. This chapter gives the opposite picture. The one religion instituted is against anything to do with the God of the Christian and Jew. Followers of God will be hunted down for execution.

What can we learn from this chapter?

1. If we reject God, we are open to all sorts of deception.
2. Whose seal or mark is on you? Are you sealed with the Holy Spirit?

Chapter 12

The Three Angels

Chapter 13 of Revelation gave us an overview of the two leaders of the final world system, and especially important was the fact that any trace of God was eliminated as much as possible. But we have also learned that there is a remnant or small group who do believe in God that escape from the grasp of the two beasts, despite their best efforts. Who are they? The 144,000 sealed in Revelation chapter 7, and other believers (mainly Jews) who have escaped to Edom.

Revelation chapter 14 begins the final judgements on the earth. This period is called '*The Day of the Lord*' in the Old Testament. Many prophets mention this time when God judges the world. This chapter gives the heavenly view of the judgements, whereas other parts of Revelation give the earthly view of the same events.

What length of time is involved in 'the Day of the Lord'? It must be at least weeks to achieve all of what is predicted to happen. But does it stretch out to a few years? In some ways, the Great Tribulation period of three and half years could refer to this. Isaiah 34:8 indicates that it could be a year.

This chapter is not chronological. The first part jumps ahead to when Jesus Christ returns to the earth after the judgements have finished. The second part jumps back to the start of the final judgements. The third part jumps ahead to the final judgement itself.

Revelation 14:1-5

The chapter starts in verse 1 with Jesus Christ '*standing on Mount Zion and with Him are the 144,000 people*' that were sealed earlier (Revelation 7:1-8). Where or what is Mount Zion? Mount Zion was one of two hills in ancient Jerusalem. It was the site of the Jebusite city that David conquered (2 Samuel 5:6-9).[1] Today the hill is called Ophel. In the Old Testament, Mount Zion refers to the city rather than the hill, especially in the Psalms.

Notice that there were 144,000 originally sealed. Not a single person has been lost. This shows the power of God to protect and preserve the people who have been sealed by Him. When Jesus prayed in John 17, he said that '*none had been lost*' (John 17:12).

Christ returns as the Lamb. Why the Lamb, and not as the glorified Christ that we saw in chapter 1? Because Christ returns as the Messiah, and the Jews recognise Him as the person they had executed about 2,000 years ago (Zechariah 12:10).

Where does this fit chronologically? When Christ physically comes back to earth, He comes to the Mount of Olives (Zechariah 14:4). This chapter happens sometime after that, and Christ is now in Jerusalem. He has established Himself as the ruler, and He is with the Jews who have been sealed to be His witness to the world during the Tribulation. That means this section must come after Revelation chapter 19.

What was the seal? It was '*the names of both Christ and God written on their forehead*'. Is it the Hebrew writing for Yahweh? This contrasts with the previous verse where the mark of the beast was put on people's forehead or right hand. We cannot serve two masters. The choice is between God or Satan.

John heard a '*sound from heaven like rushing water and thun-*

---

1. www.britannica.com/place/Zion-hill-Jerusalem

der' (verse 2). John had heard similar voices earlier (Revelation 10:3) which was an angel announcing something that John was not allowed to record. John now gives more detail, and he likens the sound to '*harps being played*'. This seems a strange mixture of sounds: turbulent water, thunder, and harps. This sound is associated with worship. Maybe this is some form of music that is unique to heaven. If John was to describe modern church music, how would he describe it?

The 144,000 Jews sing a new song in verse 3. Notice the groups that they are singing before: the throne (God?), the four living creatures, and the elders (twenty-four?). Only they can learn the song because they have been redeemed from the earth in a unique way. Is this because they can sing about an experience they had that no one else has ever experienced?

Many songs are about experiences the writers have had. The first song recorded in the Bible is Exodus 15 where they celebrate the Egyptian army being drowned in the Red Sea. What are most of our church songs about?

Is this in heaven or on earth? They are before the throne of God, the four living creatures, and the elders. The last time we saw these together they were in heaven (Revelation 7:11). Maybe these people are taken into heaven between verses 2 and 3? Maybe Christ's throne and the others come to earth to help enforce Christ's rule? I suspect the last option given that we had been told they were at Mount Zion.

We are given a description about the mental or moral attitude of these 144,000 people.

Verse 4 tells us that these people '*did not defile themselves with women, for they kept themselves pure*'. Does this mean they were never married? Or does it mean they were married only once? During a time of persecution, it is easier to survive if you are not married. There is only one of you to hide, provide food for, or look after. Two people together makes it harder to hide, escape, or feed adequately.

Or does it mean spiritual purity? This is often symbolised by virginity (Jeremiah 31:4, Lamentations 2:13, Amos 5:2, 2 Corinthians 11:2).[2] Both options are feasible because of the conditions they live through. We read later that they are blameless.

Whatever that means, these people are dedicated to following Christ. '*They follow the Lamb wherever he goes*'. The reason for this devotion is given. They were purchased from among men and offered as firstfruits to God.

We usually think of Christians being purchased and offered to God. Christians are spoken of as being '*bought with the blood of Christ*' (Acts 20:28, 1 Corinthians 6:20, 7:23, 1 Peter 1:18-19). Paul talks about believers as '*the firstfruits of Christ*' (Romans 8:23, 16:5, James 1:18). So why is this group referred to as 'bought' and 'firstfruits'? Could it be because these are the first group of Jews to recognise their Messiah as crucified and raised in a manner similar to how we recognise Jesus?

What is the significance of the firstfruits? Leviticus 23:9-14 tells us about the Festival of the Firstfruits. The first lot of food harvested is presented to the priest who waves the grain before God. They were not allowed to eat any of the crop until the firstfruits had been offered to God. (Similar to tithing?) All this is done on the first Sunday after the Passover and Festival of Unleavened Bread.

Christ is the firstfruit of the resurrection (Colossians 1:18, Revelation 1:5). What day was Jesus resurrected? On the Sunday after the Passover, on the Festival of Firstfruits. He was the ultimate fulfilment of the Festival of Firstfruits. He was presented to God as an offering, and we can now enjoy the rest of the har-

2. *Bible Knowledge Commentary: New Testament*, p 964.

vest. Jesus was the first person to be resurrected to eternal life. All believers will also be resurrected to eternal life at some point.

So how are these people the firstfruits? These people are the first of many who will turn to Christ when he physically returns to earth (Zechariah 12:10, Romans 11:26-27).

Verse 5 informs us that '*no lie was found in their mouths*'. This contrasts with the lies and deception used by the rulers during that time. They were totally free from deception, both from their own lips and from other people's lips. They were blameless. The Greek word is *amomoi*, which means 'without blemish'.[3] It is the same word used to describe the sacrificed animals that had to be without defect.

These people lived up to a very high standard. We are called to the same standard (1 Peter 1:13-16, 2 Peter 3:11-12). Do we live to that standard? That is our challenge every day of our lives.

Revelation 14:6-13

We now have three angels with three important announcements to the people on the earth.

Verse 6 describes the first angel as it '*flies in mid-air and proclaims the eternal gospel to every person on earth*'. What is the gospel? Paul gives a concise summary in 1 Corinthians 15:1-4. This proclamation allows everyone on the earth to know about Christ who will soon come to reign on the earth. They will hear that the Christ that the two beasts tried to eliminate, is the truth, and therefore the two beasts are liars. They hopefully realise they have been totally deceived.

The message going to the entire world fulfils Jesus' prediction in Matthew 24:13-14. Jesus talked about enduring to the end as these 144,000 people did.

---

3. *Vine's Dictionary*, p 69.

But the word gospel also means 'message'.[4] The angel proclaims a message in verse 7 for the people to fear God and worship the creator '*because the hour of His judgement has come*'. Notice they are told to worship the God of creation, not the God of salvation. For many people it will be too late to turn to God for salvation (Revelation 14:9-10). But they will realise the power of the God who will be judging them.

Why are they told to worship the God of creation?

Paul tells us that it is possible for people to find God from the creation (Romans 1:18-20). This should be much easier today when we can learn about the sophisticated biochemistry that happens inside every cell in our body. Evolution cannot explain how such a precisely engineered system can arise by chance. No one apparently has any excuse for not finding God in some way. Any person with an open mind will see that everything in the universe is designed, and not the result of random chance.

Notice also the fourth category in the creation; '*the springs of water*'. Water had become scarce through the famine and one third had become bitter (Revelation 8:10-11, 11:6). A new era would soon begin where water would no longer be a rare or dangerous commodity.

The second angel announces the fall of Babylon in verse 8. We will cover this in more detail when we consider Revelation chapters 17 and 18. It probably refers to the political, economic, and religious system that had been developed. It has fallen apart and will be replaced by one that Christ introduces. But it could also refer to the physical city.

Babylon has been associated with rebellion against God from its beginning. It was founded by Nimrod (Genesis 10:8-12), and it was said to be associated with the worship of Semiramis, the

---

4. *Vine's Dictionary*, p 275.

female deity.[5] But Semiramis lived much later, and she was the queen regent of the Assyrian Empire in 811-806 BC.[6]

The third angel announces the punishment for those people who have rejected God (verse 9). Everyone who worships the beast and receives his image will know the fury of God. Remember that these actions were voluntary.

They will be tormented with burning sulphur (verses 10-11). This is the ultimate punishment for rejecting God. They had warning from the two witnesses, from believers on earth before the Tribulation started, and from the 144,000 people who God sealed. They chose to reject God and worship Satan instead. Now they reap the consequences (Hebrews 10:26-27).

The punishment is described as tormented with burning sulphur and having no rest. Sodom and Gomorrah were destroyed with burning sulphur (Genesis 19:24). But this refers to the Lake of Fire (Revelation 19:20, 20:14-15). Is this a literal sulphur fire? Or is it symbolic of extreme suffering? Sulphur burns with an intense heat and results in a smell that causes choking. Whichever option you choose, this will not be a nice place to end up.

John adds a comment for his readers in verse 12. The theme for believers all through Revelation is '*patient endurance*'. Although the Tribulation lasts for only seven years, it seems a long time when you are being oppressed or under threat of execution.

John encourages his readers to patiently endure because the end result is worth it. Remain faithful to Jesus. Do not get deceived by Satan.

In verse 13, John is now told what to write by a voice from

5. This association seems to have originated from a book published in 1853 called *The Two Babylons*, by a Christian minister, Alexander Hislop. See en.wikipedia.org/wiki/Semiramis.
6. www.ancient.eu/Semiramis

heaven. '*Blessed are they who die in the Lord from now on.*' Why? Because they will go straight into their reward without going through Hades first. The Holy Spirit says they will rest.

This contrasts with the people being tormented who will have no rest. For the people martyred during this time, the rest in God's presence will be a marked contrast from the persecution, torture, and trial they had experienced.

Their deeds will follow them (1 Timothy 5:24). Our deeds always follow us. We will be judged for our work because our sin has already been judged (1 Corinthians 3:12-13, 2 Corinthians 5:10, 1 John 4:17). The judgement seat for believers is the *bema* seat[7]. The *bema* seat was used in the athletics stadiums to judge who was the winner of the races. It is a judgement of merit, not a judgement of status. What deeds will follow you to heaven?

Revelation 14:14-20

In verse 14 John sees a person sitting on a white cloud. Who is this person? It must be Christ (Daniel 7:13). Here he is shown as the glorified Christ instead of the Lamb. He is acting as a judge, so he wears a gold crown to show his divine authority. Matthew uses the title '*Son of Man*' more than 25 times.[8]

Christ holds a sharp sickle in his hand (verses 15-16). The sickle was the implement for harvesting crops. In the Bible, sickles are associated with judgement. What is He going to harvest? People. Another angel came out of the temple and told Christ that it was time to harvest the earth. So, the earth was harvested.

The harvest is said to be ripe. The Greek word (*xeraino*)[9] is used

---

7. *Vine's Dictionary*, p 337.
8. *Bible Knowledge Commentary: New Testament*, p 965.
9. *Vine's Dictionary*, p 536.

for grapes that are overripe and starting to wither. In other words, past the best condition and beginning to spoil.

Another angel came out of the temple with another sickle (verses 17-18). Another angel tells him to gather grapes from the earth. This angel is in charge of the fire. Which fire? The fire of the altar in God's temple? Or the fire with the burning sulphur? I suspect the angel is in charge of the burning sulphur because these angels are involved with judgements.

These grapes are also ripe. This is a different Greek word (*akmazo*)[10] that means to be fully grown and in prime condition. But these grapes are reserved for God's punishment.

Are there two different harvests? Why would there be two harvests? None of my books even attempt to discuss this. Any ideas? What happens to the first harvest?

What is meant by '*harvesting the grapes from the earth's vine*'? Jesus told his disciples that He is the vine and we are his branches (John 15:5). We are supposed to bear fruit (John 15:2). Grapes are therefore symbolic of fruit from our lives. God is removing the sinful deeds of mankind from the earth.

The winepress (verses 19-20) is symbolic of dealing with judgement, especially judgement of the nations (Joel 3:12-13, Revelation 19:15). The nations are judged outside Jerusalem with Christ being the sole judge (Isaiah 63:2-4, 6).

There will be a final battle of the nations against God Himself at Jerusalem (Daniel 8:25, Zechariah 12:2-3, 14:2-3, Revelation 16:16, 19:19). Here Christ Himself enters the battle and fights against the nations. The bloodshed by the armies is great with no survivors. The area covered by the battle will extend for 300 kilometres.

Does this mean a lake of blood 300 kilometres across and deep enough to reach a horse's bridle? Not likely. That is a large amount

10. *Vine's Dictionary*, p 536.

of blood, and it would cause a major environmental catastrophe. It more likely means there is so much bloodshed that the blood is splattered to the height of a horse's bridle (about 1.5 metres). This will be the result of the final war before Christ returns (Revelation 16:14-16).

This chapter begins the last short period of time immediately Christ returns in judgement. This time of judgement and turmoil on the earth is called *'the Day of the Lord'*. We will cover it in more detail in the next chapter.

One final interesting verse. Proverbs 16:4. God uses even wicked people for his own ends. What does He use wicked people for? At least two reasons. First, to fulfil his purposes. For example, the rulers of nations that conquered Israel as a punishment for their turning away from God (2 Kings 15:29, 25:10-12). Second, to be a lesson to people who have the ability to learn from other people's mistakes.

Chapter 13

The Bowls of God's Wrath

The previous chapter of Revelation introduced us to '*the Day of the Lord*'. This is the time of final judgement for the earth before Christ returns to reign on the earth. It showed us three different aspects to the Day of the Lord: the 144,000 witnesses worship God, three angels proclaim three messages (judgement is coming, Babylon is fallen, and people who worshipped the beast will be punished), and a judgement is performed on the nations outside Jerusalem. Chapters 15 and 16 continue with the Day of the Lord and add a lot of detail.

Revelation 15

In verse 1, John sees something that he describes as '*a great and marvellous sign*'. There are seven angels with the seven last plagues. The good news is these are the last because with them God's wrath is completed.

As an exercise, go back through Revelation and count the plagues that have been sent to earth so far. They cover every aspect of human activity and impact upon every part of the environment.

John sees in verse 2 a sea of glass mixed with fire. We said earlier the sea of glass is clear as crystal (Revelation 4:6). Is this the same sea? This time the sea is mixed with fire. If the sea of glass is the Word of God, this time it means the Word of God in its ability to judge. Fire is symbolic of judgement. The scriptures can wash us from our sin. But if we don't get cleansed from sin, we will get judged by the scriptures.

Standing beside the sea were the people who were victorious over the beast and his image. They had not succumbed to his deceptions, nor taken his mark. They had survived his persecutions.

Notice these people are beside the sea. The people in chapter 4 were standing on the sea. We stand on the scriptures for cleansing, but not for judgement. These people do not need judgement, but they are standing by the place of judgement. They have been separated from those who had worshipped the beast.

These people are given harps[1] from God (verses 3-4), and they sang the song of Moses and the song of the Lamb. Two songs of Moses are recorded. The first is in Exodus 15 where the Egyptian army was destroyed by God after they crossed the Red Sea. The second is in Deuteronomy 32 which gives a review of God's faithfulness to Israel.

Both these songs can be meant here.[2] The Egyptian army is analogous to the beast who tried to enslave the world but is destroyed. During the Tribulation period, God is faithful to His followers who do not align themselves with the beast.

The song of the Lamb is similar to the song sang by the four living creatures and the twenty- four elders in Revelation 5:9-10. The words are completely different, but the sentiment of God doing things for all nations is in both songs. God is praised for His great deeds, justice, truth, glory, and holiness.

Notice this song looks forward to Christ's reign, not back to

1. Harps are the only musical instrument mentioned in Revelation. Are they the sole instrument in heaven, or are they symbolic of instruments in general?
2. *Bible Knowledge Commentary: New Testament*, p 966.

the cross. It predicts that all nations will come and worship before God (Zechariah 14:16).

The temple in heaven is opened in verses 5-8. Out of the temple come the seven angels with the seven plagues. They are dressed in clean, shining linen. What does that signify?

Clean linen signifies pure and righteous beings (Revelation 19:8). The shining linen means they are in the presence of God. God is described as shining in chapter 1. Moses' face shone when he had been with God.

The golden sash around their chest is probably a symbol of status or position, and it is usually associated with glorified Christ (Daniel 10:5, Revelation 1:13). Are these angels associated with Christ somehow?

One of the four living creatures gives the angels golden bowls filled with the wrath of God. What is gold symbolic of? Notice verse 7 describes God as '*who lives for ever and ever*'. Why is this description here? What relevance does it have?

The wrath of God is obviously great because He is pouring more plagues upon the earth that is already in a sorry state. And it is probably over a very short time period. Why is God's wrath so great? Because of God's hatred of sin? Because of God's holiness? Because people have had hundreds of years to learn about God's requirements and put them into practice? Because people have deliberately chosen to rebel against God in taking the mark of the beast? Any other reasons?

Smoke filled the temple (verse 8) so that no one could enter the temple until the seven plagues had been completed. This visible glory of God is called the *shekinah* glory. We see this when the tabernacle is completed (Exodus 40:34-35) and when the temple was completed (1 Kings 8:10-11).

We also see the cloud whenever God is either pleased or angry at some activity of mankind (Exodus 16:9-10, Numbers 16:41-42,

Ezekiel 10:18). It also appears whenever God is showing His glory to mankind (Exodus 24:15-18, Ezekiel 1:28, Mark 9:7). It will appear over Jerusalem during Christ's reign (Isaiah 4:5).

The *shekinah* cloud is always associated with holiness. The tabernacle and temple were holy places. God was maintaining His holy standards in many of the other places. In Mark, Jesus was seen in his glorified state.

Revelation 16

The chapter starts with a loud voice that tells the seven angels to go and pour out God's wrath upon the earth. Chronologically these plagues are close to the time for the second coming of Christ. I cannot find any time frame for these last judgements. Is it days, weeks, or months? The last plague prepares the world for the final showdown with God.

The word used for 'loud' is *megales,* and it is used frequently in this chapter. But the same word is used for intense heat (verse 9), severe earthquake (verse 18), and huge hailstones (verse 21). The judgements are increasing in intensity as they proceed.[3] 1 Thessalonians 5:3 describes this time as '*increasing labour pains*', which go in intensity and frequency.

It is interesting to compare these plagues with the earlier ones.

The first bowl (verse 2) results in ugly and painful sores on the people who have worshipped the beast and his image. The previous plague of sores lasted five months (Revelation 9:10). There is no end for this plague until these people are judged by God.

The sequence of bowls is similar to that of the trumpets. There are differences. The trumpet judgements generally affected a third of the earth. The bowl judgements generally affect the whole earth

3. *Bible Knowledge Commentary: New Testament*, p 966.

and are more severe.[4] The trumpet judgements are spread over a time of about three and a half years, whereas the bowl judgements all fall within a more concentrated time period, probably much less than a year.

The second bowl in verse 3 causes the sea to turn into congealed blood and every living thing in the sea dies. The earlier plague (second trumpet) had resulted in one third of the sea being affected (Revelation 8:8-9). Most of the earth's surface is covered with sea water, and many countries rely on fishing for a good proportion of their food.

A result of high water temperature is less oxygen in the water, and this allows red-coloured protozoa to breed. This not only makes the water look like blood, but the decaying algae further reduces the oxygen level in the water to the point where fish die.[5] God is judging the whole world.

The third bowl results in all fresh water turning to blood (verse 4). The third trumpet had resulted in one third of the water turning bitter and many people died from drinking this (Revelation 8:10-11). This plague affects all fresh water, and it turns it into blood.

Rivers have also been subject to algal blooms, but the causes are normally different. River blooms are caused by high mineral contents allowing the algae to multiply. This is obviously a supernatural event because it happens worldwide, and not in isolated rivers.

The angel in charge of the waters says these judgements are just (verses 5-7). Why? Because the people of the earth had shed the blood of the saints and prophets of God, and now they have blood to drink. The altar in heaven responds with an agreement with the angel. The false prophet made the image of the beast talk, and here we have the altar in heaven talking.

---

4. *Bible Knowledge Commentary: New Testament*, p 967.
5. en.wikipedia.org/wiki/Red_tide

Verse 5 seems to indicate an angel is in charge of the fresh water on earth. We know God can use the weather to punish people who disobey Him (Deuteronomy 28:23-24, 1 Kings 8:35-36, James 5:17-18). We also know from Daniel 10:20 there are angels (and demons) assigned to nations. Does God also use angels in charge of parts of the environment to accomplish what He wants?

The fourth bowl in verses 8 to 9 causes the sun to increase its heat so that people are scorched. This is the ultimate global warming scenario. The fourth trumpet resulted in the sun losing a third of its light so that the days are gloomy. Now the heat output is increased resulting in temperatures much higher than usual. Will the days still be gloomy but very hot? Isaiah 30:26 predicts a seven-fold increase in the light intensity. Is that a prediction of this judgement, or a prediction of a later event or the new heaven?

Notice the people curse God and do not repent. Their deception is so great that they recognise that this is God's doing, but they still refuse to repent.

The fifth bowl (verses 10-11) is a judgement specifically against the Antichrist. His kingdom or country of origin is plunged into darkness. Is this a physical or spiritual darkness? We already know the people are in spiritual darkness because they refuse to repent.

I think this is a physical darkness to complement their spiritual darkness. It is also another obvious plague. This has happened before (Exodus 10:21-23, Matthew 27:45). But this judgement is different. The temperature is elevated but without any daylight.

People are in agony because of the heat, thirst, and sores, but they still refuse to repent. This shows the stubbornness of sin that can occur in people. It is reminiscent of the Pharaoh in Moses' time whose heart was stubborn and he would not let the Israelites go until God had destroyed the economy of the country.

The sixth bowl in verse 12 dries up the River Euphrates to prepare the way for the kings of the east. We had a hint of this with the sixth trumpet where four angels were released at the River Euphrates (Revelation 9:13-16). Those angels prepared an army of two hundred million troops.

The river is dried so there is no geographical impediment for these troops to travel to Israel. Isaiah 11:15 predicts the Euphrates River will be dried up. It almost has dried up today because of hydro and irrigation dams, but this will be a supernatural event.

In verses 13 to 14, John saw three evil spirits that look like frogs come out of the mouth of the dragon, the beast and the false prophet. Frogs are an unclean animal (Leviticus 11:10-12). The job of these demons is to gather the nations of the world for battle on the great day of God Almighty.

This is another example of deception as we will find out in the next chapter. The nations think they are fighting against the Antichrist, but Satan is congregating them to fight against God. And God is congregating them for a final judgement (Zephaniah 3:8).

Verse 15 is a warning for the believers still alive at that time. God will appear like a thief – at an unexpected time for the nations. But the believers should know from the signs that the time is near. The clothing probably refers to living righteously as elsewhere in scripture. This is an encouragement to continue to live righteously and not give up.

Verse 16 gives the name of the place for the last war before Christ returns. It is at Armageddon. It has been the place of many battles over the centuries (including one involving New Zealand troops), and it will be the starting location of this war. This series of events is discussed in Appendix 9.

The seventh angel pours out his bowl into the air in verses 17 to 18. The result is felt in heaven and on earth. A loud voice from the temple proclaims that '*It is done!*' Once again there are lightning, rumblings, thunder, and an earthquake. A number of actions are included in this final bowl.

This earthquake is stated to be bigger than any that has occurred since man has been on earth (verse 19). The great city is split into three parts. Is this a reference to Jerusalem, or does it refer to another city? Jerusalem is called 'the great city' previously in Revelation 11:8.

Many events from this time are predicted in the Old Testament, but nowhere in the Bible does it say that Jerusalem will be split into three parts. Is this Jerusalem?

The cities of the nations will also be destroyed. The infrastructure of the entire world is destroyed in preparation for Christ to reign and rebuild the world on righteousness.

Now God pours out his fury on an entity called 'Babylon the Great'. There are various theories about what this Babylon is,[6] and we will discuss this in the next chapter. For now, it is sufficient to say that whatever this refers to, it is something that has been blatantly anti-God for centuries.

There are also massive geographical changes. Islands and mountains are no longer found. The sixth seal had already resulted in the displacement of mountains and islands (Revelation 6:14), but now they disappear.

Does this mean the entire world will become one land mass similar to what scientists think was the original Gondwana? Maybe God is re-creating the original land mass of Adam's time? Whatever it does mean, there are massive topographical changes on the earth so that parts of it will be unrecognisable. Remember, New Zealand is a country of islands.

Verse 21 has the final part of the judgement. Hailstones weighing 40 to 50 kilograms will fall. Isaiah 32:19 talks about hail that flattens a forest. These are larger than even the heaviest hailstones in modern history. (And they occur when the sun's heat is seven times normal!) But despite all the changes, men still curse God

6. *Bible Knowledge Commentary: New Testament*, p 969.

and do not repent. Their hearts are eternally hardened, and so will be eternally punished.

The Day of the Lord will not be a nice time to be on earth. It is the time of God's final judgement on man for their sin and their rejection of Jesus Christ.

There are some interesting parallels between this chapter and Jesus' death on the cross.

1. Both are a judgement for sin.

2. Both involve a period of darkness. When Jesus was taking our sin, there were three hours of darkness in Judea. The fifth bowl will cause darkness over the throne of the beast.

3. Immediately before Jesus died, he said, '*It is finished*'. Before the seventh bowl is poured out, a voice from the throne says, '*It is done*'. Both signify that the work of judgement for sin is complete.

4. Both events happen outside Jerusalem. Jesus was crucified at Golgotha on Mount Moriah. The world armies will gather at Armageddon (Mount Megiddo) for the final war which occurs in the Kedron Valley.

5. Both events involve ugly and painful sores. Jesus' sores were from his whipping before the crucifixion, the nails through his wrists and feet, and the spear after he died. The first bowl will cause sores to break out people.

6. Blood is involved in both judgements. Jesus shed his blood for our remission of sin. The second and third bowls will cause all water to turn to blood.

7. Only a few people are saved from each judgement. Jesus' death results in a low percentage of people turning to Him for salvation. The Tribulation period will be a further testimony to how men prefer to continue with their sin instead of repent and get God's forgiveness.

8. Both events involve an earthquake.

9. Both events involve resurrection of people. People were raised to life at Jesus' death (Matthew 27:52-53). The executed believers from the Tribulation will also be resurrected (Revelation 20:4-5).

Chapter 14

The Woman Riding the Beast

Revelation chapters 17 and 18 are an interlude while more is explained about what will happen during the *Day of the Lord.* Remember that it does not all happen in a single day.

Chapter 16 predicts the demise of the final world leader, commonly referred to as the Antichrist.

Chapters 17 and 18 fill in a lot more detail about what happens in Revelation 16:19. It describes the destruction of other structures in place. These two chapters talk about Babylon. It is an entity that has somehow earned God's wrath, but it is not the ancient city of Babylon. Who or what is Babylon?

Revelation 17

In verses 1 and 2 John is summoned by one of the last group of angels to look at a woman called '*the great prostitute*'. The angel also gives John some facts about this prostitute. She sits on many waters. The kings of the earth committed adultery with her. The inhabitants of the earth were intoxicated with her.

What does all this symbolism mean?

The many waters are explained in verse 15. It is the mass of humanity. Whatever this prostitute represents is based on mankind or rules over mankind. And it has integrated itself into the political system which God calls adultery by the rulers.

Adultery in the Bible always assumes that one person or entity has left their spouse to go after someone or something else. Israel is often accused of adultery. Israel is described as backsliding when it commits spiritual adultery (Jeremiah 3:8). It is often connected with following the Canaanite gods of Baal and Molech (Jeremiah 7:9, Ezekiel 23:27, Hosea 1:2).

It is associated with a decline in public morality and a rise in crime (Jeremiah 7:9, Hosea 4:2, Romans 13:9). What does that indicate about New Zealand? Adultery is also associated with a lack of wisdom, similar to being intoxicated (Proverbs 6:26, 32).

Whatever this prostitute represents is something that can draw us away from God and His truth. The kings of the earth had committed adultery with this woman. That implies the woman is a false god, and the politics had combined with the woman to become part of the religious system that she symbolised. We have already read about this in Revelation 13.

The prostitute is in a desert, sitting on a scarlet beast that was covered with blasphemous names and that had seven heads and ten horns (verse 3). Does that sound familiar? It sounds like Revelation 13:1 where the first beast comes out of the sea. It also sounds like Revelation 12:3 where the enormous red dragon falls from heaven with seven heads and ten horns. Whatever this prostitute represents is Satanic. The beast will be a real person, but he is inspired and empowered by Satan. Is the woman another symbol of the false prophet or the second beast from chapter 13?

Is the desert location literal or symbolic? If it is literal, the prostitute could be the Islam religion, based in Mecca. If it is symbolic, the desert could refer to the lack of spiritual life or growth from this religion.

Verse 4 describes the prostitute as dressed in expensive clothing and is obviously powerful. Purple and scarlet were the colour of rulers and the wealthy (Judges 8:26, Esther 8:15, Ezekiel 23:6, Matthew

27:27-29, Luke 16:19). The colours themselves are also symbolic. Purple symbolises royalty and kingship, while scarlet symbolises the sacrificial ministry of the cross (Hebrews 9:19). Some versions use crimson, which is symbolic of sinfulness (Isaiah 1:18).

The woman is also dressed expensively with different types of stones and jewels. She had a gold cup filled with abominable things, that is things that God hates. This woman is trying to look good, but this is another deception.[1]

The clothing description is similar to the clothing of the top hierarchy of some traditional denominations. This has led many commentators to say the woman represents a church, and especially the Roman Catholic Church.[2]

Various types of women in scripture are symbolic of different things:

- Israel is symbolised as a wife to God (Jeremiah 3:20, Hosea 11:1).

- The church is symbolised as a virgin bride (2 Corinthians 11:2, Ephesians 5:25-27).

- Both Israel and the church have a special but different relationship with God. He rescued Israel from slavery in Egypt (Exodus 15:16, Psalm 74:2). He purchased the church with His blood (Acts 20:28, 1 Peter 1:18-19). When Israel turned to other nations instead of relying on God, it is referred to as prostitution (Ezekiel 23).

---

1. For a discussion on the prostitute, see the video of a *Prophecy Watchers* discussion with Bill Salus (www.youtube.com/watch?v=CVRuWKr5Y9Y).
2. *A Woman Rides the Beast*, pp 51-66.

- The prostitute here is a false religion. She looks like a ruler and has a facade of sacrifice, but it is not the real thing. She survives by trading religion for money.

Is this the final false religion that we read about in chapter 13 set up by the false prophet? Or is it a current religious system that already enslaves and deceives people? There have been several suggestions made over the years that could fit the descriptions.

The title of the woman is given in verse 5, and it tells us that she is a mystery. A mystery in the Bible is a teaching or idea that was hidden in the Old Testament times, but it has been revealed since the time of Jesus.

She is now being revealed for who or what she really is. She is based on Babylon, the city that was filled with pride. She is the source of all prostitution and abominations on the earth. This title again shows the prostitute is something Satanic.

Babylon was the first city to be established after the flood (Genesis 10:8-12). Nimrod tried to rule over the world but God thwarted that plan. The tower of Babel was man's first attempt to approach God by human means (Genesis 11:4). Babel means 'gate of God'. Babel is the Hebrew and Babylon is the Greek.

Babylon sounds like the Hebrew word for 'confused', *bosheth*. It was man's first act of directly disobeying God. God had told Noah and his sons to scatter over the earth, but Nimrod tried to keep them in a single region. Throughout the Bible, Babylon is seen as the source of false religion.[3] See Appendix 10 for the history of Babylon and the Biblical prediction of its fate.

In verse 6 the woman, or the entity she represents, is drunk with the blood of the saints. The definition of the saints is expanded to identify them as people who bore testimony to Jesus. This entity

3. *Bible Knowledge Commentary: New Testament*, p 970.

is extremely anti-Christian and/or anti-Jew. She has caused so many to be killed that she can drink to excess to be drunk.

False religion has always been antagonistic to the truth of God. The history of Israel shows Satan repeatedly tried to kill the line of the Messiah, starting with the Egyptians killing all male babies. Every scheme was unsuccessful. The history of the church shows that Christians of all beliefs were killed, often by other Christians with slightly different beliefs.[4] Islam has killed millions of non-adherents over the centuries. It is currently the most active persecutor of Christians and Jews, and fights other Islamic sects with different interpretations of the Quran.

This again shows us that the final days on earth will be dangerous days to be a believer in God. This should not be surprising. Satan is against anything to do with God, and he is always trying to lead believers away from God. Jesus promised us that we will have persecution (John 15:20, 16:33). We need to be prepared to have persecution in our life and persevere through the persecution. There comes a reward from being persecuted – the crown of life (James 1:12, Revelation 2:10).

The angel now begins to give John some understanding as to what or who this woman is. Verse 7 tells us the woman rides the beast with the seven heads and ten horns. We saw in chapter 13 that this is a political and economic system that will exist. It is based on a one-world government system run by the first beast or Antichrist. It is supplemented by a single world religion based around the deception of the beast's image that is made to speak. This woman represents the total of a single political, economic, and religious system combined into a single entity.

4. See, for example, *A Woman Rides the Beast*, p 392. This is a short list of some Papal campaigns against Protestants. There have also been Protestants murdering Catholics.

Who is the beast? Several ideas are possible:

1. It could be Satan. The final world system is designed and implemented by Satan. He was once the ruler of the nations (Matthew 4:8-9, Ephesians 2:2). The problem with this possibility is that it does not tie in with verse 11 that says the beast is the eighth king. But verse 8 describes the beast as '*once was, now is not, and will come out of the Abyss and go to his destruction*.' That is an accurate description of Satan if this chapter is chronologically after the final destruction.

2. It could be the Antichrist (the first beast). He once was in that he ruled for around seven years. He now is not because he is in the lake of fire (Revelation 19:20-231). What does the phrase '*and yet will come*' mean (verse 8)? The Antichrist will never leave the lake of fire, and he does not come out of the Abyss. Can that apply to the Antichrist?

3. It could be a combined system of politics, economics, and religion. It once was when the Antichrist ruled in conjunction with the false prophet (Revelation 13). It now is not in that it has been dismantled as described in chapters 17 and 18. It yet will come when Christ sits on the throne of David and reigns on the earth, but it will be a totally different system. Personally, I doubt this possibility because verse 8 tells us that people will be astonished when they see who this is, implying that it is an actual person.

However, the beast is specifically described as having seven heads and ten horns. From chapter 13, we know this is the first beast described, known as the Antichrist. This woman is a religious system that is used to establish political power.

The doomed and deceived inhabitants of the earth will be astonished when they see the beast. Revelation 13:3 tells us the world will be astonished at the Antichrist when he receives a fatal wound but recovers. Isaiah 14:16-17 says people will be amazed when they see Satan. The tone in this passage is one of derision. They will realise that they have been deceived.

There seems to be a play on the Greek words used here. The beast will come out of the Abyss (Greek *Apoleia*), which is related to the Greek god, Apollo. Apollo was the 'promised seed' in Greek mythology, and he can be seen as a forerunner of the Antichrist.[5] The Antichrist could present himself as the offspring of Apollo.

The reference to the Book of Life is interesting (verse 8b). We have another reference to it in Revelation 20:12-16 where it is used to determine people's final destiny. Anyone whose name is not written in the Book of Life will be thrown into the lake of fire. When are names written in the book? Verse 7 sounds like they were written at the time of creation. This ties in with other verses, such as God choosing us (Ephesians 1:4), and God knowing us (1 Peter 1:20). Or is the book filled up as people are born and die? Or is our name included when we decide to accept Jesus as our saviour?

Verse 9 starts with a hint that this is going to be difficult to understand. It calls for a mind with wisdom. The verse goes straight into the explanation, although again it is heavily coded.

'*The seven heads are seven hills on which the woman sits*'. Five have fallen, one is current, and the other will arrive in the future but not last long. There are a few theories about what these seven hills mean.

Can the heads be symbolic of people? If they are, then which five people do you pick out of the numerous leaders prior to this time?

---

5. *Exo-Vaticana*, p 528.

Five empires had preceded John's era: Egypt, Assyria, Babylon, Persia, and Greece. The major empires at John's time were the Roman Empire west of the River Euphrates, and Parthia to the east. There was still one that is yet to come at that stage. The Ottoman Empire succeeded the Parthian Empire, and could qualify as the one still to come. Or the empire of the beast could be referred to as an empire based somewhere in the Middle East.

Rome was known as the city on seven hills, so many commentators say the woman is the Roman Catholic Church.[6] They point to the numbers of people killed by the Catholic Church during the Inquisition,[7] the Crusades, and various attempts to eliminate various branches that did not follow the religious teaching of the Catholic Church. The Roman Catholic Church has often called for a 'new world order' to try to introduce an institutional form of Christianity.[8] But the next bit stumps them because they disagree on how to explain it.

The final world religion may be based on the Roman Catholic Church, or it may be an amalgamation of the Catholic and various other religions, based on a New Age model.[9] It will teach all types of abominations.

- The Roman Catholic Church teaches that Mary is the person to pray to,[10] that Mary is the Mother of God, that priests can forgive sins, and that dead saints can perform miracles. None of these ideas are found in the Bible. The Vatican has declared that Muslims are saved because they worship one god.

---

6. *Bible Knowledge Commentary: New Testament*, p 970; *A Woman Rides the Beast*, pp 67-85.
7. *A Woman Rides the Beast*, pp 229-262.
8. www.wnd.com/2021/03/4900164/
9. *Prophecy 20/20*, pp 221-227.
10. *A Woman Rides the Beast*, pp 454-457.

- It has historically done all it can to distance itself from the Jewish background. It changed Passover to Easter,[11] introduced Christmas,[12] and changed the day of worship to Sunday.[13]

- New Age teaches that we are a god and god is us, that there are many ways to find god, and that the earth itself is a goddess to be worshipped.[14]

- Is there any false teaching that the Pentecostal and Protestant churches teach? Some groups would classify the Rapture, gifts of healing, miracles, and tongues as false teaching. The 'prosperity gospel' has been widely discredited as false.[15] What else?

Another possibility is that the city could be Mecca and the religion could be Islam. Babylon in the Bible is identified as the centre of anti-God activity. Islam is the most anti-God and anti-Israel system on earth today. If the Islamic empire is the final empire, its spiritual capital is Mecca, although the political capital could be Istanbul, Tehran, or another city.

The seven hills may be seven spheres of influence controlling the world. These are the government, education, media, economy, arts and entertainment, family, and religion.[16] Although each of these areas used to be independent, they are becoming increasingly integrated and increasingly anti-God.

---

11. www.catholic.org/encyclopedia/view.php?id=4117
12. www.catholic.org/encyclopedia/view.php?id=2933
13. en.wikipedia.org/wiki/Sabbath_in_Christianity
14. en.wikipedia.org/wiki/New_Age
15. en.wikipedia.org/wiki/Prosperity_theology
16. www.generals.org/the-seven-mountains

The seven heads are seven kings (verse 9). Who are they? Does the reference to seven kings mean rulers of the seven empires? If we were to choose five rulers from the past empires, who would we choose? The Roman Emperor at the time of writing was Domitian, but he was not a historically significant leader compared with many other emperors. So, I think the kings are synonymous with empires.

The '*one to come*' has two possibilities. One possibility is the revived Roman Empire. The second possibility is the revived Ottoman Empire. See Appendix 5. Either of these could be revived in our lifetime. But the last empire will last only a few years instead of centuries.

Only the Assyrian Empire does not exist in some form today. Babylon was based in Iraq, and Persia was based in Iran. The Assyrian Empire was based in Iraq and Syria. Does that have any relevance to the comment '*now is not*'? It is interesting the Assyrian empire is also the only one that did not allow for the release of the Jews. Jews left all the other empires, but not the Assyrian empire.

The beast is identified as a king in verse 11. He belongs to the seven in that he rules an empire. He is going to his destruction because he will be put into the lake of fire. This identifies him as either the first beast (Revelation 13), or Satan as the power behind the Antichrist.

According to verses 12 to 14, the ten horns are ten kings or co-rulers who will rule with the beast. Are these ten rulers from within the final empire (Daniel 7:24)? Or are they ten rulers of major countries from around the world who agree to cooperate with the beast for political reasons? They receive their authority for one hour, a short period of time. They give their power and authority to support the beast, and they have one purpose. They will unite against Jesus Christ and make war against the Lamb, but the Lamb will overcome them. Does this refer to Armageddon or the Day of the Lord?

Verse 12 specifically states that the ten kings '*have not yet received a kingdom*', but they will for a short period of time. Traditionally, these are thought to be ten rulers contemporaneous with the first beast. The Greek word for 'king' is *basileus*,[17] and is applied to people with significant power that can be leveraged to the advantage of the top rulers. For example, the herods were vassal kings under the control of the Roman Empire. So, it can apply to rulers over entities other than land. In modern language, we would call them 'influencers'.

One recent suggestion is that the ten kings are the leaders of ten commercial corporations that agree to provide their services to the beast ruler.[18] These services could provide the database of all people on earth and allow their intimate surveillance. We are already aware that companies like Google, Facebook, Twitter, etc already gather information about where we live and work, what we buy, what we watch on YouTube or search on Google, who we bank with, and a host of other information. We see CCTV cameras everywhere watching what we do. Facial recognition allows these to identify who the watchers are observing. These services will be essential for the final rulers of the world to have complete control over everyone.

Another suggestion is they could be ten mega-wealthy people whose companies are involved in technology helping to support the beast system.[19] These companies could cover a wide range of emerging services or technologies such as nanotechnology, quantum computing, genetic manipulation and hybridisation, the

---

17. *Vine's Dictionary*, p 343.
18. 'Who Are The Ten Kings In Daniel And Revelation?', Gary Stearman in *The Prophecy Watcher*, Nov 2020, pp 4-10, 16-17. See also a video discussion at www.youtube.com/watch?v=eKxkoXwv884
19. 'Are the Ten Kings Actually Ten Oligarchs?', Mondo Gonzales in *The Prophecy Watcher*, April 2021, pp 18-19, 32.

internet of things, and satellite internet technology. Two examples suggested are Elon Musk (Tesla electric vehicles, Space X rockets, Starlink satellites, Neuralink computer/brain connectivity) and Bill Gates (Microsoft computers, vaccine technology, microchip nano-vaccine implants, genetically modified farming, and many other technologies).

Notice that there are three qualifications to the people with the Lamb in verse 14. They are '*called, chosen and faithful*'. Many Bible teachers do not like the idea of predestination, that is the idea that God chose us to be his disciples (Ephesians 1:4-5, 11). But it does seem to appear in the Bible.

We are given the meaning of the water on which the prostitute sits in verse 15. They are '*people from every nation, language, and ethnic group*'. This false religion will be found in every part of the world. A possibility is that the religion will be so innocuous that it will be acceptable to almost anyone.

The beast and his ten underlings will come to hate the religious system, and ultimately destroy it (verses 13-17). This seems strange when you remember that it is the religious system that compels people to worship the beast (Revelation 13:14-15). What causes these rulers to turn against this religion? When does this happen? Does this prostitute religion need to be destroyed before the beast religion can be established? If that is the case, the timing is probably half-way through the seven-year agreement when the beast's image is installed in the temple.

Whatever the reason for its destruction, the prostitute religion will be utterly destroyed. It will be stripped of its grandeur and positions of influence. Its properties will be dispersed among the nations. Does this refer to the Roman Catholic Church with its vast wealth, properties, and financial dealings?

What does '*eat her flesh*' mean (verse 16)? We know that burning with fire was the Israelite punishment for fornication (Leviticus

20:14, 21:9). Verse 3 told us the woman was in a desert – a place which cannot sustain life. Is this a reference to Mecca? If the desert is figurative, it is an apt description. Any religion that ignores or substitutes God does not give any spiritual life, and it can be likened to a spiritual desert.

Whose plan was it to destroy the false religion? Verse 17 tells us that it is God's plan. God plants the idea in these rulers' hearts, even though they are controlled by Satan. This shows again that God is always in ultimate control of the politics of the world (Romans 13:1, 4). Here God plants ideas in people's hearts that they fulfil. In Exodus God hardened Pharaoh's heart (Exodus 9:12, 10:20, 11:10).

The final verse tells us the woman is a great city that rules over the kings of the earth. Rome certainly ruled over the kings of Europe during the Dark Ages, but it cannot be said to directly rule over the earth now. Mecca is the centre of worship for the Islamic peoples. But is there a city that rules over the earth? Probably the best candidate today is New York with the United Nations headquarters and the Wall Street stock exchange. The problem is that it is not based in the Middle East.

Will Rome be once again a world-ruling city under a revived Roman Empire? Or will there be an Islamic empire reign from Mecca? Or will Babylon (verse 5) be rebuilt, and the world system be governed from Babylon? I am inclined to think the last scenario will eventuate (see Appendix 10).

Revelation 18

Verses 1 to 3 begin with another angel with great authority and splendour announcing that Babylon is fallen. Much of what the angel says about the inhabitants of Babylon has already been covered in Isaiah and Jeremiah. But the description of why the world mourns its demise is given. The nations had embraced what Babylon had to offer them, and the merchants grew rich from trading with her. Further details are given in verses 11-20. But the end result for Babylon is a home for evil spirits and birds.

Another voice from heaven tells believers to get out of Babylon so they are not destroyed with the city (verse 4). Lot was given a similar warning in Genesis 19:12. It also sounds like Jesus in Matthew 24 and echoes Jeremiah 51:6, 9, 45. Verse 5 shows how sinful the city has become. The new Babylon will be as sinful as the old Babylon. Pride continues to be a part of the city (verse 7). But she will be destroyed by fire in one day (verse 8). Is that literal, or figurative of a short period of time?

The impact on the political world is described in verses 9-10. The world's rulers will mourn its destruction. Their power was derived from Babylon and its systems, but that is now removed as God moves in to take control of the world. Its destruction will be sudden, but there does not seem to be any surprise in their comments. It almost seems that they were expecting it to happen at some stage. Maybe they are relieved at the destruction?

Notice a phrase used to describe the relationship between politics and religion. '*The kings of the earth committed adultery with her*' (verse 9). Are religion and politics supposed to be separated? Ancient Israel had their political leaders come from a different tribe to their religious leaders. Melchizedek is one person where the combination meets with approval (Genesis 14:18), and he becomes the standard for the future (Hebrews 7:14-17) which will be fulfilled by Jesus Christ.

The economic results of Babylon's destruction are listed in verses 11 to 17. Ancient Babylon was involved in the trade of every commodity, as is Babylon is also. Money, gems, clothing, building materials, food, livestock, and people. Notice verse 13 details both the bodies and souls of men. How can you trade the souls of people? What does this mean? Whatever it is, there is an economy surrounding it.

Maybe the Roman Catholic Church practices of indulgences and payments to get people out of purgatory could be trading in the souls of people. These practices involved paying money to either have your sins forgiven or to reduce the time spent in purgatory.[20] But we know that forgiveness of sins is possible only through Jesus Christ (1 Peter 1:18-19), and the concept of purgatory does not appear in the Bible. Both these practices cause people to think their spiritual condition has been improved, whereas the reality is that nothing has changed.

Similarly, Islam teaches a combination of being saved by Allah and doing things to earn merit. Actions such as praying toward Mecca, giving alms to the poor and pilgrimage are all said to help get access to paradise.

The economic impact is mourned by the traders who distribute the goods being traded in verses 17 to 19. Their livelihood has been suddenly destroyed. By way of contrast, people in heaven will rejoice because this destruction is seen as God's judgement for the way believers were treated by the people running the city (verse 20).

An emerging possibility is that Babylon is symbolic of Saudi Arabia. Isaiah 21 is an oracle against Babylon. The names used are all areas in Arabia: the Desert by the Sea (Red Sea?), Dumah (near Medina), Dedan (an ancient name for Saudi Arabia), Kedar (a descendant of Ishmael).[21]

Isaiah 13 is another prophecy about Babylon. Verse 20 specifically mentions that Arabs will not pitch their tents there again. This means that Babylon cannot be Rome because no Arab shep-

---

20. *A Woman Rides the Beast*, pp 179-197
21. *God's War on Terror*, pp 395-397.

herd would be in Rome. Isaiah 34:8-10 talks about burning pitch (crude oil, used to build the tower of Babel). We saw this happen during the first Gulf War when Saddam Hussein set oil wells on fire in Kuwait. Notice that the '*smoke of her burning*' is repeated (Revelation 18:9, 18).

Another mighty angel gives a demonstration of how quickly the city is destroyed in verses 21 to 24. A large boulder is picked up and thrown into the sea. The destruction of Babylon is violent, quick, irreversible, and complete (see Isaiah 13:19).

Many occupations will never again occur there – musicians (entertainers?), tradespeople and food processors (cafe culture?). Electricity will be eliminated. Marriages will no longer occur. The traders of the various commodities were recognised as the world's great people (why not the political rulers?). Even today the news media exalts business leaders more than political leaders: probably because of their length of service in their chosen careers, and probably because the power of many multi-national corporations is greater than most countries.

The Greek word in verse 23 for magic or sorceries is *pharmakeia*.[22] The world was drugged by religion and economic trade, and it led them astray. The world system pictured in Babylon is responsible for the killing of the believers in God (prophets and saints), and everyone else.

This almost brings to a close the end of life on earth under Satan's rule. Remember in chapter 5 the scroll with the seven seals. This was the title deed to the earth. Christ is now ready to return to the earth and regain control of the earth.

---

22. *Vines Expository of Words*, p 587.

Chapter 15

The Return of the King

There is a line by us unseen that crosses every path,
the hidden boundary between
God's patience and His wrath.
- *J.A. Alexander, 1827*

Revelation chapters 14 through to 18 are about God pouring out His judgement on the earth on what the Old Testament prophets called '*the Day of the Lord*'. This is the time predicted when Jesus will finally judge the world for its rejection of Jesus Christ as their Messiah or Saviour.

Chapter 14 finishes with people being judged and God harvests the earth of people. Chapter 15 has angels preparing the seven bowls to be poured out on the earth. Chapter 16 shows us seven bowls of God's wrath, and the armies gathering at a place called Armageddon. Chapters 17 and 18 show us the destruction of man's political and economic system with the destruction of Babylon. Man's attempt to run the world began and ends at Babylon.

Chapter 19 begins a new era. Christ returns to reign on the earth, but it is not without a fight. This chapter destroys many people's mental picture of God as a meek, mild, tolerant, and largely uninvolved grandfather figure. This chapter shows the side of God that most people ignore. A God who hates sin, does punish evil, and does judge wickedness.[1] This pictures God dealing out his fury on unrepentant mankind. This battle will be the bloodiest ever seen in the history of mankind.

Revelation 19:1-10

Verses 1 to 10 are about events that happen in heaven.

After the destruction of Babylon and all that it represents, a multitude is heard shouting praise to God in verses 1-3. Who makes up this multitude? At different times, we have heard of multitudes of angels or multitudes of people saying or singing different things. There is no description given as to who this multitude is. Is it the combined group of people and angels?

People are obviously involved because the multitude talks about salvation. Angels do not seem to have any chance for salvation. (Have you found any verse in the Bible that talks about any angel repenting, or even having a chance at repenting?) It is a concept that seems to be available only to people. The multitude praises God for condemning the prostitute who had corrupted the earth, and for avenging the blood of His servants in verse 2.

The twenty-four elders and the four living creatures fall down and worship God in verses 4 to 5. It is interesting that these two groups are associated throughout Revelation. (Why are they associated?)

We met them in chapter 4 and they worshipped together then by falling down. In chapter 5 they worship together again by falling down. The 144,000 sing a new song before them in chapter 14.

This is the last mention of the twenty-four elders. From here on, they are merged with all the resurrected believers and lose their identity as church believers.

---

1. *Agents of the Apocalypse*, p 195.

The one time they do not worship together is chapter 11 where they worship God because He has finally begun to reign. The word '*Hallelujah*'[2] is found only four times in the New Testament, and all of them are in chapter 19.

I personally find it interesting that every time these two groups worship, they fall face down. Is this relevant to us today? Are we doing our worship wrong? Or is it because they are in heaven in front of God that they worship like this?

A voice came from the throne encouraging all God's servants to praise God. Whose voice is this? God? Christ? An angel?

John hears a voice he has trouble describing (verse 6). We have heard this description in parts before, but never combined. The four living creatures have a voice like thunder (Revelation 6:1). God has a voice like the sound of rushing water (Revelation 1:15). Daniel heard a voice that sounded like a multitude (Daniel 10:6). John hears a sound from heaven in Revelation 14:2, but he does not say what or who the sound was.

Their shouting introduces a new era in verse 6. For the first time, they say that God Almighty reigns. Up until now, man has ruled himself and has failed to establish lasting peace and justice on earth. God now takes over the world and begins to reign. This is the point at which rejoicing and gladness occurs. All the events recorded so far have involved death, destruction, and sadness.

The wedding of the Lamb (verse 7) is covered in Appendix 3. It is the time when God celebrates with all his believers or saints. His bride has prepared herself. The church is referred to as a virgin bride waiting for the bridegroom to come (Romans 7:4, 2 Corinthians 11:2, Ephesians 5:25-33, Is the church the only group to be here? The language suggests that it is.

The bride has made herself ready (verse 8). How? On earth by

---

2. *Vine's Dictionary*, p 287. Means 'praise you Jah'.

having her sin forgiven, and by living righteous and spiritually productive lives. In heaven by being judged for her actions and being rewarded for her works. The final stage of making herself ready is the fine linen to wear. Fortunately for us, this symbol is interpreted as the righteous acts of the saints (verse 8). Our righteous acts are our clothing (James 1:22-25, 2:14-18). It is the thing we are judged on and rewarded for (1 Corinthians 3:10-15).

The angel tells John in verse 9 to record in writing that the people invited to the wedding supper are blessed. When were we invited? Everybody has been invited.

1. We have been chosen by God. Ephesians 1:4, 5, 11.
2. God wants everybody to come to Him and gives everyone plenty of time. 2 Peter 3:9.
3. God accepts everyone who turns to Him. John 1:12.
4. We accept the invitation when we turn to God. John 3:16-18.

The angel emphasises the importance of the wedding supper by adding '*these are the true words of God.*' The angel is repeating exactly what God has told it to say.

For some reason John decides to worship the angel in verse 10, but he is warned not to. The angel says that he is a fellow servant with John. Both believers and angels are working for God. Angels do not have autonomy to do their own thing, but only serve God. Satan tried to do his own thing, and he was punished for it. The angel tells John to worship God. God alone must receive our praise. No one else is worthy of our praise. Saying a 'Hail Mary' means that we disobey God because it praises Mary instead of God. Should we worship the Holy Spirit?

The final sentence (verse 10b) is interesting. The angel tells John that the '*spirit of prophecy is the testimony of Jesus*'. All prophecy throughout the Bible is about Jesus. Even the prophecy in Revelation is about Jesus, although we cover other topics and other people. Ultimately Jesus is the conclusion of all prophecy. If our prophecies in church do not draw us closer to Jesus, they are false prophecies.

There are two aspects to prophecy: the Hebrew view of prophecy, and the Greek view of prophecy. The Hebrew view is based on pattern; the Greek view is based on prediction.

- Every aspect of Hebrew life is based on a pattern that shows how God works salvation.
- Every aspect of the tabernacle and the temples are a pattern that shows how God works salvation for everyone.
- All the festivals show God's salvation and plan for people.
- People's actions were often prophetic. Examples include Abraham (Genesis 22), Noah, Moses (obtaining water from rocks, bronze serpent). See 1 Corinthians 10:11 for an explanation.
- The Hebrew wedding process is also symbolic of how God interacts with the church.

The Greek view says prophecy is prediction. We tend to have a Greek view, but we must also learn to appreciate the Hebrew view.

Revelation 19:11-21

Verses 11 to 18 are about events that happen on earth. This is the climax of the War of Armageddon. John sees heaven open, and a white horse with a rider. We saw another white horse and rider in Revelation 6:2.

- The first rider is not given a name, but this rider has two names to identify him; '*Faithful and True*' (verse 11), and '*Word of God*' (verse 13).

- The first rider went out to conquer, but this rider goes out to judge.
- The first rider was given a crown, but this rider wears many crowns. They are his by right.
- The first rider holds a bow, but this rider has a sword coming out of His mouth.

Who is this rider? Jesus Christ. We know from Joshua that one of Jesus' names is *'the Captain of the army of the Lord'*. He gave Joshua the strategy for conquering Jericho (Joshua 5:13-6:5).

What is the significance of the blazing eyes in verse 12 (Revelation 1:14)? Eyes are symbolic of knowledge and fire is symbolic of punishment. When we combine the symbols, they represent punishment for actions and motives of people. Who will God judge? The people who still refuse to acknowledge God (verse 21).

On His head are many crowns. I think this is the first reference to Christ wearing crowns (other than at Calvary). It shows His authority over various aspects, but they are not explained.

He has a name that no one knows except He himself. This differs from all other times when Jesus reveals himself. He always gives a name so that we know who He is. Sometimes the names are descriptions of what He does, such as *Jehovah Rapha – The Lord that heals* (Jeremiah 30:17, Exodus 15:26). Sometimes the names are descriptions of who He is, such as *El Elyon – The Most High God* (Genesis 14:18, Psalm 57:2, 78:35). But this time it is different. This time, Christ is the indescribable one. Language fails to adequately describe God.

He is described in verse 13 as dressed in a robe dipped in blood. A better description would be 'splattered with blood'. This is because Christ has been judging the armies gathered at Jerusalem (Isaiah 63:1-6). When was the other time Christ wore a robe with blood on it? On the way to Calvary. Blood is symbolic of our salvation, which is achieved only through the blood of Jesus Christ (Isaiah 45:22, 1 Peter 1:18-19).

His name is *'the Word of God'*. John gives Jesus' divine genealogy in John 1, and this introduces Jesus as the Word of God (John 1:1-2, 14). Does this verse contradict verse 12 where His name is unknown?

Jesus' second coming is a great contrast from his first coming.[3]

- He was born in obscurity (Philippians 2:5-7). He will be seen by everybody at this return (Revelation 1:7).
- He was wrapped in cloth (Luke 2:7). He will be clothed in a royal robe (Revelation 19:13).
- He was surrounded by farm animals (Luke 2:16). He will be accompanied by a heavenly army (Revelation 19:14).
- The doors of the inn were closed (Luke 2:7). The doors of heaven will be opened (Revelation 4:1).
- He had the voice of a new-born baby (Luke 2:12). He will have a voice with the sound of many waters (Revelation 1:15).
- He was the Lamb bringing salvation (John 1:29). He will be the Lion bringing judgement (Revelation 5:5).

The armies of heaven follow Christ on white horses and wearing fine linen, white and clean (verse 14). Who are these armies? What do they do? If we go by their clothing, the armies are Christ's saints, the believers. 1 Thessalonians 3:13 says, *'our Lord Jesus Christ will come with all his holy ones.'* Are the holy ones here angels or believers? Jude 14 quotes from Enoch about Jesus coming with his holy ones to judge everyone. These armies could be either angels

3. *Agents of the Apocalypse*, p 198.

or believers. Or a combination of both. So, if you are a believer, you and I may be among this army.

Out of Christ's mouth comes a sharp sword with which to strike down the nations (verse 15). Notice who does the fighting. It is not the armies of heaven. It is Jesus Christ alone who will strike down the nations. When he confronts the first beast (the Antichrist), he will '*overthrow the lawless one with the breath of his mouth and destroy by the splendour of his coming.*' (2 Thessalonians 2:8).

Nations will be judged on how they respond to Jesus Christ. Some people believe Matthew 25:31-46 is a judgement on nations because all the nations are gathered before God. But that may just mean everybody is gathered there, irrespective of the nations they come from. If it is a judgement on nations, the criteria is on how the nation treated the poor, the foreigners, the sick and the disadvantaged. These are the things that Sodom and Gomorrah were judged for (Ezekiel 16:49-50).

Next is a quote from Psalm 2:9 stating that Christ will rule the nations '*with an iron sceptre*'. Why iron? Because it is strong and will withstand pressure. Remember the fourth beast in Daniel's visions (Daniel 2:40, 7:7). It was predominantly iron, and it ruled the world. Similarly, Christ's reign will be total, and He will rule the world.

The '*winepress of the fury of the wrath of God*' is the valley of Jezreel. This has already been covered in Revelation 14:17-20. Matthew 24:30 tells us that all nations of the earth will see Christ returning to the earth. Does this mean the Christ will be physically visible to everyone on earth simultaneously through a miracle? Or does this mean by TV?

The rider's name is written on his robe and on his thigh in verse 16. '*King of Kings and Lord of Lords*'. This leaves no doubt that it is Jesus Christ. Why on the thigh? When you see a rider on a horse, the thigh is the natural place to put your insignia. Everyone will be able to read the thigh.

Verse 17 has an angel calling the birds[4] of the air to eat the flesh of the people who have been killed. This is in preparation for the slaughter that will soon occur. How many people will be killed? John mentions the figure of two hundred million troops in Revelation 9:16.

What is the reason for the massive slaughter of people on an unprecedented scale? The answer may be in Isaiah 24:5-6. '*The earth is defiled by its people; they have disobeyed the laws, violates the statutes, and broken the everlasting covenant. Therefore a curse consumes the earth; its people must bear their guilt.*' The punishment is described in verses 21 to 23. '*In that day the LORD will punish the powers in heaven above and the kings on the earth below. ... the Lord Almighty will reign on Mount Zion.*'

Is this a loving God if He kills so many people? Yes. But people have had many, many chances to get right with God, especially if they are living in this era. Paul talks about three ways everybody has an opportunity to know God, even if they never hear a gospel message.

- We can know God through creation (Romans 1:18-20).
- We can know God through our conscience (Romans 2:13-16).
- We can know God by believing in what Jesus Christ did for us (Romans 3:21-26).

For the people of this era, they have had the example of the 144,000 Jews, they have had the two special witnesses, and they have had the various plaques and natural disasters. These latter

4. The Greek word is *orneois*, which means vultures (*Vines Dictionary of Old and New Testament Words*, p 67). This differs from the birds used in Jesus' parables about the mustard seed and the sower. That word is *peteinon*, which refers to any bird that can fly.

events were all designed to show the power of God and to get people to run to Him. But they didn't. Now they reap the consequences. God has given mankind plenty of time to repent, but it has been ignored (2 Peter 3:9).

Zechariah 14 gives us some more details about this time:

- Verse 4. Christ will come on to the Mount of Olives, and that it will split in two from east to west.

- Verse 5. The armies of God (saints) will arrive after the earthquake.

- Verse 6. The environment will change – '*there will be no light, nor cold or frost*'. Is this an indication that it will happen during the summer? There is no light during the day, but it will be light at night-time. Does this mean the earth's rotation is changed, or its axis is flipped because of the geographical changes? Is this temporary for the day, or does it become a permanent 12-hour change?

- Verse 8. Living water will flow from Jerusalem.

- Verse 10. The whole land will become fertile farmland.

- Verses 12 to 15. The people fighting against Jerusalem will die almost instantly. Is this a nuclear attack? It sounds more like a Peter Jackson horror movie.

The last three verses (19-21) of this chapter are some of the most amazing verses in the Bible. The beast and the false prophet have controlled the world for at least seven years. During that time, the world population has halved, the environment has degenerated with one third of all fresh water going bitter, and the sea dying. The light has decreased to about one quarter of normal resulting in low crop yields and subsequent famine. The world economy has been destroyed, and there have been murder attempts on the Antichrist or war against him.

Despite this, the beast or Antichrist and the world rulers gather their armies to make war against God. We already know the signs that accompany the return of Christ, but still mankind is arrogant enough to think they can fight against God and win. People are so deceived that they believe they have a chance to beat God in a war.

What could make mankind think about making war on God? What weapons will they use? Will there be weapons that are not developed yet? Do they think that God and the host of people coming with Him are an alien invasion?

This may not be as silly as it sounds. The media has a lot of stories about semi-spiritual beings, such as vampires, UFOs, search for alien life, etc. The American armed forces have repeatedly given information about UFO encounters that show that this phenomenon is using technology that is foreign to us. Some people say that they are coming from another dimension. The Roman Catholic Church is expecting alien visitors,[5] and is prepared to baptise them into the Church.

Isaiah 24:21-22 describes changes in the angelic realm. The '*powers in heaven above*' are the spiritual forces that are vying for control on earth. We already know from Daniel that there are spiritual beings controlling the nations. These are now taken prisoner and punished.

The result is that the beast and false prophet are captured and are thrown alive into the lake of fire in verse 20. This is hell, and they seem to be the first to be sent there. It was not meant to be

---

5. *Exo-Vaticana*, pp 529-532.

for people, but it was prepared as the final punishment for Satan and his demons (Matthew 25:41). The rest of the people rebelling against God are killed by military action and their bodies are eaten by the birds. Thus, ends man's reign on earth, and sets the stage for Christ's reign.

Here is something for you to think about. Daniel ends with two dates that don't make sense (Daniel 12:11-12). We know the sacrifices are prohibited in the second half of the 70th week, so the number of days should be 1,260. But here Daniel says there will be an extra 30 days. Is there a 30-day period from Christ's return until the beast and false prophet attack Christ and are captured?

D-Day marked the invasion of Normandy on 6 June 1944. But the battle for Normandy went well into August. Paris was liberated on 25 August 1944. But Daniel says people must wait another 45 days to reach 1,335 days. What is happening during that time?

Chapter 16

Satan's Destiny

Destiny is not a matter of chance;
it is a matter of choice.'
- *Winston Churchill, 1874-1965, English politician*

Chapter 19 saw the end of man's rule on earth and Christ's return to reign on the earth. The reign of Christ is covered in the Old Testament but is largely brushed over in a few words as part of one verse in Revelation. This is covered in Appendix 11. Chapter 20 now deals largely with Satan's fate.

Revelation 20

To set the scene, the beast and the false prophet are in the lake of fire, and Christ has judged the nations. Now an angel comes down from heaven with a key to the Abyss and a great chain. Satan is chained and thrown into the Abyss for a thousand years (verses 1-3).

Presumably all his demons are chained with him. The reason is to prevent the nations from being deceived. They had been deceived for roughly 6,000 years, and the world had been ruined as a result.

Now the world would have 1,000 years of righteous rule with no deception from the rulers. But after the thousand years have ended, he must be set free for a short time.

Who is this angel? No name or rank is given. Is this an angel of important rank? Or is it an angel selected by God for this purpose? Satan was an archangel before pride caused him to rebel against God. Satan was in a position of authority until he rebelled against God when his authority and power were removed. He is now imprisoned for one thousand years.

What is the Abyss? The Greek word is *abussos*, which means 'great depth'.[1] It is a place of punishment for demons. When Jesus removed a group of demons from a man at Gerasenes, they begged Jesus to not send them to the Abyss (Luke 8:31). Demons asked Jesus if He was going to torture them before their time (Matthew 8:29. Luke 4:33-34, 8:27-28).

There is another place of punishment for angels called Tartarus (2 Peter 2:4). This place is described as '*gloomy dungeons*'. This is the only place this word is found in the Bible, but it was commonly used in Greek literature. The Greeks thought Tartarus was the ultimate place of punishment, and they called it 'the dark abode of woe'. They said it was as far below Hades as Hades was below the earth.[2]

Are these the same place? They may be, but the Greek words are different. Wherever they are, they are not nice places to be imprisoned. The angels in Tartarus also seem to be a specific group. They are described as '*angels that sinned*'. Does that describe the angels in Genesis 6:2-4, as opposed to the angels who joined Satan in his rebellion?

Why will Satan be held for only one thousand years? The answer is in verses 7 to 10. God is going to demonstrate that even after a thousand years of perfect rule in a perfect environment, and even with Satan bound, man is still sinful enough to rebel at his first opportunity.

---

1. *Vines Dictionary*, p 74.
2. en.wikipedia.org/wiki/Tartarus

Various people have been given authority to judge in verses 4-6. Or are they angels? These people sat on thrones. Jesus promised his disciples that they would sit on thrones and would judge the twelve tribes of Israel (Luke 22:28-30). I presume the rest of the judges are people who have achieved some rewards from God for their service (Matthew 25:14-30, esp 29). The church is described as a kingdom of priests. Believers from the church age may be the judges.[3]

Who is being judged here? The church had been judged and rewarded before the wedding supper in the previous chapter. The believers who survived the Tribulation will automatically be ushered into the 1,000-year reign of Jesus Christ. The people who had taken the mark of the beast were dead, either from the plagues or killed by Jesus (Revelation 19:21).

Another group of people arrives on the scene. These are the martyrs from the Tribulation period who are resurrected. They have been beheaded, which is the usual Islam method of execution. They had not worshipped the beast or received his mark. They will reign with Christ during the one thousand years.

This is said to be the first resurrection. So, what about church age believers from the Rapture? Was that a resurrection? Yes, but not everyone who was raptured was resurrected, because many of them were still living at the time. The difference this time is that all the people that are resurrected had been killed.

Many writers think the Old Testament believers are resurrected at this time. The reason is that these believers did not have an opportunity to believe in Jesus Christ and His blood that was shed for our sin. They achieved salvation from a relationship with God. This is similar to the Tribulation believers who achieved sal-

3. 'Life During The Millennium' by Larry Ollison. In *The Prophecy Watcher*, November 2020, pp 26-27, 32-34.

vation by recognising Christ as their Messiah. See Isaiah 26:19-21, Ezekiel 37:12-14, Daniel 12:2-3.

An alternative thinking is that Old Testament believers were raised with Jesus at His resurrection. The thinking is that Ephesians 4:8 describes the believers held captive in Hades were freed at the same time that Jesus freed Himself.

John writes, '*blessed and holy are those who take part in the first resurrection*' (verse 6). The second resurrection is those who have never believed in God, and they are therefore destined for hell. Everyone who is resurrected up to this point are priests of God and reign with Jesus Christ. The Old Testament says a lot about the time when Jesus reigns on earth, but this is not mentioned in Revelation. We cover this in Appendix 11.

Verse 7 tells us after the thousand years has been completed Satan is released and will again deceive all nations from all parts of the earth.

Who are Gog and Magog in verse 8? Gog is called '*the chief prince of Rosh, Meshech and Tubal*' in Ezekiel 38:3, 39:1. He is obviously a demonic power behind the nations. The Septuagint has an interesting translation for Amos 7:1. It says, '*The Lord showed me a swarm of locusts, and one of the locusts was Gog the king.*' Physically, locusts do not have a leader because they are swarming insects. So why does Amos refer to a leader and give it a name? It must be important information. Is it to prove the identity of Gog?

Locusts are symbolic of demonic destruction, and the leader of the demons does have a name (Revelation 9:1-11). Rosh, Meshech and Tubal are sometimes said to be the patriarchs of the Russian and eastern European nations, but they can also be traced to regions around Turkey. Maybe Gog is the demonic power behind Europe or the Middle East?

There is a saying that people who do not know their history are doomed to repeat it. The people born during the 1,000-year reign still need to make a choice about whether to accept Christ's rule or reject it.

Over the decades and centuries, memories of how bad things were on earth during the Tribulation will fade from the collective memory.[4] In each generation there will be people who reject the rule of Christ. After a thousand years, there will be a large number who will happily rebel.

Once again, a massive army is gathered in verse 9. No numbers are given but the description is '*like sand on the seashore*'. That gives an indication of the birth rate and the ability of the planet to support the population.

Given that war had not occurred for 1,000 years, I wonder what sort of weapons they will try to use. They will surround Jerusalem, the city God loves. More important, Jerusalem is the city where Jesus reigns as king. But fire will come down from heaven and devour them.

This time, it sounds like not a shot is fired. God launches a pre-emptive strike. There is no mention of any damage to Jerusalem. There are no earthquakes or other signs as in previous times. There may not be any warnings from Christ.

Fire coming down from heaven was often associated with God's judgements, especially when people died as a result. And it seems to be a sudden punishment with no or little forewarning. This has happened previously:

- Sodom and Gomorrah (Genesis 19:24)
- the plague of hail was associated with a large lightning storm (Exodus 9:23-24)
- the death of Aaron's sons for disobeying God (Leviticus 10:2)

---

4. 'Life During the Millennium' by Larry Ollison. In *The Prophecy Watcher*, November 2020, pp 26-27, 32-34.

- Israelites complaining (Numbers 11:1), and
- Elijah's sacrifice when confronting the prophets of Baal (1 Kings 18:38).

The result of this is that the devil is captured and thrown into the lake of fire where the beast and false prophet are (verse 10). From now they suffer torment forever. What sort of torment? I believe it will be mental as well as physical. Everyone is given multiple chances to find God. The biggest torment will be for these people to remember their chances to find God; or in Satan's case to remember back to when he had a choice but chose to rebel against God.

What does this episode prove? That mankind still has a sinful and rebellious nature inside us. We can live in a perfect environment, without Satan tempting us, have perfect leadership throughout our lives, but we will still rebel given the opportunity.

That is the basis of our salvation through Jesus Christ. We cannot save ourselves because we cannot deal with our sinful natures. Only Jesus Christ can deal with our sinful nature and present us as holy and spotless before God. We will always have sin in our lives and will always struggle to do what God wants us to do. But Jesus Christ has paid our debt to God, and the Holy Spirit lives within us to guide us in God's ways.

Immediately after God's defence of Jerusalem, a great white throne appears with God sitting on it (verse 11). The earth and sky flee from God's presence and cease to exist. The throne is floating in space somewhere between what used to be heaven and earth.

The names given to this throne are significant. *Great* speaks of the infinite One who is the judge. *White* speaks of divine holiness, purity, and justice. *Throne* speaks of the majesty of the One who has the right to determine the destiny of his creation.[5]

---

5. *Agents of the Apocalypse*, p 253.

We tend to think of the universe as permanent and fixed in time and space, but the Bible describes it differently:

- The heavens can be shaken (2 Samuel 22:8, Isaiah 13:13, Joel 3:16, Haggai 2:6).

- The heavens are stretched out (Job 9:8, Psalm 104:2, Isaiah 40:22, 42:5, 44:24, 45:12, 48:13, 51:13, Jeremiah 10:12, 51:15, Zechariah 12:1). The Hebrew word usually translated firmament (KJV) or waters (NIV) is *raqia*. It strongly suggests an originally super dense medium stretched out very thin (*'like a tent'*) on the second day of creation week. This means that what God created on day one and two was time, matter, energy, and space. These are the building blocks from which He constructed the universe.[6]

- The heavens had a distinct beginning and will have a distinct end (Genesis 1:1, Job 14:12, Colossians 1:16, Hebrews 1:10). The Big Bang Theory finally caught up with the Bible.

- The heavens can tremble (Isaiah 13:13).

- The heavens can be measured (Isaiah 40:12, Jeremiah 31:37). They are not infinite.

- The heavens and earth will melt with a great heat (Isaiah 34:4, 51:6, 2 Peter 3:12-13)

Over the last 200 years, science has shown that the heavens or

6. www.ldolphin.org/update.html, reprint of *Personal Update*, February 1997 from Koinonia House.

the universe has physical properties. It has dielectric permittivity, magnetic permeability, impedance, elasticity, and zero-point energy (the amount of thermal energy in an absolute vacuum).[7] It has a mass and volume.[8] They had a definite start time and will have a definite end time.

These have been the greatest discoveries of the twentieth century. Before that, the universe was thought to be infinite in time and space. These verses confirm what mathematical physics thinks when it predicts that we live in a ten-dimensional universe.[9]

Why destroy this universe and build a new one? Why not simply purify the existing one? I believe it is because of sin. Everything sinful has to be destroyed. The existing universe (not only earth) is contaminated with sin.

The new heaven and new earth as described in the last two chapters is unlike the existing universe. But despite the descriptions, we still cannot fully imagine what it will be like.

We now have the last resurrection in verse 12 – all the unbelievers. Jesus spoke about this in John 5:28-29. They stand before the throne ready for judgement. The sea gives up all the people who have drowned. Death and Hades give up the people in them. The people alive at the end of the thousand years will also be standing there. Is there any reason the Old Testament believers are not resurrected at this time?

Jesus is the judge on the throne. Jesus said that all judgement has been delegated to him (John 5:22, 27). Paul tells us that our secrets are judged by Jesus Christ (Romans 2:16). Peter said that Jesus was ordained by God to be '*the judge of the living and the dead*' (Acts 10:42).

---

7. www.ldolphin.org/update.html, reprint of *Personal Update*, February 1997 from Koinonia House.
8. en.wikipedia.org/wiki/Observable_universe
9. phys.org/news/2014-12-universe-dimensions.html

Judgement begins when the books are opened (verse 12). These books are records of what everyone has done. God has the biggest database of them all, and it covers every person who has lived. One book has a title, '*the Book of Life*'. Anyone with their name in this book will go to eternity with God, while everyone without their name in the Book of Life is punished in the lake of fire (verse 15).

I think this is the time when what I think is the scariest part of the Bible is fulfilled. Matthew 7:22-23 says that many people will recall the prophecies, deliverances from demons, miracles, and other acts done in Jesus' name. But He will reply, '*I never knew you. Get away from me, you evil doers.*' Many religious people will be in this group, simply because they never asked Jesus Christ to be their saviour.

There are other books at the judgement throne. We are not told what these are, but the Bible does mention other books that God has.[10]

- The Book of the Law. The Jews thought they could earn salvation by keeping the Law. But no one was capable of keeping the Law perfectly (Romans 3:20, 23).
- The Book of Works. God keeps a complete record of what we do, and are judged accordingly (Matthew 16:27, 2 Corinthians 11:15).
- The Book of Secrets. We can keep secrets from other people, but we cannot keep anything hidden from God (Ecclesiastes 12:14, Luke 8:17, Romans 2:16).
- The Book of Words. We will give an account for every idle word we speak (Matthew 12:36-37).

Winston Churchill once said, 'I am ready to meet my maker.

10. *Agents of the Apocalypse*, pp 256-259.

Whether my maker is ready for the ordeal of meeting me is another matter.'[11] Jesus is more than ready to meet the greatest English politician of the twentieth century. Will Winston really be ready to meet God? If he is included in this resurrection, he won't be. What about you? Will you be at this resurrection, or the earlier one?

The lake of fire is the final destination for every person who has not believed in God (verses 14-15). It is the final destination of every angel that rebelled against God. A list of people who end up here is given in Revelation 21:8. The first category is the cowardly. We don't think of cowardice as a sin, but God does. Why? The second category is the unbelieving. You don't have to be a great sinner to get into the lake of fire. You can simply not believe anything you have heard or seen about God.

The Greek term for this place is *gehenna*,[12] and is usually translated as 'hell'. This is the place where the fire never goes out (Matthew 5:22, 10:28, 18:9). Gehenna was originally a name for the place where refuse was burnt in the Valley of Hinnom, south of Jerusalem.

Death and Hades are thrown into the lake of fire (verse 14). This removes all signs of sin. Death is the result of sin (Genesis 2:16-17, 3:19). With death being destroyed, there is no longer any sign of sin, nor any result of sin.

Hebrews 9:27 tells us that man is destined to die once, and then to face judgement. Which judgement will you face? The previous one, or this one? The previous judgement is for people who have had their sin dealt with by Jesus Christ, and it is a reward for our actions. This judgement is for people who have not accepted Jesus Christ as the remedy for sin, and they are punished because they still carry their sin.

---

11. www.keepinspiring.me/winston-churchill-quotes/
12. *Vine's Dictionary*, p 300.

Make sure you have had your sin forgiven and are ready for the first judgement. That is the only way to avoid this judgement. More information is at the end of chapter 18.

Chapter 17

The New Jerusalem

Don't give up! Don't get discouraged!
I have read the end of the book! We win!
- *Desmond Tutu, 1931-2021, South African bishop*

Chapter 21 introduces a new era. Jesus Christ has reigned for 1,000 years while He ruled over the earth. During this time, Satan was bound in The Abyss. Despite this, men still rebelled against God when Satan was released and tried to battle it out with God. But ultimately, sin was put down. Satan finally gets his final punishment by being thrown into the lake of fire.

Chapter 21 starts a completely new and totally different era. The last two chapters reflect the first two chapters of the Bible.

- A new world is created.
- Sin is absent.
- New systems are put in place.

Revelation 21

Verse 1 reminds us that the first heaven and earth passed away (Revelation 20:11). This is brushed over here, but this event is mentioned in other places. We tend to think the universe is so big that nothing can destroy it. We think the universe has been around for so long that it is permanent. But the Bible tells us that God will destroy it and start a new universe.

- Psalm 102:25-27 says God will roll up the heaven and earth like a piece of clothing. This point is interesting. How do you roll up a three-dimensional object? What other dimension is it rolled into? You can roll something into another dimension only when it is thin in that dimension.

- Isaiah 65:17-19 talks about God creating a new heaven and earth, and calling it Jerusalem. He specifically states that the former earth will not be remembered, and that weeping and crying will not be heard here. Everyone will be free from all the effects of sin and evil, death, hunger, trouble, or tragedy.

- Matthew 5:18. Jesus says that heaven and earth will pass away. Until that happens, the scriptures will remain in force.

- 2 Peter 3:10-13. The heavens will disappear with a roar. The elements will be destroyed by fire. Earth will be laid bare. Everything will be destroyed. The elements can be translated as 'building blocks'.[1]

- Revelation 6:14 talks about the heavens receding like a scroll being rolled up.

The Greek word for '*new*' is *kainos*.[2] This word does not mean 'new' as opposed to 'old'. It means it will be completely different. Paul uses the same word in 2 Corinthians 5:17 when he says, '*if*

---

1. *Vine's Dictionary*, p 196.
2. *Vine's Dictionary*, p 430.

any man be in Christ, he is a new creature'. It speaks of a complete change in quality or nature.

The new heaven and earth do not have any sea. Sea is symbolic of nations and people groups. In the new heaven and earth, there are no divisions. God divided the world into languages in Genesis 11:7-9. The world may have been divided geographically in Genesis 10:25. The Hebrew text indicates the division of the earth, the land mass.[3] Was this the start of continental drift?

The sea was a source of fear to seafaring people until a few centuries ago when it was discovered that you can circumnavigate the earth. The flat earth people thought that eventually you could fall off the edge.

Why no sea? Because there is no division among God's redeemed people (Galatians 3:28-29). All divisions disappear because the Christ is the leader.

We are not given any description of what the new heaven and earth will look like. Our current environment is totally different from the world that existed before Noah's flood, as evidenced by the fossil record. So, it should be no surprise when the new environment is totally different again. Would John be able to describe it in a manner that we could understand?

We can infer from verse 23 that there is no sun, moon, or stars. These were originally created to '*mark days, seasons, and years*' (Genesis 1:14). But there is no time in eternity, so we do not need any demarcation of time.

But verse 2 does have a description of the new city, the New Jerusalem. It comes '*down from God out of heaven, beautifully prepared as a bride for her husband*'. Was this city in existence earlier? It may have been the millennial home of the resurrected believers.

---

3. www.ldolphin.org/daysofpeleg.pdf. This is a reprint of the article that was published in *Bible and Spade*, 22.2, 2009, pp 51-64.

It is not said to be created. The wording makes it sound like it already existed and simply came down from heaven. In that case, it may already exist and be sitting in heaven waiting for it to be moved to its final destination.

This is the city that Abraham was looking for. He was seeking '*the city whose architect and builder is God*' (Hebrews 11:9-10). Paul says we are '*enrolled in heaven*' (Hebrews 12:22-23), and this is our final destination. Did Jesus refer to this city in John 14:2-3?

It is '*prepared like a bride for her husband*' (verse 2). This signifies perfection and no expense spared. Brides tend to want everything perfect on their wedding day. The New Jerusalem is perfect in every way. It is the perfection that only God can make.

The New Jerusalem is called '*The Holy City*'. The original Jerusalem was compared with Sodom in Revelation 11:8. Jerusalem has never been a holy city as there was always sin there. This city comes down from heaven, and it is therefore free of any sign or hint of sin.

Isaiah 65:18-19 describes a new heaven and new earth. The New Jerusalem is described as a delight, and its inhabitants are a joy. God himself will rejoice over this Jerusalem.

From this time on, God dwells with people (verses 3-4). Previously God was in heaven and men were on earth. God was present through the Holy Spirit. But now a new era starts where men and God live together. Every cause for sorrow is now removed. Death, mourning, crying, and pain are all abolished from this time. A new order of things is again introduced.

Notice that God will wipe people's tears away. Does that mean that there will initially be some sorrow? About what? But God comes to comfort and reassure people.

The person sitting on the throne says, '*I am making everything new*' (verse 5) Who is this person? Jesus Christ. This is at least the fourth re-creation of the earth.

- Genesis 1 was either the first or second, depending on the interpretation of verse 2.[4]
- Genesis 9 during Noah's flood.
- Revelation 20 at the beginning of the 1,000-year reign.
- This one.

But only the original creation and this one involves a total remaking of the universe. The others were a remodelling of the earth.

John is told to write down a statement from Jesus Christ (verses 6-8):

1. '*It is done.*' Christ's work on earth is completed.

2. '*I am the Alpha and Omega, the Beginning and the End.*' This is a reference to his eternal nature. This title was first used in Revelation 1:9. It is implied in the title given to the church at Smyrna (Revelation 2:8).

3. '*Whoever is thirsty will be given to drink without cost from the spring of the water of life.*' We saw a similar spring of water bringing life to the desert and the Dead Sea coming from under the temple in Ezekiel 47. It brought life to everywhere it went, and produced fruit and food.

   Jesus told the Samaritan woman that anyone who drinks His water will not be thirsty again (John 4:13-14). This living water will be free because all sin would have been dealt with. I do have one question about this verse. Living water

---

4. Genesis 1:2. The Hebrew word for '*was*' can also mean '*became*'. Many commentators think that Satan's rebellion resulted in the destruction of the original creation, and the record in Genesis 1 describes the first re-creation of earth.

is usually associated with salvation from sin and a new life in Christ. Why is this mentioned here when sin had been judged a long time ago? No one needs salvation in this scene.

4. Anyone who overcomes will inherit what the new heaven and earth have. What do we have to overcome to inherit? First, we have to overcome our flesh. It is what prevents many people receiving salvation, and it causes us to regress during our daily lives. Second, we overcome the temptations we encounter by not giving in to them and sinning. Third, we may have to overcome our natural tendency to choose life if we are faced with the option of dying for our faith.

5. Next is a list of people who will not inherit the new creation. First listed are the cowardly, and then the unbelieving. The cowardly are distinguished from the unbelieving. They may believe everything about Christ and His salvation, but never had the courage to take that step and accept it for themselves. That is worse than being an unbeliever, because you almost got there but failed at the final step.

   A list of sinful behaviours of people is given. These are a broad list of sin categories that God will punish people for. The list covers all areas of sin. The punishment is the lake of fire as told in the previous chapter (Revelation 20:11-15).

6. Their ultimate destination is the same place that Satan ends up – the lake of fire. Hell was prepared for Satan and his demons, but not originally for people. People end up there as their final destination simply by refusing to acknowledge God. The second death is eternal separation from God.

Our inheritance is not the same as our rewards. Our rewards are what we get because of what we have done for Christ. Our inheritance is what we get because of our relationship with God. Romans 8:15-17 tells us that God adopts us as His children, and He makes us heirs. Our inheritance is because of our new birth in Christ.

Paul goes further and says that we are all '*joint heirs with Christ*'. Under Jewish law, the eldest son got a double portion of the inheritance. But under Roman law, all children were entitled to equal shares. Paul is telling us that we are all equal in God's sight because of our new birth.

John is invited to see the bride, '*the wife of the Lamb*' (verse 9). The church is called the bride of Christ in 2 Corinthians 11:2. But the description here does not include any mention of people. This chapter gives a description of the city.

In verse 10, John was carried to a high mountain to see Jerusalem descend. Where is this mountain located? Is it a physical mountain? Or is it symbolic of some point where John can see everything?

The city shone with the glory of God (verse 11). It is described as being '*like a jasper that was clear as crystal*'. Most jasper stones are not clear. This description seems to indicate the unique nature of this city. It is a picture of incredible beauty and brilliance. Diamonds were unknown in John's time, so today we might describe the city as resembling a diamond.

The description of brightness and clarity suggests that there are no shadows or mists. Darkness represents sin and shame, and the fact that there is something to hide from God. But this is a sinless environment, and all sin has been dealt with previously. Nothing can be hidden in this city. There is no need to hide anything.

The city has a high wall with twelve gates and twelve angels at the gates (verses 12-14). Why does this city need walls? They were needed to keep enemies out, but there are no enemies at this time. The walls symbolise security. Our eternal security is in Jesus Christ.

What is the role of the angels at the gates?

- Angels have been guardians (Genesis 3:24, Exodus 23:20, 2 Kings 19:35, Psalm 34:7, Isaiah 37:36, Daniel 6:22, Acts 5:19). So what are they guarding against?

- Angels have been messengers (Genesis 16:9-11, 21:17-18, Exodus 3, Numbers 22:32-35, Judges 6, 13, 2 Kings 1, Zechariah 1, Matthew 1, Luke 1, Acts 10, 27:23 plus numerous examples in Revelation). What message do they need to pass on?

The twelve gates are named after the twelve tribes of Israel. There are also twelve foundations named after the twelve apostles. Will Judas have his name there? If not, then who will replace him? Two men were selected, and Matthias was voted as his replacement (Acts 1:26). Is his name on the foundations?

I find it interesting that this is the first time that Israel and the church are mentioned in the same context. Obviously, all the redeemed believers in this Jerusalem are there because of either Israel or the church. Christianity and Judaism are finally amalgamated.

Previously, Israel and the church were separated. They had different beginnings, different roles, different structures, and different destinies. Now they are finally combined into a single entity of believers.

The gates are distributed around the city with three gates on each side (verse 13). Similarly, when Israel camped in the wilderness, there were groups of three tribes on each side of the tabernacle (Numbers 2), except that the tribe of Levi was camped in the centre. Notice the compass points. There are directions in this city, but are they the same as on earth?

The city is measured and found to be 2,200 kilometres long, wide, and high (verses 15-21). Is the shape a cube or pyramid? Chapter 22:1-2 could suggest a pyramid shape as the river flows down the street. But a river can still flow down inside a cube.

New Zealand is about 1,600 kilometres from Cape Reinga to Stewart Island. 2,200 kilometres is the distance from Auckland to Sydney. The City of London (not the greater city) has an area of 2.9 square kilometres and a population of around 9,400.[5] On that basis, this city can hold over 100 billion people on one level alone. It is big enough to hold everyone who has been conceived since the beginning of time.

Its height extends far into the sky. The International Space Station orbits around 420 kilometres above earth.[6] So the top of this city extends six to seven times further into space.

In Solomon's temple, the Holy of Holies was a cube of 20 cubits or about 10 metres (1 Kings 6:20). That was the holiest place on earth at that time. The New Jerusalem is the Holy of Holies for eternity. It the sanctuary of God Himself.

The city has a wall 65 metres thick (verse 17). What is the wall for? Does the city need protection? From what?

Next comes a description of the city, and its foundations (verses 18-21). It sounds like all the materials are transparent and allow light to be transmitted. Even the gold is described as being as clear as glass. So how is it recognised as gold?

The twelve foundations are described as twelve gems. When you compare the stones used in this foundation and the stones used for the high priest's breastplate (Exodus 28:15-20), there are

---

5. en.wikipedia.org/wiki/City_of_London#Geography
6. en.wikipedia.org/wiki/International_Space_Station

seven in common. But the order in the two lists is different. Is this significant?

The twelve gates are made of pearl. But pearls are produced by oysters which are an unclean fish according to Leviticus 11:9-12. So why are the gates made from pearls?

You would be tempted to think that everything is in the New Jerusalem. But there are some things missing!

John tells us that there is no temple in this city (verse 22). There is no need for a temple because God is now living with his people. Both God and the Lamb are mentioned here. Where is the Holy Spirit? There is no need for the Holy Spirit here. He was given to us on earth to help us (John 14:16-17, 26).

There is no sun or moon (verse 23). The source of light is described as the glory of God. All people will walk in the light that is there. The nations will walk by its light. Does this mean that we still have national identities in this city? The kings of the earth will bring their splendour into the city. Their splendour will probably look rather pale compared to the splendour of the city. What will they bring? Does this mean that there will be people living on the new earth? If so, who are they?

One idea is that there will be people living outside the city. These are people who have been saved from their sin, but they lived a life unworthy of any rewards. They do not receive any rewards at the judgement seat after the Rapture.

Jesus told five parables where people are sent to the '*outside darkness where there will be weeping and gnashing of teeth*'. One of these parables is Matthew 22:1-14. A king prepares a wedding banquet for his son, but the invited guests refuse to attend. The king sent servants out to ask anyone to come. But one man came to the wedding but did not have the appropriate clothing. He was cast out into the outside darkness.

This is seen to be symbolic of people who have responded to the invitation for salvation. They have accepted Jesus Christ as their saviour. But they have not done anything since to earn a reward or to get correct clothing (Revelation 19:8). They are not judged at the Great White Throne because their sin has already been dealt with. But they fell short of God's requirements for righteous living.[7] Are these people referred to in Revelation 22:15?

Because they are outside the city, they live in comparative darkness. There will be weeping because they realise the opportunities that had been lost. See Appendix 3 for a discussion on this idea.

There is no security system! The gates of the city will never shut (verse 25). Ancient cities shut the gates at night to prevent enemies entering undetected during the night. But in the new creation, there will be no night, and there will be no enemies wanting to enter the city.

There is a lot of information not given to us. Can we leave the city when we want to? Maybe we can because there are open gates in the walls. Where will we go and what will we do outside the city?

The glory and honour of the nations will be brought into the city (verse 26). How does this compare with the kings bringing splendour two verses ago? What exactly will the nations bring in?

Whatever enters the city, it will be pure (verse 27). Nothing that will defile the place will enter. No impure person will ever enter this city. The new creation will be characterised by purity. The only people in the city will be redeemed people; people whose names have been recorded in God's Book of Life (Revelation 20:11-17).

Revelation 22

John continues his tour of the New Jerusalem with the angel in chapter 22. He is now shown a river of the water of life which flows

7. *The Kingdom, Power and Glory*, pp 83-95, 266-275.

from the throne of God down the middle of the main street. The water is described as clear as crystal.

Notice that everything in this new world is transparent:

- Revelation 21:11 – the city is clear as crystal.
- Revelation 21:18 – the walls are pure as glass.
- Revelation 21:21 – the streets are like transparent glass.

What does this mean? The purity of the water symbolises the holiness and purity of God. But it could simply mean that there is no need to hide anything. Sin caused Adam and Eve to hide their bodies behind fig leaves and to hide themselves from God. Because this environment is sinless and pure, there is nothing to hide and no need to hide from anyone else.

The river has been mentioned before. Chapter 21:6 tells us that the river is for drinking, and it is without cost. A similar river existed during the millennium (Ezekiel 47:1, 12 and Zechariah 14:8).

On this earth, all rivers eventually flow into the sea. But the new earth does not have any sea (Revelation 21:1). So where does this river go to?

The throne from which the river originates is called '*the throne of God and of the Lamb*'. Both God the Father and God the Son now share the throne. Where is the Holy Spirit and what is His role at this time? This is the first time that Christ sits on a throne with God. Currently, Christ is not on a throne. Jesus is seated at the right hand of God (Hebrews 1:3, 10:12). It is this throne the prophets mean when they say that Christ's reign will never end.

Verse 2 tells us that on each side of the river is '*the tree of life*'. The trees have 12 crops of fruit, one for each month. This shows God's continued provision for His people. The trees fruit monthly. Does this mean that there will be time in the New Jerusalem? The leaves of the tree are '*for healing the nations*'. What does that mean?

The Greek word for healing is *therapeia*,[8] which is best translated as a medical service that gives health. There is no sickness in this environment, but somehow these leaves seem to contribute to the physical well-being of everyone. Do we eat the leaves as well as the fruit?

Is this the same tree mentioned in Genesis 3:22 and 24? Both trees are in places where sin is absent. Sinful people cannot eat from this tree. The church in Ephesus was promised that if they overcome, they will earn the right to eat from the tree of life (Revelation 2:7). Only people who are obedient to God can eat from this tree (verse 14). It is free for people to eat from. God has provided the price through Jesus Christ. The fruit is continually available. The moral is that God wants us to live a life of obedience free from sin. This is what brings eternal life.

There is no longer any curse (verse 3). No healing for illness is necessary. The curse was introduced by Adam's sin, and this introduced pain, toil, weeds, sweat, sickness and death. But this has been eliminated when everything sinful was put into the Lake of Fire.

The throne of God and of the Lamb are in the city. The previous chapter told us that God and the Lamb are the temple (21:22). Now we are told that His servants will serve God. What will they be doing?

We will have a privileged place because we will see God's face (verse 5). This indicates that we will be under God's good favour. Moses was not allowed to see God's face, but he was allowed to see God's back (Exodus 33:21-23). God's name will be on the servant's foreheads. We have come across this expression before, and it means that we are sealed by God for His purposes. We will have the freedom to be in God's presence because of our resur-

8. *Vine's Dictionary*, p 294.

rection bodies which will be without any form of corruption (1 Corinthians 15:42-44, 49).

Once again John tells us in verse 5 that there will be no lamps or sun for light. God is the source of light. This is a repeat of 21:23-24. John repeats we will reign with Christ for ever and ever. What or who will we be reigning over? These two facts seemed to make a great impression on John.

This finishes the description of the New Jerusalem. The remainder of the chapter has an encouragement from Jesus with some supplementary comments from John.

There is still one question to be answered. What will we do in the New Jerusalem? There is no mention of us lying on clouds playing harps. We must be busy doing something. Will we be praising God and worshipping for eternity? Or are there other things to do? Can we go in and out of the city? If so, to do what?

The angel guiding John now tells him that these things are trustworthy and true (verse 6). Did John have some doubts about what he had seen? Or was it simply too great to be believable? Whatever the reason, we are told that everything we have read is true.

The purpose for John seeing this vision is stated again (verse 6). The Lord showed John '*things that must soon take place*'. This verse alone shows that we must take the book of Revelation literally. The things described will happen.

We may not understand all of it, but we are given enough information to be able to recognise the signs when they occur. We are warned about things to avoid to ensure we enter the New Jerusalem. In chapter 1 we were told about things to happen. Now a timeframe is given for us.

Christ now seems to speak in verse 7. He reiterates that He is coming soon, and He states this three times before the end of the chapter. What does soon mean? After all, these words were written over 1900 years ago. 2 Peter 3:9 tells us that God delays things to give people time to repent. The word translated soon is *tachu*,[9] and can mean 'quickly'. We know that when God acts, He acts quickly.

The promise of a blessing for keeping this book is repeated in verse 7. The first mention of blessing for reading Revelation is in chapter 1:3. Now we are told we will be blessed if we keep to the words of prophecy in this book. Keep what? Keep to the principles of God, and do not capitulate to the beast system. This will mean hardship and possible martyrdom, but ultimately, we will be blessed as a result.

When John had seen the things revealed to him, he fell down to worship the angel who was his guide (verse 8). What was it that made John worship the angel? Was it the total revelation? Or the last part about the New Jerusalem? John had made this mistake previously (Revelation 19:10).

The angel reprimands John in verse 9, and repeated what he said previously almost word for word. We are told to not worship angels or created beings (Exodus 20:3-6). Angels are servants of God. They have a similar relationship to what we do. They are God's servants, like the prophets and we are.

Angels have many of the attributes that we do. They have intelligence, a will, and feelings. They have a personality. But they are still only created beings like we are. The only entity we should worship is God.

John is now told to not seal up the book because the end is near (verse 10). This contrasts with Daniel who was told to seal up his book (Daniel 12:4, 9). Daniel's words will be sealed until the end of the times, and then the wise will understand what Daniel wrote about (Daniel 12:10).

9. *Vine's Dictionary*, p 503.

Note Daniel says the wicked people will never understand what he wrote. They do not have the understanding that is given by the Holy Spirit.

Revelation is an open book. Many symbols are explained for us as we read it so that we can understand it. We are given enough information to know God will intervene in the affairs of mankind and judge the world, then bring in His kingdom. We are given instructions about what God expects from his church.

Verse 11 is puzzling. Why does God want wrong and vileness to continue? The point here is not to continue doing wrong, but to point out that if people do not heed this prophecy, they will continue in their wickedness. The judgements of God are always designed to turn people to Him. Mankind is so stubborn that they will continue to disregard God when He does bring judgement.

The flip side is that if we are doing right and being holy, we should continue doing those things.

Christ now speaks (verses 12-16) and repeats that He is coming soon. His reward is with Him, and He will give to everyone according to our actions. This refers to every judgement. It refers to the judgement seat of Christ (2 Corinthians 5:10-11) where rewards are given to believers for their actions. It refers to any judgement seat.

Unbelievers are judged at the great white throne based on their works (Revelation 20:11-12). The main work we are judged on is how we respond to Jesus Christ. If we accept Christ, we are rewarded with eternal life. If we reject Christ, we are rewarded with the Lake of Fire. See the last chapter for how you can accept Christ if you have not already done it.

Christ again describes himself as '*the Alpha and Omega*' (verse 13). This is the same person who introduced the book in the first chapter (verse 8). This whole book is a revelation from Jesus Christ. He is at the beginning and is at the end. He existed before creation, and He will continue to exist after the new creation.

Christ now pronounces a blessing on those who wash their robes (verse 14). This could be a reference to Revelation 7:14 where people from the Great Tribulation have washed their robes in the blood of the Lamb. It could refer to the bride at the wedding of the Lamb where clean linen was worn (Revelation 19:8). Washing your robes is symbolic of obeying God and living by his standards. These people have the right to eat the tree of life and to come in through the gates of the city.

This contrasts with the unbelievers who are said to be outside of God's blessings and rewards (verse 15). The rest of the verse describes the sins of the unbelievers. The final description is symptomatic of all unbelievers – they love and practice falsehoods to the extent they do not accept the truth about God. But if the unbelievers have been sentenced to the lake of fire, who is outside the city? Are they the people we discussed earlier?

Jesus tells John in verse 16 that He had sent the angel to show John the message for the churches. He gives another description of himself. The historical Jesus was descended from David by both sides of his earthly family.[10] The title '*Root of David*' has been used in Revelation 5:5, but ultimately refers to Isaiah 11 where the title is used twice for the person who will rule the world with righteousness.

The '*bright Morning Star*' is a new title. The morning star is a star that shines brightly shortly before the sun rises. Maybe this title suggests that Christ is going to arrive shortly to begin His judgements. This will usher in a bright new day for the world.

Different groups now join in asking Christ to return (verse 17). The first group is the Holy Spirit and the bride. The bride is probably the church (2 Corinthians 11:2), but it could include other believers who are going to be at the wedding of the Lamb (chapter

---

10. Matthew's genealogy is to Mary. Luke's genealogy is to Joseph.

19). People who hear the message of this revelation want Christ to come and judge the world.

An invitation is given for anyone who is thirsty to come and drink from the water of life. Jesus told the Samaritan woman that only He can give living water (John 4:10-13). Isaiah 55:1 tells us to get water that comes from God. The water is a free gift. It is free because Jesus paid the price with His death at Calvary. See the final chapter for how to access this.

There is a final warning from Christ in verses 18-19. If anyone adds to these words, the plagues described will come upon them. If anyone subtracts from these words, they will not partake in the holy city. Rejecting the word of God is rejecting God Himself. We are strongly encouraged to take these words seriously.

That means we cannot allegorise this book. We cannot think that this is a good story, or that it has already been fulfilled. We must be ready to be a participant; either as a believer in God and finally enter the New Jerusalem, or as an unbeliever going through the judgements and ultimately being sent to the Lake of Fire.

Christ says again He is coming soon in the last two verses. John closes the book with a simple request to come as promised. He gives a short benediction to close the book.

Chapter 18

Final Thoughts

If man is not made for God,
why is he only happy in God?
If man is made for God,
why is he so opposed to God?
– Blaise Pascal, 1623-1662, French mathematician

Revelation is a book of different themes, but it is integrated in many ways. The main theme throughout Revelation is Jesus Christ:

- Chapter 1 opens with a picture of the glorified Christ.

- Chapters 2 and 3 give Christ's messages to the seven churches. Although they were for specific churches at that time, they are relevant to churches all through history, including today. Every individual church today will correspond to at least one of these churches, and therefore will probably have some area to improve in.

- Chapter 4 gives us a picture of Christ being worshipped in heaven.

- Chapters 5 and 6 show the crucified Christ accepting the scroll and opening its seals. This is the only time Christ appears as the crucified Lamb. This is His last act regarding salvation. From here on He is depicted as being victorious, and shows Christ acting as the ultimate king and judge.

- Chapters 7 to 19 show a judging Christ who is punishing mankind for their rejection of Him. But throughout this time, he is also a redeeming Christ who is picking out groups of people who will follow Him.

- Chapters 19 to 22 show us an eternal Christ. He is shown as the centre of the new Jerusalem.

Another theme throughout Revelation is 'overcoming' or 'patient endurance':

- Every message to the seven churches has a reward for the overcomers. These are: the right to eat from the tree of life (Ephesus), will not be hurt by the second death (Smyrna), a new name (Pergamum), authority over the nations (Thyatira), name to remain in the book of life (Sardis), be a part of God's temple (Philadelphia), and be given the right to sit on Christ's throne (Laodicea).

- The 144,000 people sealed in chapter 7 overcome the dangerous circumstances they live in, and they are with Jesus Christ on Mount Zion in chapter 14.

- The two special witnesses are given power to repel and overcome anyone trying to hurt them for three and a half years. They are resurrected three and a half days after their assassination to enter heaven (chapter 11).

- The Jews who flee to God's prepared hiding place are protected from the attacks of the dragon (chapter 12).

- Jesus Christ overcomes the armies that come against him twice. The first time is in chapter 19 when the first beast and the worldwide coalition fight against Jesus. The second time is after the millennial kingdom when God does a pre-emptive strike against the rebellion (chapter 20).

- Many believers overcome surviving without the mark of the beast to help populate the millennial kingdom (chapter 20).

Another theme is the judgements that God will perform:

- First, God judges the seven churches that represent all churches throughout history. Each church is given a report on what they are doing well, what they are doing wrong, and how to improve. This judgement is an assessment rather than punishment.

- Second, God judges (punishes) the people on earth for their sin and rejection of Jesus Christ. Many of the judgements seem to repeat with an increasing intensity. They are designed to persuade people to turn to Jesus for forgiveness, but most people continue to behave as though Jesus does not exist.

- Third, God punishes Satan and his demons for deceiving people and the nations throughout history.

Remember what Paul wrote to the people at Corinth. '*We must all appear before the judgement seat of Christ, that each may receive what is due to him for the things done while in the body, whether good or bad*' (2 Corinthians 5:10). If you have asked Jesus to forgive your sin, the judgement will be a reward for how well you have been a disciple (see Appendix 3). If you have never had your sin forgiven, you will appear at the second judgement, and there will be no time for changing your mind (see chapter 16). The choice is yours.

The last three chapters of Revelation are a mirror image of the first three chapters of Genesis:

- A new heaven and earth are created in Genesis. This is destroyed in Revelation and a new heaven and earth are created.
- The world was created as a sinless environment, and the new world will finish as a sinless environment.
- Sin enters the world in Genesis 3, and it is eradicated in Revelation 20.
- God has daily fellowship with his creation in Genesis, and He will be the centre of the New Jerusalem in Revelation.
- Sinful people are denied access to the tree of life in Genesis, but redeemed people are given free access to the tree of life in Revelation.

Can you think of any others?

I have asked a lot of questions through this book. There are still many aspects that I do not understand. But these questions do not have any material impact upon the meaning and predictions in Revelation. What is predicted will certainly happen. The Bible has proved its ability to predict events by correctly predicting numerous events in the past. As a result, we can be certain that future events will happen as described.

As a believer in the truth of the scripture, we can repeat the last phrase John wrote, '*Come, Lord Jesus.*' Although we do not know when the predicted judgements will begin, we must be prepared for them to begin at any time.

I guess the main question is, 'Am I ready to face Jesus Christ?' Each of us must do an audit of ourselves to see how we compare with God's standard. If you are ready to face Jesus Christ, we need to get busy getting other people ready to face Christ.

If you have never accepted Jesus Christ as your saviour, you need to do it now. There are four principles that you need to know.[1]

1. **God loves you and has a wonderful plan for your life.** '*God loved the world so much that He gave His one and only Son, so that everyone who believes in Him will not perish but have eternal life.*' (John 3:16). Jesus said, '*I came that they may have life and have it to the full*' (John 10:10).

2. **Man is sinful and separated from God.** Therefore, people cannot know and experience God's love and plan for their lives. Paul wrote, '*Everyone has sinned; we all fall short of God's glorious standard*' (Romans 3:23) and '*the wages of sin is death, but the gift of God is eternal life*' (Romans 6:23). That means eternal separation from a holy and perfect God.

3. **Jesus Christ is God's only provision for sin.** Jesus Christ died as our substitute to pay the penalty for our sin. '*God showed His great love for us in this: while we were still sinners, Christ died for us*' (Romans 5:8). Jesus said, '*I am the way, the truth and the life. No one comes to the Father except through me.*' (John 14:6).

4. **We must individually receive Jesus Christ as Saviour**

1. These are from a tract titled 'The Four Spiritual Laws'.

and Lord. Only then can we know and experience God's love and plan for our lives. '*To all who believed Him (Christ), He gave the right to become children of God*' (John 1:12). We receive Christ through faith. '*It is by grace that you are saved, through faith – and this is not from yourselves, it is the gift of God – not by our works, so that no-one can boast.*' (Ephesians 2:8-9).

If you want to accept Jesus as your saviour, pray this:

God, I acknowledge that I am a sinner and need your salvation. I believe that Jesus was crucified as the sacrifice for my sin. I believe that he was resurrected to prove that He is the Son of God. Please forgive my sin. Cleanse me from unrighteousness. Make me your child. Fill me with your Holy Spirit to lead me and guide me through my life.

If you have prayed that prayer, you are now safe from the judgements and plagues described in Revelation. But now you need to ensure that you will be rewarded and enter the New Jerusalem. You now need to find a local church that teaches the Bible seriously, join an encouraging small group, and live a life that is pleasing to God.

Appendices

Appendix 1

Symbols Used in Revelation

Bronze	The metal involved in judgement. The bronze altar in the temple and tabernacle are bronze because it can handle fire.
Crown	Authority.
Eagle	Swift action.
Eyes	Knowledge.
Feet	Symbolic of judgement, especially when something or someone is placed under the feet.
Fine linen	Righteous acts of believers.
Fire	Judgement resulting in purity.
Five	The number associated with man's work or actions.
Four	The number associated with the earth.
Gold	The metal associated with God. It is the only metal found as a pure element in nature. All the furniture inside the tabernacle and temple is gold.
Head	Intelligence.
Horns	Leadership and/or strength.
Incense	Prayers of the saints (believers).
Lampstands	Churches.
Mountains	Kingdoms.
Olive trees	Israel.
Purple	Royalty, kingship.

Red	War, bloodshed.
Rock	Jesus Christ, the Messiah.
Scarlet	Sacrificial ministry on the cross.
Sea	Mankind. Raging sea symbolises mankind is a state of unrest. Calm seas symbolises mankind at peace. Usually refers to Gentile nations.
Seven	The number of completeness. The heavens and earth were created in seven days.
Six	The number associated with man.
Stars	Angels (including fallen angels or demons).
Sword	Truth.
Ten	The perfection of God's order.
Twelve	The number of God's people.
Trumpets	Used for announcements and proclamations, especially judgements.
Twenty-four	The number associated with priests.
Walls	Security, safety.
Water	The Word of God (scriptures).
White	Purity and righteousness.

Appendix 2

What is the Rapture?

Has this world been so kind to you
that you should leave with regret?
There are better things ahead than any we leave behind.
- *C.S. Lewis, 1898-1963, author*

In Revelation chapter 4 we saw the church was in heaven and involved in worshipping Jesus Christ. How and when did this happen? How can we be sure the church is removed from earth before most of the events that happen in Revelation?

One point of clarification. The church is defined in the Bible as all people from the resurrection until now who have believed in Jesus Christ, had their sins forgiven, and acknowledge Jesus Christ as their Saviour and Lord. It does not refer to the church as an institution such as Anglican, Catholic, Baptist, etc.

Organisations cannot be redeemed, only people can be. There are people in almost all local churches who have not had their sins forgiven, or do not believe in a resurrected Jesus Christ. Many institutional churches have non-believers in leadership roles. We need to make this distinction clear to avoid confusion later.

Jesus Christ's Returns

When we read about Jesus Christ returning it is possible to get confused. Some verses say He will appear in the clouds and come to meet the believers in the air while others say He will land on the Mount of Olives. Some verses refer to a war while others don't.

Jesus predicted that He would return to the earth after His death and resurrection (Matthew 26:64; Mark 14:62 John 14:3, 18; 16:16; 21:22). There were numerous references in the Old Testament about the Messiah taking up David's throne. The angel Gabriel told Mary that her son would be given David's throne (Luke 1:26-33). Paul writes in the New Testament about Jesus' return (1 Corinthians 15:51-54; 1 Thessalonians 4:13-18).

As you study this topic, you will find many inconsistencies until you realise that Jesus will return twice. The table lists some of the differences.

First Return	**Second Return**
Coming to meet believers and take them to heaven. (John 14:1-3, 1 Thessalonians 4:16-17, Hebrews 9:28)	Returning with resurrected believers. (Colossians 3:4, 1 Thessalonians 3:13, Jude 14)
No judgements.	Earth is judged. (Daniel 7:27, 2 Thessalonians 1:8)
Imminent, could happen at any time. (2 Peter 3:10, Revelation 22:7, 12, 20)	Occurs after a period of 7 years after many detailed events. (Revelation 19:11)
Not mentioned in the Old Testament.	Predicted in the Old Testament. (Daniel 2:44-45)
Occurs before the day of wrath. (1 Thessalonians 1:10, 5:9, Revelation 3:10)	Concludes the day of wrath. (Matthew 24:21-22)

No reference to Satan.	Satan is bound for 1,000 years. (Revelation 20:2-3)
Jesus comes to meet believers in the air. (1 Thessalonians 4:16-17)	Jesus comes to the earth. (Daniel 7:13-14, Zechariah 14:4)
Jesus claims His bride.	Jesus comes with His bride. (Jude 14)
Only believers will see Him. (1 Thessalonians 4:16-17)	Everyone will see Him. (Matthew 24:27, 30, Revelation 1:7)
Tribulation begins sometime after.	Millennial kingdom begins immediately. (Acts 3:21)
Believers (saints) go to heaven. (1 Corinthians 15:21-23, 52, Colossians 3:4)	Saints return to earth with Jesus. (1 Thessalonians 3:13, Jude 14)
Jesus does not set up a kingdom.	Jesus sets up His kingdom. (Matthew 24:26-31)
No immediate physical changes on the earth.	Big physical changes on the earth. (Isaiah 40:4, Zechariah 14:4, 8, 10)

In this appendix we will cover the first return of Jesus, and the timing aspects. This event is called 'The Rapture'. Appendix 3 covers what happens immediately after the Rapture. We cover the second return in chapter 15. This whole topic is very controversial, so I will try to cover all the various scenarios that have been suggested. But please do your own research and decide for yourself what you believe is correct.

What is 'The Rapture'?

Most studies of the end times recognise that Jesus' coming triggers a series of events. The first coming is called the 'Rapture'. How does it get its name? This term is not in the English Bible. There are two possible and related explanations for this term.

1. From the Latin *rapiemur* which is a translation of the Greek word *harpazo*, which means 'to be forcibly snatched, to be taken away'.[1]
2. From the Latin *rapturo* which means 'caught up'.

The original reference to this event was Jesus speaking to his disciples in the Upper Room before going to Gethsemane in John 14:1-3. Jesus told his disciples three things:

1. Do not be troubled,
2. He was going away to prepare a place for them in His Father's house, and
3. He will come again to take them to be with Him.

Did Jesus take the disciples to the Father's house? No. So this is still to happen. When Jesus ascended to heaven after the resurrection, he went alone and left his disciples standing and watching (Acts 1:9-10).

Why is the Rapture needed? Isaiah 57:1 talks about righteous people being taken away to protect them from evil. That makes sense when we read about what will happen during the Tribulation period.

---

1. *The Rapture*, p 8.

How Will The Rapture Happen?

The main references to this event are in 1 Thessalonians and 1 Corinthians 15:51-52.

1 Thessalonians 4:13-15. Some of the believers in Thessalonica were concerned that the people who had died would not see the return of Christ. Paul reminds them Jesus died and rose again. So every believer who dies will be raised at some point. Remaining alive does not impact upon the resurrection of those believers who have died. Paul gives a description of how it will happen.

1 Thessalonians 4:16-17. Jesus himself will descend from heaven with a loud command. There will be the voice of an archangel. There will be a trumpet call of God. With these three sounds, the dead believers will rise first, then the living believers will meet Jesus in the air. From this point all believers in Jesus Christ will be with Him forever.

These verses contain a lot of information, and some unanswered questions.

1. Jesus will leave heaven to come to the earth, but not stand on the earth. He will meet the believers in the air (verse 17). This makes a distinction between this return and when Jesus returns to stand on the Mount of Olives (Zechariah 14:4, Revelation 19:11-21).

2. Jesus will give a command. What will that command be? Will it be a command for all believers to meet Him? Will it be a command for the earth to give up the dead believers? (Luke 7:14, John 11:43, 5:28-29) The Greek word *keleusma* means a shouted command as used in the military.[2]

---

2. *Vine's Dictionary*, p 572.

3. There is a voice of an archangel. One archangel is mentioned in the Bible – Michael (Jude 9). Michael is the angelic prince over the nation of Israel (Daniel 10:21, 12:1). Is the archangel Michael involved in taking believers to heaven? Or is this another archangel who has not been named? Or does Jesus speak with the sound of the archangel? Do angels accompany God for the Rapture as they did for His ascension (Acts 1:9-11)?

4. The trumpet call of God means a new beginning. The first time the trumpet call of God was heard was at Mount Sinai (Exodus 19:16). At that time God was introducing a new order. He gave a new way of life with defined ways of living and interacting with God. The trumpet call at the Rapture introduces a new way of life. Believers are taken to heaven (1 Corinthians 15:52) while unbelievers are left in a sinful world.

5. The dead believers will be resurrected before the living believers are taken up. The verse says, '*the dead in Christ*'. This does not refer to Old Testament believers in God who will be raised at a later resurrection (Daniel 12:2, Revelation 20:11-15). Only people after Jesus' resurrection are called '*in Christ*'. Why not all believers?

6. Paul believed that he and his readers might well be alive when the Rapture takes place. He used the term '*we*' meaning that he expected Christ's return at any time. There is no prediction that needs to be fulfilled before Jesus Christ returns to take us to be with Him.

7. All believers in Christ will be with Him forever. We will be taken to the place that He is preparing for us (John 14:2-3).

But the important thing for Paul was who we would be with, not the where.

1 Corinthians 15:51-52 is a summarised version, but it does add information:

1. We will be changed at the Rapture. We leave our earthly bodies behind and get heavenly bodies. Our bodies of sin, death and decay are changed for incorruptible bodies (verses 40, 42-44, 53-54). As we read through this chapter, we find our resurrection bodies will undergo seven transitions:

   - Perishable to imperishable (verses 42, 53)
   - Dishonour to glory (verse 43)
   - Weakness to power (verse 43)
   - Physical to spiritual (verse 44)
   - Earthly to heavenly (verses 48-49)
   - Flesh and blood to transcendent (verse 50)
   - Mortal to immortal (verse 53)

2. This event happens extremely quickly; '*in a flash, in the twinkling of an eye*' (verse 52). The twinkling of an eye is not a blink. It is the time it takes for light to travel the thickness of your eye. It is about 10^{-43} seconds, which is the smallest quantum of time possible. The Greek word for '*flash*' is *atomos*, which means that which cannot be cut or divided, the smallest possible quantity.[3] The Greek word for '*twinkling*' is *rhipe*, which means to hurl, and was used for any rapid movement.[4]

---

3. *Vine's Dictionary*, p 414.
4. *Vine's Dictionary*, p 648.

Jesus told two parables that may be related to this event. Matthew 13:24-29 talks about the story of the wheat and weeds (specifically tares, which look like wheat when not mature). The separation takes place at harvest time. The Rapture is the harvest time when Christ will separate true believers from professing believers. Jesus gave His explanation in Matthew 13:36-42.

A similar story is the parable of the fishing net (Matthew 13:47-50). But there is another harvest time when Christ will again separate believers from unbelievers (chapter 15), and the parables may relate to then.

Is Anything Preventing the Rapture?

Does any prediction need to be fulfilled before Jesus returns at the Rapture? No. There is nothing stopping Jesus returning for His church. Jesus is waiting for His instruction from the Father.

Some people quote Revelation 7:9-10 and say this means every nation and language must be reached with the gospel before Jesus returns. Two points:

1. This passage refers to the time between Jesus' first and second comings.
2. The twenty-four elders say they already belong to every tribe, language, people, and nation (Revelation 5:9).

Jesus himself told his disciples that no one knows when the Rapture will occur. Only God the Father knows when this will happen. Jesus himself does not know the time. See Matthews 22:42, 22; 25:13; Mark 13:32; Luke 12:40. There are some events that can happen at any time, and they are important to the unfolding of the end time events. They can happen before or after the Rapture, but do not prevent the Rapture from happening. These are:

1. There are two invasions predicted for Israel. Psalm 83 seems to predict an invasion of Israel by its immediate neighbours. Ezekiel 38 and 39 predict another invasion of Israel by countries more distant. Ezekiel 38:8 mentions two descriptions that do not currently apply to Israel. They have recovered from a war, and they all live in safety. Many writers think this could be the War of Armageddon (see Appendix 9).

2. Rebuilding the temple at Jerusalem. Seven different groups are preparing for the rebuilding. The Dome on the Rock (mosque) is a current hindrance, but recent archaeology suggests the mosque is not built on the original temple site.[5]

3. The possible rebuilding of Babylon. Saddam Hussein began reconstructing Babylon, but progress effectively halted when the American forces landed in Iraq. We will cover this in Revelation chapters 17 and 18.

4. Some people think Psalm 83 describes an invasion of Israel. Verses 5 to 8 describe an alliance of Jordan, Gaza, Lebanon, Syria and Iraq. Their aim is to destroy Israel as a nation. This aligns with the aims of the Palestinians and Iran.[6] Is this the war that precedes Ezekiel 38?

5. Damascus will get destroyed as detailed in Isaiah 17. This chapter seems to describe Israel as being very weak, but Damascus is turned into a pile of ruins. It becomes a place for animals to rest. The last verse implies the destruction

---

5. 'Temple' by Bob Cornuke, in *Personal Update*, January 2015, pp 17-24. *Epicenter*, pp 189-201.
6. *God's War on Terror*, pp 242-243.

happens overnight. Is it the result of Israel destroying it because of continuous militant attacks? The ISV translation of verse 2 is interesting: '*terrorism will be no more*'. Jeremiah 49:23-27 may be describing the same event.

6. A disaster in Iran, described in Jeremiah 49:34-39. Elam was a minor party in the Persian Empire. The people of Elam will be dispersed to every nation, but they will eventually be restored.

7. Jordan will be toppled. Jeremiah 49:1-22.

8. Disaster in Egypt, including civil unrest, lack of water, unemployment, and a partial take-over by Israel. But there is eventually a restoration when they worship God. Isaiah 19.

Rapture in the Old Testament

Although the Rapture is not predicted in the Old Testament, some people think that it does show up in patterns or 'types'. Note that most of these examples are preludes to judgement for sin and rebellion. These imply the Rapture will be before any worldwide judgement. Examples quoted are:

1. Enoch was taken before the flood (judgement) (Genesis 5:21-24). There are three groups of people involved in the flood; those who were judged and drowned, those who were saved, and those who were removed prior to the judgement. Enoch is seen in this as a picture of the church being removed before the judgement began.

2. Noah and his family were taken into the ark for protection during the judgement by flood (Genesis 7:6-10). The judgement could not happen before Noah's family was safe inside the ark.

3. Lot and his family were forcibly removed from Sodom and Gomorrah before its destruction (Genesis 19:15-17). 2 Peter 2:7 describes Lot as righteous, and he had to be removed before the judgement could begin.

4. Isaac is not mentioned after being offered as a sacrifice (Genesis 22:1-13) and before his marriage (Genesis 24:62-66). He can be seen as a picture of the church because he obeyed his father, and he was loved by his father. A substitute sacrifice was made for Isaac's life.

5. Rahab was given a red ribbon to ensure her safety when Jericho was destroyed (Joshua 2:17-18; 6:23). She was given this protection at least 20 days before Jericho was destroyed.

6. Daniel was not present when his friends were sentenced to the blazing furnace (Daniel 3).

Alternative explanations can be made for some of these.

Enoch is a picture of our salvation from God's judgement for sin. Our relationship with God saves us from eternal damnation because our sin has been forgiven.

Isaac is a picture of Jesus Christ. Isaac was loved by His father. He volunteered to be sacrificed. Except this analogy fails because of the ram being sacrificed.

There is an interesting passage in Isaiah 26:19-21 that seems to be describing the Rapture. These verses talk about the dead living again, their bodies rising, the earth giving up bodies, hiding until the wrath has passed, and the Lord punishing the people of the earth for their sins. Verses 19 and 20 can be seen to describe the Rapture as discussed above. Verse 21 can be understood as the judgements in Revelation. Note the instruction for the resurrected people to '*...enter your rooms*'. Everyone seems to have their individual living space, remarkably similar to what Jesus said in John 14:2.

Will the Church Go Through the Tribulation?

There are four verses that indicate the church will not go through the Tribulation. These verses are:

> Romans 5:8-9. *But God demonstrates his own love for us in this: while we were still sinners, Christ died for us. Since we have now been justified by His blood, how much more shall we be* ***saved from God's wrath*** *through Him.*

> 1 Thessalonians 1:10. *Wait for his Son from heaven, whom he raised from the dead – Jesus, who* ***rescues us from the coming wrath.***

> 1 Thessalonians 5:9-10. *For God* ***did not appoint us to suffer wrath,*** *but to receive salvation through our Lord Jesus Christ. He died for us so that, whether we are awake or asleep, we may live together with him.*

> Revelation 3:10. *Since you have kept my command to endure patiently, I will also* ***keep you from the hour of trial*** *that is going to come upon the whole earth to test those who live on the earth.*

In addition, the church is in heaven in Revelation chapter 4 (as represented by the twenty-four elders) prior to the seals being opened in chapter 6. If we look at Revelation as a mostly chronological sequence, we see the church is in heaven prior to the Tribulation that starts with the seven seals being opened.

When Will the Rapture Occur?

This is probably one of the most controversial points in the study of end time events. Various ideas have been put forward for when the Rapture will occur. These ideas are:

1. Before the Tribulation. That is, before the opening of the seals (Revelation 6).

2. In the middle of the Tribulation (before Matthew 24:15 and Revelation 11).

3. When Christ returns at the end of the Tribulation and before the 1,000-year reign (end of Daniel 9:27, Matthew 24:30 and Revelation 19). This period is called '*the Day of the Lord*'. In other words, the Rapture and Jesus' second coming are a single event.

4. At the beginning of Christ's 1,000-year reign (Revelation 20).

5. That Christ will not return at all. The end times teachings are all allegories to events that have already happened, or they are currently happening.

Let's deal with the last one first. This view is held by many of the major denominations, including the Roman Catholic Church and many Protestant denominations. A lot of Pentecostal people also believe this. They believe that Jesus Christ will not literally return to earth to reign as King, but it means that He will reign in our lives. So the line in the Lord's Prayer '*your kingdom come, your will be done on earth as it is in heaven*' will never be fully answered.

To be blunt, these people deny the truth of the Bible and deny the reliability of God. The Old Testament has 1,845 references to a final judgement (called the '*Day of the Lord*') and to the Messiah ruling through Israel, and 17 books mention these events. In the New Testament, there are 318 references in 216 chapters, and 23 books mention it. This means that denying the literal return of Jesus means that you do not believe what the Bible says about what it sees as a major event.

There is another and more important problem with allegorising the Bible. What do you decide is an allegory? And why is it an allegory and not fact? What about the creation? Adam and Eve? The virgin birth? The resurrection? These all have important issues for our salvation, and for our understanding of the Bible. Calling these teachings 'allegories' is essentially making the Bible the equivalent of a fairy tale book.

Pre-Tribulation Rapture says Christ will return before the seven-year period known as the Tribulation starts, or before the first of seven seals is opened. Most conservative Bible teachers have this opinion. It was believed by the majority of early church leaders.[7]

- The church is in heaven in Revelation 4 and 5 before the judgements on earth begin in Revelation 6.

- Paul writes the '*man of lawlessness*' will not be revealed until

7. *Daniel's 70 Weeks*, pp 86-88.

the spiritual influence on earth is removed (2 Thessalonians 2:1-3, 7). That spiritual influence is either the church and/or the Holy Spirit.

- The judgements on earth are because of sin. Believers in the effectiveness of Jesus Christ's blood to forgive and atone for sin are removed from the earth before these judgements are given. Their sin has already been judged.

- Revelation 1:19 – John is told to write '*what he has seen, what is now, and what will take place later.*' If chapter 1 is what John saw (the glorified Christ) and chapter 2 and 3 are what is now (the churches), chapters 4 onwards is what is to take place later. The churches are not in this category. They have been removed from the earthly picture.

- Revelation 3:10 – Christ promises the churches to keep them *from* the hour of trial coming to the whole earth. He does not promise to keep them *through* the trial.

Mid-Tribulation theory suggests the Rapture occurs in the middle of the seven-year period:

- It recognises that the judgements are related to sin, and believers are removed because their sin has already been dealt with. Thus, believers will go through some Tribulation, but will be spared the Great Tribulation.

- Many of the arguments for the pre-Tribulation period apply. The timing is different. The problem is the '*man of lawlessness*' in 2 Thessalonians 2 is not identified until the church is removed. But he is obviously working during the first half of the Tribulation. He is the rider on the white horse when the first seal is opened. He is the '*Beast from the sea*' in Revelation 13.

Post-Tribulation and millennial theories are similar:

- They recognise Jesus Christ returns to earth to set up His kingdom based around Israel. Most people who believe the church is a replacement for Israel tend to believe this timing.

- The believers are given responsibility in the kingdom (1 Corinthians 6:2, 2 Timothy 2:12, Revelation 20:4).

- The difference is timing. In post-Tribulation, Christ takes the church immediately before the final judgement on the nations but after the bulk of the Tribulation has been completed. Believers are not caught in the final judgement at Armageddon. Two famous people who believed this are Martin Luther and Sir Isaac Newton.

- In the millennial Rapture, the Rapture occurs at the beginning of the millennium. Believers go through all the judgements.

There is another side to the question, 'when will the Rapture occur?' This is based around the events associated with the Feast of Pentecost. Pentecost occurs fifty days after the Feast of Firstfruits, which we know as the Day of the Resurrection (Easter Sunday).

We have already mentioned the trumpet at Mount Sinai (Exodus 19). This happened on '*the third day of the third month*', and Jews say this was on the Day of Pentecost. Deuteronomy 16:9-10 also says the Day of Pentecost is at the beginning of the corn harvest.

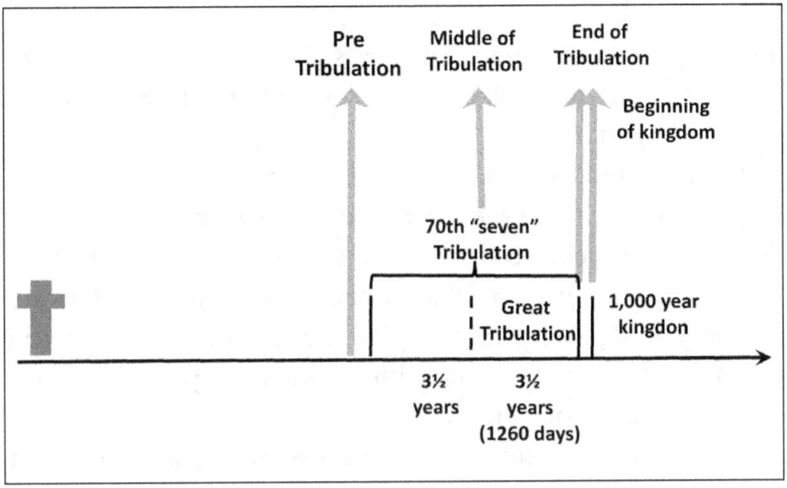

This fits the pattern. The Rapture is the time when Jesus returns to harvest the earth of people who are ready for his return. But there is more to the pattern than a similarity to harvesting.

Both giving Israel the Law and the Rapture involve a trumpet call from heaven. Exodus 19:19 tells us the trumpet call was long and grew louder. The trumpet was blown by someone in heaven. The Rapture will also involve a trumpet call from heaven (1 Thessalonians 4:16).[8]

The early church leaders thought because Jesus ascended to heaven during the Pentecost season (the time between resurrection and ascension), he would most likely return at a similar time. This is summer in the northern hemisphere, and it is the time when food is harvested and stored.

Two people from the Old Testament were raptured. The first was Enoch (Genesis 5:21-24). Jewish tradition says that Enoch

8. 'The Pentecost Prophecy' by Gary Stearman, *The Prophecy Watcher*, May 2021, pp 4-7, 10, 16-17, 40-41.

was born and raptured on Pentecost.[9] Elijah was also taken into heaven (2 Kings 2:11), but no date was given. If Enoch is a pattern for the church, can we expect the Rapture to occur on Pentecost to fulfil the pattern?

I believe the Rapture will occur before the Tribulation, and this book is based on that view. But you do your own research and decide for yourself. I believe it fits the predictions best. But the most important question is not 'when will this happen?', but *'are you ready for it to happen?'* If the Rapture does happen in the next minute, will you be taken up with Christ? Have you asked Jesus Christ to forgive your sin and become your saviour?

There is another topic that continues from this point. What happens to the believers when they reach heaven? That topic is very briefly mentioned in Revelation, and it is covered in more detail in Appendix 3.

9. *The Rapture*, p 97.

Appendix 3

After the Rapture

To go to heaven, fully to enjoy God,
is infinitely better than the most pleasant
accommodations here.
- *Jonathan Edwards, 1703-1758, theologian*

In Appendix 2 we covered the Rapture, the event where Jesus Christ meets the believers in the air with a shout, and all believers are taken to heaven. Dead believers are resurrected first, and the living believers meet them in the air (1 Thessalonians 4:14-17). This appendix looks at what happens to the church after the Rapture. What happens once we are in heaven and before Revelation 4 where we saw twenty-four elders as representatives of the church worshipping God? In summary, there are two major events:

1. We are judged and rewarded for our actions.
2. We will have '*the wedding supper with the Lamb*'.

1. Judgement and Reward

Everyone who has lived will be judged at some point (Hebrews 9:27). There are two judgements of individuals – one for believers and one for unbelievers. Different things will be judged at these two judgements.

We as believers cannot be judged for our sin. That has been dealt with when we believe on the atoning work at Calvary. Jesus Christ forgives our sin, so there is no sin to be judged (John 3:18, 5:24, 6:37, Romans 8:1, Hebrews 9:13-14, 10:17-18, 22).

But we are rewarded for our actions (Revelation 2:10, 2:17). We are all judged for our actions and we must give an account of our lives before God (Hebrews 9:27, Romans 14:10-12, 1 Corinthians 4:5, 2 Corinthians 5:10, Ephesians 6:7-8).

1 Corinthians 3:11-15 talks about '*building on the foundation of Jesus Christ*'. What we do after our salvation is rewarded. Using '*gold, silver and costly stones*' refers to building something of lasting value, something that will endure. Using '*wood, hay or straw*' refers to building something that will not last for eternity, as these materials all decay or can be burned.

The day of judgement will show what is the quality of our work. If our work stands up to Christ's scrutiny, we will receive our reward. If it does not stand up to Christ's scrutiny, we will suffer loss, but we will not lose our salvation. Our loss at this stage is the loss of a reward. And this affects our inheritance later.

The above passage refers to judgement by fire. In John's description of Jesus Christ, he describes Christ's eyes as '*like blazing fire*' (Revelation 1:14). Jesus Christ sees and records everything and judges everything (Revelation 20:12). He judges according to impartial standards (1 Peter 1:17).

Jesus talked about this in the parable of the servants (Matthew 25:14-29). Some servants were given more to work with than others. Some prospered with what they were given, but some squandered the opportunity they were given. The rewards were based on *how* the servants used the opportunity given to them (verses 21, 23), not on the quantity of what was achieved. If we do not use our spiritual opportunities, they risk being taken away from us and we risk punishment (verses 29-30).

Paul says a similar thing in 1 Corinthians 3:8. Making an analogy to gardening, he says, '*The man who plants and the man who waters have one purpose, and each will be rewarded according to his own labour.*' Planting is a higher skilled task than watering, but the reward given to each person will reflect how well they did at each task.

Where are we judged? Before the judgement seat of Christ (2 Corinthians 5:10). This is a different seat from that used at the final judgement (Revelation 20:11). The word used for judgement is *bema*.[1] This bema seat was used in the stadiums by judges to determine who the winner of the race was. Pilate sat on a *bema* seat when deciding what to do with Jesus. This judgement is not a judgement of status – it is a judgement of merit, a judgement of our actions.

What will we be judged for? There are 12 areas of judgement:

1. How we treat others. Hebrews 6:10; Matthew 10:41-42; 1 Peter 1:13-15.
2. How we exercise our authority over others. Hebrews 13:17; James 3:13.
3. How we employ our God-given abilities. 1 Corinthians 12:4, 11; 2 Timothy 1:6; 1 Peter 4:10.
4. How we use our money. 1 Corinthians 16:2; 2 Corinthians 9:6-7; 1 Timothy 6:17-19.
5. How we spend our time. Psalms 90:12; Ephesians 5:16; Colossians 4:5; 1 Peter 1:17.
6. How much we suffer for Jesus. Matthew 5:11-12; Mark 10:29-30; Romans 8:18; 2 Corinthians 4:17; 2 Peter 4:12-13.
7. How we ran the particular race that God has chosen for us. 1 Corinthians 9:24; Philippians 2:16, 3:13-14; Hebrews 12:1.
8. How effectively we control our old nature. 1 Corinthians 9:25-27.

1. *Vine's Dictionary*, p 336.

9. How many souls we witness to and win for Christ. Proverbs 11:30; Daniel 12:3; 1 Thessalonians 2:19-20.
10. How we react to temptation. James 1:2-3; Revelation 2:16.
11. How much the doctrine of the Rapture means to us. 2 Timothy 4:8-9.
12. How faithful we are to the Word of God and the people of God. Acts 20:26-28; 2 Timothy 4:1-2; 1 Peter 5:2-4.

The Bible talks about five books that record our lives, our motives, our service, etc.[2] These books are *The Book of the Living* (Psalm 69:28); the *Lamb's Book of Life* (Revelation 3:5, 13:8); the *Book of Tears* (Psalm 56:8, 2 Kings 20:5); the *Book of Deeds* (Daniel 7:10, Revelation 20:12); and the *Book of Remembrance* (Malachi 3:16).

The New Testament mentions five crowns given to believers for various rewards:

1. The Crown of Righteousness for everyone who looks forward to Christ appearing (2 Timothy 4:8).
2. The Crown of Life is a reward for endurance and perseverance, especially during trials (James 1:12, Revelation 2:10).
3. The Crown of Glory for willing and fruitful church leaders (1 Peter 5:4).
4. The Incorruptible Crown is a reward for overcoming, self-control and having victory over our flesh (1 Corinthians 9:25-27). Also called the Victor's Crown.
5. The Crown of Rejoicing for winning souls for Christ (1 Thessalonians 2:19-20).

Are these physical crowns, or are they symbolic of something?

---

2. *The Kingdom, Power and Glory*, p 112.

They may be symbols of rank or achievement. They are probably important to determine our role in the kingdom of God. But notice that we can lose our crown. Revelation 3:11 tells us to '*hold on to what you have so that no one will take your crown.*'

This judgement has very important implications for us:

1. Are you sure that you are a believer in Jesus Christ? Have you repented of your sin, asked Jesus for forgiveness, and live a life as blameless as possible? If you have not done this, you will stand before Jesus Christ at the second judgement (Revelation 20:11-15), not at this judgement. The rewards at that time will be eternal punishment. See chapter 18 for how to get right with God.

2. Am I living a life that makes the most of every opportunity? Am I living a blameless life as a believer? Am I putting right the areas of my life that God is challenging me on? Am I using my spiritual gifts to benefit other people? Do I do things with the right motives? These are the types of things that God will judge believers for.

2. The Wedding Supper

The church is pictured as the bride of Christ. Israel was pictured in the Old Testament as a wife and was often unfaithful by rejecting God and embracing various forms of idolatry. John the Baptist was the first person to use the bride analogy (John 3:29). Paul often refers to the church as a bride (Romans 7:4, 2 Corinthians 11:2, Ephesians 5:25-33, James 4:4).

The wedding feast is announced in Revelation 19:6-9. Why are we covering this now? Because it ties in with what Christ is doing with His church.

After the judgements have been completed, Christ now has a bride who has been prepared and is clothed in her wedding garments (Revelation 19:7-8). The unrighteous acts have been dealt with and only the righteous acts are rewarded. Now is the time to celebrate our relationship with Jesus Christ. All impediments will be gone. All shame will be gone. We can worship God as we should.

Go back to Revelation 4:10-11. Who are the twenty-four elders? What do they do? Why? Because their reward comes from God, but they give them back because it is only God's grace and Holy Spirit that enabled them to receive those rewards.

The Wedding Model

The ancient Jewish wedding procedure is a model for the church and its reunion with Jesus Christ.[3] Throughout the New Testament, the church is called the bride of Christ (Ephesians 5:22-23, Romans 7:4, 2 Corinthians 11:2, James 4:4).

The first step in a Jewish wedding was the betrothal. This was when the marriage covenant was initiated. The prospective bridegroom took the initiative and negotiated the price he must pay to purchase his bride.

Once the bridegroom paid the purchase price, the marriage covenant was established, and the young man and woman were regarded as husband and wife. From that moment on, the bride was declared to be consecrated or set apart exclusively for her bridegroom. As a symbol of the covenant relationship that had been established, the groom and bride drank from a cup of wine over which the betrothal had been pronounced.

After the marriage covenant was established, the groom left his bride and returned to his father's house where he remained sepa-

3. *The Kingdom, Power and Glory*, pp 121-126.

rated from his bride for approximately twelve months. This gave the bride time to get herself ready for married life.

During this period of separation, the groom prepared a dwelling place in his father's house to which he would later bring his bride. At the end of the period of separation, the bridegroom came to take his bride to live with him – usually at night. The groom, the best man, and other male escorts left the father's house and conducted a torch-light procession to the home of the bride.

Although the bride was expecting the groom to come for her, she did not know the time of his coming. As a result, the groom's arrival was preceded by a shout which announced the imminent departure to be with him.

The groom and his bride, her attendants, and the wedding party returned to the groom's father's house for the marriage feast, which often lasted for seven days. The bride is shown publicly as a wife at the end of the week.

How does this apply to the Rapture?

1. The price has been paid for His bride: Jesus' blood, death, and resurrection at Calvary (Hebrews 9:11-15, 1 Peter 1:18-19).
2. The church (believers in Jesus Christ) is in the betrothal stage: we have been promised to Christ as a bride and are waiting for His return.
3. The covenant has been established between Christ and His church. Jesus sealed the covenant with a cup of wine at His last supper (Matthew 27:27-29, Mark 14:23-25, Luke 22:20).
4. The Bridegroom has departed, and His return could happen at any time. He has gone to prepare a place for you and me (John 14:2-3).
5. The Bridegroom will appear suddenly when most people are not anticipating His return, and He will take His bride back to His house (Matthew 25:1-13).

6. The marriage supper will take place with Christ and His bride.
7. Christ's bride will accompany Him when He returns to earth (Jude 14, Revelation 19:14).

Outer Darkness

There are a few parables that seem to imply some believers will go to hell. These all refer to people going to the '*outer darkness where there is weeping and gnashing of teeth*'. How does this relate to the judgement and wedding feast?

Jesus told the parable of the wedding banquet in Matthew 22:1-14. In this story, the king prepared the banquet. But the invited guests did not attend. The king commanded his servants to bring in anyone who would come to the banquet. But one guest was not wearing wedding clothes, and he was thrown outside into the darkness.

This person was a believer. He accepted the invitation to come to the wedding and was allowed into the wedding venue. This is equivalent to someone accepting Jesus as their saviour. They will be taken to heaven in the Rapture, but they will not have any rewards.

Revelation 19:7-9 tells us the people invited to the wedding of the Lamb are given clothes to wear. The explanation in verse 8 tells us that our future clothes are based on our acts. Not having the appropriate clothing means the man in the parable accepted the offer of salvation but did nothing else of merit to earn proper clothing, or to earn a reward. He had no fruit from his salvation.

A similar scenario plays out in the parable of the talents in Matthew 25:14-30. The master has three servants who are given varying amounts of talents (money) to use while the master is absent. When the master returns, he rewards the first two servants who doubled their talents with increased responsibility in his business. The third servant did nothing with his talent, so he is punished with being cast outside in the darkness.

Again, this servant is punished for a lack of fruit. He was a trusted servant who his master thought should be able to handle the responsibility. His master had given him something to work with, but it was wasted.

What or where is the darkness outside? It seems to imply that only people who have shown spiritual fruit in their lives will enter the marriage feast with Jesus. They will have earned the appropriate clothing based on their works since their salvation.

People who are judged to have insufficient works or fruit will be outside the marriage banquet in relative darkness, weeping because they finally realise that they have lost their opportunity for greater rewards. It is the darkness outside the light of God's presence.[4] The term 'darkness' seems to have a relative meaning: the darkness is relative to the light where God is. It does not seem to mean darkness because of an absence of light.

The parable of the ten virgins is similar (Matthew 25:1-19).[5] Five virgins were not ready when the bridegroom came unexpectantly and were locked outside. All ten virgins represent born-again believers who are undefiled, chaste, and pure. But five of them did not maintain their faithfulness to the very end. They had allowed their relationship with the Holy Spirit (symbolised by oil) to run out. The moral of the story is that we must always be ready for any opportunity that God brings us.

I think the scariest part of the Bible is Matthew 7:21-23. Here people stand before the judgement seat and give an account of themselves. These people have given God's messages (prophesied),

4. *The Kingdom, Power and Glory*, p 88.
5. *The Kingdom, Power and Glory*, pp 126-135.

expelled demons and performed miracles. But Jesus calls them '*evil doers*' and casts them out. He says that he does not know them. These people were busy doing the work of God, but they did not have a relationship with God. The important question is not 'Do I know God?' The question we should all ask is '*Does God know me?*'

Personal Application

Where will you be when the Rapture occurs? Will you be taken into heaven? Or will you be left on earth? The first step is to acknowledge that you need Jesus Christ to forgive your sin, fill you with the Holy Spirit, and become a disciple of Jesus. See the last part of chapter 18.

What are you doing to build a reward in heaven? Are you working at what God wants you to do? Or are you following your own agenda? Is your relationship with God growing continually?

Remember Hebrews 9:27. '*Man is destined to die once, and after that to face judgement.*'

Appendix 4

Daniel's Overviews

Almost certainly we are moving into an age
of totalitarian dictatorships – an age in which
freedom of thought will be at first a deadly sin
and later on a meaningless abstraction.
The autonomous individual is going
to be stamped out of existence.
- *George Orwell, 1903-1950, author*

Daniel had five different insights into the future of Middle Eastern history. The first one sees history from a human viewpoint, whereas the others see history from God's perspective. Many have had a partial fulfilment, but still wait for their complete fulfilment. Some of these have close similarities to the briefing Jesus gave his disciples in Matthew 24.

1. The Multi-metal Statue

Daniel chapter 2 records that King Nebuchadnezzar had a vision one night, and he was greatly troubled about what it meant. He demanded that his wise men and advisers first relate the dream to him and then give the interpretation. Nebuchadnezzar wanted to know that whoever gave him the interpretation had exceptionally good perception, hence the reason to tell the dream first. I guess that is one way to determine who really has insight and who is a pretender.

In answer to the prayers of Daniel and his friends, God shows Daniel the same dream. It consisted of a statue of a man with a head of gold, chest and arms of silver, belly and thighs of bronze, and legs that change from iron to a mixture of iron and clay at the feet. A rock hit the statue's feet and demolished the entire statue. The rock became a mountain that filled the earth.

Daniel told Nebuchadnezzar that the golden head represents the Babylonian Empire. After the Babylonian would emerge another empire, represented by the silver body parts. After that would be a third empire, signified by the silver parts. This is followed by a fourth empire made of iron that over time changes to a combination of iron and clay.

This kingdom is described as one that will crush and break all the others. But the clay indicates that there will not be a lot of cohesion, meaning '*the people will be a mixture and will not remain united*' (verse 43). Finally, God will set up a kingdom that will engulf the entire world.

The gold part represents the Babylonian Empire (627-539 BC), with the Persian Empire represented by the silver (539-330 BC), and the Greek Empire represented by the bronze (330-63 BC). The iron legs are commonly thought to represent the Roman Empire.

The decreasing value of the metals involved is thought to be related to the power of the ruler. Nebuchadnezzar was an absolute dictator, whereas the Persian rulers had rules whereby their decisions could not be so arbitrary (Daniel 6:8, 12, 15). The Greeks invented democracy whereby the ruling class had a vote, while the Roman emperor was responsible to a senate who passed the laws.

Most commentators think the iron and clay parts represent the

Roman Empire.[1] The iron component represents the over-riding crushing of the other nations under the Pax Romana. But the subservient nations still retained their national identities in many ways, symbolised by the clay. The subservient nations could not be united to form a united empire, and the Roman army was continually trying to quell uprisings.

The Roman Empire was never conquered. It was split into two sections in 395 AD to make it easier to govern, corresponding to the two legs in the vision (Daniel 2:33, 40-43). The western part was invaded by a series of Goths, Huns, Vandals, etc at different times until it finally reverted into different nations in around 500 AD. The eastern part (known as the Byzantine Empire) lasted until 1453 when Constantinople was captured by the Muslims, who eventually became Ottoman Turks.[2]

This thinking indicates that a revived Roman Empire will emerge before God returns to establish His kingdom on earth and absorb all other empires or nations. Many people see the European Union as the forerunner of the revived Roman Empire.

But Bible prophecy is centred around Israel. And this particular dream is about the empires that are centred on Babylon (Nebuchadnezzar's kingdom), or modern-day Iraq.[3] An alternative idea is that the iron and clay legs represent the various Arab empires culminating in the Ottoman Empire. Rome never conquered large parts of the Middle East. The Romans never took over any land east of the River Euphrates or in Saudi Arabia. These lands were part of the Parthian Empire. The bulk of the Persian Empire and the Seleucid Greek Empire became the Parthian Empire, and over time formed into the Ottoman Empire.

1. *The Bible Knowledge Commentary: Old Testament*, p 1335.
2. *God's War on Terror*, p 302.
3. *God's War on Terror*, pp 312-315.

These two options will influence where people think the final ruler will emerge. We discuss this in Appendix 5.

Ultimately, God destroys all remnants of the preceding empires and establishes his own kingdom to rule the world.

2. The Four Beasts

Daniel's dream in chapter 7 happened between chapters 4 and 5 in a chronological sense (553 BC). Daniel would have been in his late sixties. He saw four beasts, the last of which was terrifying. He asked for an explanation of the fourth beast to help understand what he was seeing.

In verse 2 he sees a churning sea. This is symbolic of mankind. Like the sea, mankind is in a constant state of change; never settled, and sometimes raging violently. Revelation 13:1 has another beast coming out of the sea.

Verse 4 shows the first beast: '*a lion with wings of an eagle*', and it was given the heart of a man. This animal was a symbol of the Babylonians, and they decorated their buildings with this motif. The removal of its wings may refer to the fact that the empire did not expand after Nebuchadnezzar's death. The heart of a man could describe their attitude toward the nations they conquered.[4] They were largely left to live in their own country, they could continue their daily practices or religion, but they were forced to pay tax to the Babylonians. The brightest of the youth in each country were taken back to Babylon to train in the court (Daniel 1:3-5).

In verse 5 we have the second beast: '*a bear raised up on one side and it had three ribs in its mouth*'. The Medo-Persian Empire was a combination of two smaller empires – the Medes and the Persians. The three ribs could refer to the three battles that established it as

4. *The Bible Knowledge Commentary: Old Testament*, p 1350.

a world empire – Media (Iraq) in 550 BC, Lydia (western Turkey) in 546 BC, and Babylonians at Opis in 539 BC. They could refer to the three countries that were the origins of the empire – Media, Persia and Elam. They could refer to three nations conquered by the Persians: Babylon, Lydia, and Egypt. The city of Babylon was taken over a few weeks after the battle at Opis, as described in Daniel 5. Persian history records the party was on the night before the festival in honour of Sin, the moon god.[5]

The command to '*eat flesh*' in verse 5 is a divine command to extend its territory into a vast empire. The Persian Empire covered more land than the other empires in this dream. Its border went from Turkey in the west, to Sudan in the south, and across to western India in the east.

The Persian Empire was similarly kind to the nations under them. Slave labour was abolished, sacred objects were returned to their original peoples (Ezra 1:7-11), and rebuilding of temples was financed. They allowed exiles from the Assyrian and Babylonian deportations to return home if they wished (Ezra 1:2-4). The Persian Empire lasted about two hundred years.

The third beast in verse 6 represents the Greek Empire. Leopards are fast, agile animals and efficient hunters. The four wings symbolise the speed of conquest under Alexander the Great. When Alexander died the empire was split between four generals due to a lack of heir. This is symbolised by the four heads. Two subsequent empires that affected Israel were the Ptolemy Empire based in Egypt, and the Seleucid Empire based in Babylon.

Note the empire was given '*authority to rule*' (verse 6). By whom? By God. See also Romans 13:1-7, Daniel 2:21, 4:17. It seems that every country, nation, and leader is appointed by God to rule for a determined length of time. We sometimes find that difficult

---

5. en.wikipedia.org/wiki/Fall_of_Babylon

to understand, especially when extreme evil or incompetence is perpetrated by some of the leaders. But we need to remember that God is ultimately in control, and that every leader will have to answer to God for their actions.

Again, the Greeks allowed their subject nations to largely live undisturbed. Greek language became the major language throughout the Empire. Religious practices were generally allowed to continue with occasional outbreaks of repression. One such repression of Judaism led to the Maccabean revolt.

Verse 7 introduces the fourth empire. Daniel could not describe this animal in terms of other animals, so he describes it in terms of its effects on people. He says it is '*terrifying, frightening, and very powerful*'. It crushed and devoured its victims and trampled everything that was left.

Commentators are split on what empire is represented by this animal. The split in commentary is basically around whether the beast represents the Roman Empire, or the Arab nations represented by the various Islamic empires. Unfortunately, nothing in Daniel's dream clarifies this, except perhaps the geography of the empires.

Many writers from the last 200 years see this as the Roman Empire. The Roman Empire took over Judea and Samaria from the Seleucid Greeks. The Romans imposed their rule and customs on every nation they took over. They tried to totally assimilate most aspects of society into the Roman way of doing things. Any resistance was crushed, which was different from the other empires where they were allowed a certain amount of tolerance.

This animal could easily describe the Muslims, and this has been suggested by numerous people. Islam is a religion of submission. All other forms of religion are suppressed, especially Judaism and Christianity. Laws of the conquered countries are changed to reflect Sharia Law. Human rights that are taken for granted in western countries are removed in Muslim countries. Muslim countries are currently split between Sunni and Shi'a Islam, but they may merge politically to form a stronger world political presence.

Daniel notes that this beast '*was different from all the former beasts*' (verse 7). Different in what way? One possibility is the form of control. The other empires used politics as the form of control. The Roman Empire was characterised by emperor worship (religion). Islamic countries are characterised by submission to their religion. If this beast represents a future revived empire, it will use religion as the form of control. Is that what Daniel meant?

This beast has ten horns, symbolic of ten leaders.[6] One horn usurps three others and seems to take over the leadership of all ten. God sets up thrones to judge people and the four beasts are destroyed. Finally, God sets up a kingdom that will never be destroyed.

Throughout Revelation are beasts that have either seven or ten horns. This beast begins with ten horns, but three are destroyed or removed. Horns are symbolic of kings or authority. We have a picture of an empire that starts as a coalition of ten countries. But three countries are removed or destroyed by an emerging little horn, leaving the seven remaining rulers.

The '*little horn*' has the eyes of a man and a mouth that speaks boastfully. Eyes are symbolic of knowledge. This person will be very intelligent, and he will have a good surveillance system to know what his subjects are doing. He has an ego problem in that he is a boastful speaker. Verse 25 says that '*he will speak against the Most High and oppress his saints*'.

---

6. There are currently nine countries surrounding Israel: Iran, Iraq, Turkey, Syria, Lebanon, Jordan, Egypt, Saudi Arabia, and Yemen. Palestine is not a recognised country as at December 2020, although it does have a governmental system and a leader.

God sets up thrones to judge this empire. The beast was destroyed. His empire is replaced by Jesus Christ who is '*given authority, glory, and sovereign power. All peoples, nations, and men of every language worshipped Him*' (verse 13-14).

3. The Ram and the Goat

Chapter 8 describes Daniel's dream about a ram with two horns, one longer than the other. It was attacked by a fast-moving goat *from* the west with a prominent horn. The ram was attacked and over-powered. The goat prospered, but at its peak the horn shattered, and four horns grew in its place. Two horns fought over Israel ('*the Beautiful Land*', verse 9) until one set itself up to be God and destroyed the sanctuary.

A time of 2,300 evenings and mornings would last until the sanctuary would be re-consecrated (verse 14). This has been already fulfilled under Antiochus Epiphanes in 168 BC when a statue of Zeus was erected in the temple and a pig was sacrificed on the altar. The temple was finally cleansed 1,150 days later after the Maccabean Revolt. But it will have a second fulfilment during the reign of the final ruler.

The angel Gabriel interprets the dream for Daniel. The ram represents the kings of Media and Persia, while the goat represents Alexander the Great from Greece.[7] As described above, the Greek Empire split into four sections after Alexander's death.

One of the Seleucid kings (Antiochus Epiphanes) eventually conquered Israel and desecrated the temple. The Seleucids had an almost continuous fight with the Ptolemies based in Egypt (the second horn).

7. *Learn the Bible in 24 Hours*, p 107.

> The Talmud records that when Alexander the Great entered Jerusalem, the High Priest showed him the writings of Daniel. He recognised his own career being predicted, and he spared the city from destruction.

Another similar ruler will arise in the future who will stand against God, but he will eventually be destroyed.[8] He is commonly called 'the Antichrist' by commentators, although the Bible does not call him by that name or title. Revelation calls him '*the beast from the sea*' (Revelation 13:2).

In the explanation given by Gabriel, this ruler is described as '*a master of intrigue*'. He will '*cause astounding devastation*' and will '*cause deceit to prosper*'. He will '*take his stand against the Prince of princes*' (verses 23-25).

4. Seventy 'Sevens'

Daniel received a timeline of future events as they applied to Israel in Daniel 9:24-27. This was given verbally by the angel Gabriel as the result of Daniel praying about Israel. Depending on which version you read, the Bible talks about seventy '*sevens*' or '*weeks*' in these verses. These four verses are some of the most amazing predictions in the Bible, especially since they are tied to an extremely specific time frame.

These are weeks of years.[9] This was a concept the Jews were familiar with. The land had to be left fallow or uncultivated

---

8. *God's War on Terror*, pp 337-339.
9. *Daniel's 70 Weeks*, pp 28-30. *Bible Knowledge Commentary: Old Testament*, p 1361; *Learn the Bible in 24 Hours*, p 109.

every seven years (Exodus 23:10-11, Leviticus 25:1-7). Every seven 'Sabbath years' was a year of jubilee (Leviticus 25:8-12).

In verse 24 Daniel was told that seventy 'sevens' or 490 years are decreed for Israel and the Jews, to *'finish transgression, put an end for sin, atone for wickedness, bring in everlasting righteousness, and to seal up the vision and prophecy'*. This is a summary giving the time involved and the reasons for this time limit. The reasons are still valid. The world still transgresses God's law, still sins, still engages in wickedness, and is still waiting for righteousness to be brought in. This prediction still has not been fully enacted.

Two important time frames are given in verse 25. The time starts when the decree is given to restore and rebuild Jerusalem. The time finishes when the Anointed One comes. At this time the Jews were under Babylonian control and many had been deported by Nebuchadnezzar. Most of the Jews at that time lived in or around Babylon. Jeremiah had predicted this captivity would last 70 years (Jeremiah 29:10). This chapter was written one or two years before the seventy years were completed. The start time was approaching.

Who is the Anointed One, the ruler in verse 26? This refers to the Messiah (Psalm 2:2, Acts 4:26). The word Messiah comes from the Hebrew word *masiah* which means 'anointed one'.[10] The Greek equivalent word is *christos* from which we get our title Christ.[11]

Two time periods are mentioned together: seven '*sevens*' and sixty-two '*sevens*'. This makes a total of sixty-nine, so one '*seven*' has not been mentioned yet. Sixty-nine '*sevens*' is 483 years. What is predicted to happen during this time? The city Jerusalem will be rebuilt with streets and a trench. The word trench can mean a

---

10. *Vine's Dictionary*, p 150.
11. *Vine's Dictionary*, p 101.

moat or a wall.[12] It refers to a barrier of some type. The city will be completed, but in times of trouble.

We know from Ezra and Nehemiah that various decrees were issued. The first was in Cyrus' first year (537 BC) when he allowed the Jews return to Jerusalem to rebuild the temple (Ezra 1:1-4). The temple construction was started, but it soon stopped due to political opposition. Darius issued a second decree (522 BC) allowing the construction to continue, and it was paid for by the Persian Empire (Ezra 6:1-12). Continual trouble delayed the building until Artaxerxes Longimanus gave the Jews authority to rebuild the city walls on 14 March 445 BC (Nehemiah 2:7-9).[13] It is this third decree to rebuild Jerusalem that triggers the countdown.

The 49-year landmark is uncertain. Most writers think it refers to the original city wall and street repairs being completed.[14] Certainly, the work was done with a lot of trouble as Nehemiah describes. Jerusalem was expanded further under both the Greeks and more especially under the Roman Empire. Herod the Great (73-4 BC) did a lot of expansions and rebuilt the temple to gain favour with the Jews.

What date does the prediction finish? And why is that significant?

All the ancient civilisations worked on a lunar calendar of 30-day months, which gives a 360-day year.[15] The entire Bible is based on a 30-day month, even the book of Revelation, despite the fact the Romans (and almost the entire world) had reverted to a 365-day solar calendar by 701 BC.

---

12. *Daniel's 70 Weeks*, p 34.
13. *Daniel's 70 Weeks*, p 34.
14. See, for example, *Major Bible Themes*, p 306; *Daniel's 70 Weeks*, p 31.
15. *Prophecy 20/20*, p 46.

69 'sevens' × 7 years × 360 days = 173,880 days

What date is 173,880 days after 14 March 445 BC?

445 BC to 32 AD:	173,740 days
Leap years:	16 days
14 March to 6 April:	24 days
	173,880 days

What happened on 6 April 32 AD? Jesus rode into Jerusalem on a donkey, and He allowed the people to worship Him as a king on this day, and *only* on this day (Luke 19:37-38).[16] He was riding a donkey as predicted in Zechariah 9:9. This was 10th Nisan on the Jewish calendar; the day the Jews were presenting their Passover lambs to the priests to check their acceptability (Exodus 12:1-5).

This is the day Jesus presented himself as the Passover Lamb for all mankind.

In Luke 19:39 we read the Pharisees were upset and told Jesus to rebuke his disciples. What were they upset about?

Jesus refused to rebuke either his disciples or the crowd. He knew exactly what was happening. His next statement (verses 41-44) is very interesting. He laments the fact the Jews did not recognise the true significance of that particular day, and they did not recognise the time of God's coming.

The Pharisees especially should have known because they were the people who studied the scriptures. They had the chance for peace, but apparently let it slip. The implication is that if Israel had recognised their Messiah that day, Jerusalem may not have been destroyed by the Romans thirty-eight years later.

16. *Daniel's 70 Weeks*, pp 41-44; *Learn the Bible in 24 Hours*, p 110.

The Jewish people have not been at peace since that time. They have been scattered across the world, persecuted, blamed for various plagues or social ills, discriminated against, and occasionally been subject to elimination programmes and pogroms.

Anti-Semitism is still common around the world, and New Zealand consistently votes against Israel at the United Nations. The Muslim world still calls for the elimination of Israel. The Jews had their chance for peace, but let it slip for now.

Back to Daniel, we read in verse 26 that the Anointed One will be cut off after 69 '*sevens*' and will have nothing. The Hebrew says he will be cut off, but not for himself. The people of the ruler will destroy the city and the sanctuary or temple. The end will come like a flood, war will continue until the end, and desolations are decreed.

Jesus, the Anointed One, was executed by the very people who proclaimed him king. Four days after accepting their king, the crowd was asking for his crucifixion (Luke 23:20-23). The Hebrew word for 'cut off' is *karat* which means to be executed or to have a violent death.[17] But it was not done for himself – he had committed no crime. Jesus was crucified for me and you.

This point in this verse represents a gap in time between the fulfilment of the first 69 '*sevens*' and the 70th '*seven*'. That gap has lasted almost two thousand years.

The ruler over Jerusalem at the time was Pontus Pilate who was a Roman. Herod Antipas was a puppet ruler over Galilee, and it was also under Roman control. The Romans came to Jerusalem in 70 AD after a revolt in northern Israel and laid siege to Jerusalem for nine months.[18] Four legions were involved, all of which were from middle Eastern areas.[19] Over a million people were reported

17. *Prophecy 20/20*, p 51; *Daniel's 70 Weeks*, p 45.
18. *God's War on Terror*, pp 349-353.
19. en.wikipedia.org/wiki/Siege_of_Jerusalem_(70_CE)

killed during that time.[20] Titus Vespasian wanted to keep the temple intact, but one soldier threw a torch through a window and the wooden interior burnt. The fire melted the gold fittings inside.[21] Titus ordered the troops to take it apart stone by stone to recover the gold (see Jesus' prediction in Matthew 24:1-2). Thus, both the city and the sanctuary were destroyed. The recovered gold was used to build the Coliseum in Rome.

We are living in the last part of that verse. Wars are a continual fact around the world. Many we do not hear about because they are civil wars in countries that have little political or economic significance to us. Wikipedia lists over 50 current conflicts.[22]

4 major wars	> 10,000 deaths last year
14 wars	1,000 to 9,999 deaths
22 minor conflicts	100 to 999 deaths
19 skirmishes	< 100 deaths

Desolations have been decreed, and we will come across these in Revelation chapters 6, 8 and 9.

Verse 27 picks up the 70th '*seven*' at some point in the future. The future ruler will confirm or enforce a covenant for a seven-year period. But in the middle after just three and a half years, the ruler will force a stop to sacrifices and offerings.

This indicates the temple at Jerusalem is going to be rebuilt at some time, and it has probably been built prior to the covenant. In

---

20. *Daniel's 70 Weeks*, p 44.
21. Josephus, *The Jewish Wars*, Book 6, chapter 6, paragraph 5.
22. en.wikipedia.org/wiki/List_of_ongoing_armed_conflicts. Retrieved 19 December 2020. The list had increased since I first saw it about four months earlier.

one part of the temple, he will set up something that is an abomination to the Jews and will desolate the temple.

Whatever this is, it will cause the temple to cease being used until the end that is decreed for the ruler is fulfilled. Daniel 8:14 tells us this will be 1,150 days (three years and 55 days).

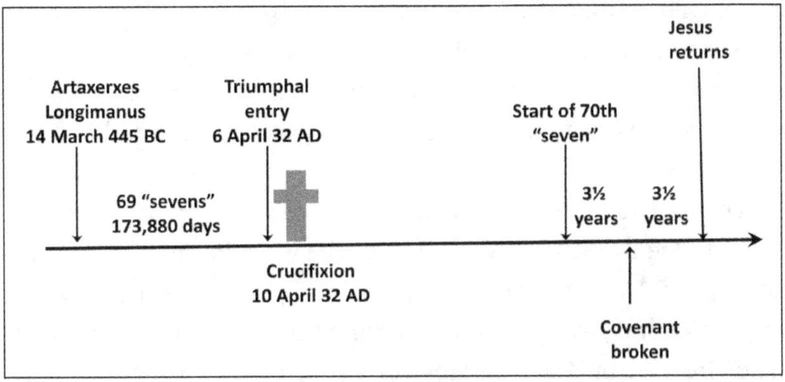

Jesus gave his disciples an outline of end time events because they asked him three questions (Matthew 24:1-3). When would the temple be destroyed? What will be the sign of Jesus coming? And what will be the sign of the end of the age? The rest of chapter 24 and chapter 25 are really answering the last question. As you read the answers Jesus gave, ask yourself, 'Is this happening today?'

Verses 4 to 8 describe life in general for both Jews and Christians. Wars, famines, and earthquakes are happening continuously. The Greek word for 'nation' is *ethnos*,[23] which can also refer to a race or people group. Many of the current conflicts are racial, for example, Kurds vs Turks, tribal conflicts, etc. But this is the beginning. Notice what Jesus said in verse 6; '...*the end is still to come.*'

23. *Vine's Dictionary*, p 426.

Verses 9 to 14 describe the spiritual conditions. Persecution and execution because of faith has always been happening somewhere, but it will increase during the second half of the 70th week (Revelation 13:7, 12, Daniel 7:25, 11:36).

Many people will turn away from their faith, and many false prophets will appear and deceive people who are unsure of their beliefs. These may well be church leaders. Notice that deception is a common item that we warned against (verses 4, 11, 24).

Verse 15 mentions the '*abomination that causes desolation*' that we found in Daniel (9:27), so this verse refers to the middle of the 70th '*seven*'.

Verse 21 has the origin of the word '*tribulation*' used for this period. The King James Version uses the word '*tribulation*' instead of '*distress*'. The term 'Tribulation' is now generally recognised as the entire seven-year period in Daniel 9:27. The last half is called 'The Great Tribulation' because of an increase in intensity of persecutions, wars, and other happenings we will cover later.

Verse 30 talks about Jesus coming '*with power and glory*'. This is His second return. This is the answer to the second question, and this corresponds to Revelation 14:1 and 19:11.

5. Kings of North and South

Daniel has a vision in chapter 10, but the interpretation is given in chapters 11 and 12. The vision is given during the reign of Cyrus (600-530 BC).

Chapter 11 verse 2 gives a summary prediction of the Persian Empire. Persia will have another four kings with the fourth being far richer than the others. This king will attack Greece, but a Greek king will arise who will dominate until his empire is split into four parts.

The fourth king was Xerxes I (485-465 AD),[24] who was the wealthiest ruler of the Persian Empire. He was the king in the book of Esther. Xerxes tried a few times to conquer Greece but was not successful. In September 480 BC, Xerxes led one of the largest ancient armies ever assembled. He was victorious at the Battle of Thermopylae because the Greek army was betrayed, which allowed the Persians to overrun most of Greece, including Athens.

But the Persians suffered a severe defeat at the naval Battle of Salamis a few weeks later, even though he vastly outnumbered the Greeks. This weakened the Persian army to the extent they never had another major military victory. This may be the origin of the saying, 'we won the battle but lost the war'. Xerxes then retreated back to Persia, where he was murdered in 465 BC.[25]

Verses 3 to 4 predict a mighty king (Alexander the Great) who will be largely unstoppable. But his empire will be broken into four parts because he will die with no heirs.

Alexander the Great became ruler of Greece in 336 BC, and he began a ten year campaign to conquer Persia in 334 BC. Between 334 and 330 BC he conquered Asia Minor, Syria, Egypt and the Persian Empire. He reached India before his troops rebelled and forced him to make his way back toward Greece. He died aged 32 in Babylon in 323 BC from malaria with complications from alcoholism.

Apparently, he was asked as he lay dying who he would leave the empire to. Alexander said to leave it to the strong. A few years after Alexander's death, his kingdom was divided among his four generals.

Seleucus took over Syria and Mesopotamia, based in Babylon. Ptolemy took over Egypt. Lysimachus took control of Thrace (modern eastern Bulgaria) and western part of Turkey. Cassander

---

24. www.bible-history.com/old-testament/persian-kings.html
25. en.wikipedia.org/wiki/Xerxes_I

took over Macedonia and Greece. The four separate kingdoms were not as strong as the total Greek Empire due to in-fighting.

Verses 5 to 35 predict the political conflicts and intrigues between the kings of the North and the kings of the South,[26] the Seleucids and the Ptolemy's. The final king was Antiochus Epiphanes,[27] who in 167 BC issued a decree prohibiting sacrifices in Jerusalem, sacrificed a pig on the altar and erected a statue of Jupiter in the Most Holy Place in the temple (1 Maccabees 1). This led to the Maccabean revolt.

Verses 31 to the end of the book are still future. They describe a future leader from the former Seleucid area who exalts himself above God and uses bribery to maintain and extend his power.[28] We cover this person in Appendix 6. He will be involved in a war with a southern alliance and conquer Egypt. But a coalition of armies from the east and north will result in his defeat in Israel.

Verses 40 to 45 describe his downfall. Despite his wide-spread leadership, there are disgruntled people. Two other kings will attack; '*the king of the South*' (an African-Arab coalition?) and '*the king of the North*' (a Russian or Turkish led coalition?). He will bring his armies through many countries, including Israel ('*the Beautiful Land*').

Why is Jordan exempt from conquest? (Does he come from Jordan?[29] Or are there geographical factors involved? Or is God protecting someone?)

---

26. For a good explanation of these verses with the historical evidence, see *The Bible Knowledge Commentary: Old Testament*, pp 1368-1370.
27. Epiphanes means 'the illustrious one' (he named himself). He was so untrustworthy that he was nicknamed Epimanes which means 'the madman'. See *The Bible Knowledge Commentary: Old Testament*, p 1369.
28. *God's War on Terror*, pp 340-344.
29. en.wikipedia.org/wiki/Hashemites

> Jordan claims it is a Hashemite kingdom. This means the rulers claim direct descent from Mohamed, the prophet of Allah. Maybe this exempts them from war. Maybe a member of the Jordanian royal family is the leader and directs his troops away from the country.

While he is capturing the Egyptian conglomerate, news from the east and north panic him, and he sets out to annihilate large armies. The final battle in Israel leads to his end.

Chapter 12 describes an initial time of unprecedented distress in Israel, followed by deliverance and resurrection. Three different time frames are given. The start point is not given, but it can be inferred from Revelation. It is commonly thought to refer to the temple sanctuary being defiled.

I assume the time frames all have the same starting time. There will be 1,260 days until an unspecified event when Israel is finally broken (whatever that means) in verse 7. From the abolition of the daily sacrifice will be 1,290 days, and people will be blessed if they can endure for 1,335 days.

Obviously there are some unspecified events that must take place during the extra 30 or 75 days.[30]

Is it during this time Jesus shows Himself to the Jews as their Messiah (Zechariah 12:10-14)?

30. A few suggestions are given in *The Bible Knowledge Commentary: Old Testament*, p 1374.

Appendix 5

Roman or Ottoman Empire?

All empires fall, eventually. But why?
It's not for lack of power.
In fact, it seems to be the opposite.
Their power lulls them into comfort.
They become undisciplined.
- *Max Barry, author*

There will be a ruler in the future who will rise to take over the leadership of three countries, and he will lead a confederation of ten countries. This is pictured as the fourth empire in Daniel's dreams. Opinion is divided as to what countries this person will rule over.

The two options are either a revived Roman Empire based in Europe, or the Muslim countries surrounding Israel.

Roman Empire

A revived Roman Empire is based on the fact that the Roman Empire conquered most of the Greek Empire. It is described as the legs of iron that gradually change to clay towards the feet in Nebuchadnezzar's dream (Daniel 2:31-33, 39-43).

In Daniel's dream in chapter 7, he saw four beasts coming out of the Great Sea (Daniel 7:2-3). The Great Sea in the Bible is what we call the Mediterranean Sea. Rome is located on the Tiber River that drains into the Mediterranean Sea, and therefore is a good candidate.

The Roman Empire had conquered most of the Greek Empire by 63 BC, and it expanded west to England to control all the Mediterranean countries. It was unable to take over the countries east of the River Euphrates. This was ruled by the Parthian Empire. However, Israel was under Roman rule and therefore could be part of any revived Roman Empire.

The Roman Empire was never conquered. It was split into two sections in 395 AD to make it easier to govern, corresponding to the two legs in the vision (Daniel 2:33, 40-43). The western part was invaded by a series of Goths, Huns, Vandals, etc at different times until it finally collapsed into different nations in around 500 AD. These formed the basis of the Holy Roman Empire which was led by the Pope and the Roman Catholic Church. The eastern part (known as the Byzantine Empire) lasted until 1453 when the capital, Constantinople, was captured by the Ottoman Turks,[1] led by Mehmet II.

The remnants of the Roman Empire still exist today. Not only in the nationalities of the countries around the Mediterranean, but in the politics, languages, and social structure. Most western European languages have a Greek and Latin background. The political and legal systems are largely based on Roman systems.

The legs and feet of clay in Daniel chapter 2 are symbolic of the different nationalities that made up the area occupied by the Roman Empire. These are distinct and have little cohesion between them. They may belong to the European Union, but there are large differences and disagreements between them. It makes a fragile mixture that can easily break.

---

1. *God's War on Terror*, p 302.

One example is the United Kingdom, which entered the EU in 1973.[2] The first two applications in 1963 and 1967 were vetoed by France. There were several referenda where the vote went against staying in the EU, and England never took on the Euro currency.[3] It exited from the EU on 1 January 2021. Scotland wants a referendum to break out away from the UK so that it can re-join the EU. But it must be remembered that Scotland was never part of the Roman Empire.

Many commentators recognise that the EU currently consists of more than ten nations. They are predicting either mergers of countries, or a disintegration of the EU before the ruler can emerge from a group of ten countries.

Ottoman Empire

The alternative view is that the ruler comes from the Muslim nations surrounding Israel. In some ways, Rome never conquered this part of the world. They installed puppet kings who were answerable to Rome, but they allowed much of the Greek culture and customs to continue as long as the subservient countries did not revolt.

This applies to what we know today as Israel. The herods in the Bible were Idumean puppet kings under Rome's control.

After the death of Alexander the Great, his generals divided up the conquered territories. Seleucus I Nicator took over the land from Mesopotamia to Afghanistan to create the Seleucid Empire in 312 BC.[4] He incorporated Greek administration with Persia's form of governance.

---

2. en.wikipedia.org/wiki/European_Union%E2%80%93United_Kingdom_relations
3. en.wikipedia.org/wiki/United_Kingdom_membership_of_the_European_Union
4. en.wikipedia.org/wiki/Seleucid_Empire

The Seleucid Empire broke the region in districts, and Parthia was one of the districts in the eastern part of the empire, based largely in what is today Iran. But Parthia would soon become its own empire.

The Seleucids were weakened by internal war and conflict with the Ptolemies in the west, and the Parni tribe made their move in the east. In 247 BC the local governor Andragorus started a rebellion against Seleucid rule. Knowing the Seleucids were distracted and Andragorus was weak, Arsaces conquered Parthia, thus becoming Parthia's first king.

The Seleucid ruler Antiochus III would retake it in 209 BC. By this time Arsaces' son, Arsaces II was on the throne. Antiochus could have killed him but, instead, he set him up as district governor.

After Antiochus left to go back to Syria, the Parthian elite, disgruntled at their subordination, deposed Arsaces II and set up Phriapatius as their third king. A series of wars followed during which the Parthians expanded eastwards to take over India and almost reached China by 168 BC. In 144 BC they took Babylon from the Seleucids. The Empire at its peak stretched from the Mediterranean Sea to China.

After losing territory to the Romans, the Romans invaded Parthia near Carrhae in 53 BC under the Roman triumvir Crassus. Crassus was comprehensively defeated by the Parthian archers on horseback.

This was a psychological blow to Rome, and it was reinforced with the defeat of Mark Antony in 32 BC. These defeats caused Caesar Augustus to negotiate a long-term peace agreement with Parthia in 20 BC.

The boundary between the Romans and Parthians was the River Euphrates, although the Romans tried three times to invade

Parthia with little long-term success. The continual Roman invasions and internal conflicts led to the Parthian Empire being taken over by the Sasanian Empire in 224 AD.[5]

The Sasanian Empire lasted until 651 AD when it was overthrown by the Arab Rashidun Caliphate.[6] The Empire rivalled the western Roman Empire, and sustained trade relations with the Tang Dynasty of China. The Rashidun Caliphate was founded by one of Muhammad's earliest converts, Abu Bakr.[7] It began in Arabia and spread to Iraq and Syria. It was succeeded by the Islamic Caliphates which eventually became the Ottoman Empire.

The Ottoman Empire began in the 11th century when the Seljuk Turks conquered first Persia, Anatolia (central Turkey), and had taken over the Balkans by the 14th century.[8] At its peak, the Ottoman Empire surrounded the Mediterranean Sea, including Spain, Portugal and part of southern France, and several east European countries. The Ottoman Empire was destroyed in 1922 in the aftermath of World War 1.

If the Muslims recombine to re-form the Ottoman Empire or a Caliphate, the fourth animal in Daniel's dream (Daniel 7:7-8) could easily describe the Muslims. Islam is a religion of submission, corresponding to the iron teeth. All other forms of religion are suppressed, especially Judaism and Christianity, but all religions could eventually be absorbed. This could correspond to the beast crushing and devouring its victims.

Laws of the conquered countries are changed to reflect Sharia Law. Human rights that are taken for granted in western countries

---

5. www.ancient.eu/Parthia_(Empire)/
6. www.ancient.eu/Sasanian_Empire/
7. www.ancient.eu/Rashidun_Caliphate/
8. www.ancient.eu/Ottoman_Empire/

are removed in Muslim countries, including current 'woke' rights such as homosexuality and gender diversity. This corresponds to being trampled under the feet.

Muslim countries are currently split between Sunni and Shi'a Islam with a few other minor sects, but they may merge politically to form a stronger world political presence.

Which one?

Most commentators predict the future ruler will come from the Roman Empire. These include Chuck Missler,[9] John Walvoord,[10] Lewis Chafer,[11] and most conservative commentators.

But there have been many people in the past who see the final ruler coming from an Islamic country. These include John Wesley, Martin Luther, John Calvin, Jonathan Edwards, and a range of other people spanning several hundred years.[12]

At this point in time, we cannot know whether the Roman or Ottoman Empire is the origin of the final ruler. Political events can happen quickly. Either option seems feasible. But as we get closer to the predicted events, we will have greater clarity.

I believe the final ruler will come from the Ottoman Empire. He seems to come from the countries under the Seleucid Empire, so that covers from Turkey east to Iran (Persia) and south to Egypt. If he comes from Turkey,[13] he will come from both Empires.

9. *Prophecy 20/20*, p 69.
10. *Bible Knowledge Commentary: Old Testament*, pp 1335, 1354.
11. *Major Bible Themes*, p 315.
12. *God's War on Terror*, pp 322-331.
13. For a discussion on why Turkey should be a serious contender, see *God's War on Terror*, pp 419-443.

There is an organisation that consists of ten countries. That is ASEAN (Association of South East Asian Nations). The countries involved are Indonesia, Brunei, Thailand, Malaysia, Laos, Singapore, Philippines, Vietnam, Cambodia, and Myanmar. There are too distant to be part of the prophetic picture, but they act similar to the final empire. They do not have a common currency. They use English as their 'joint' language, which makes it difficult for some of these nations.

This type of structure could be a template for the future leader to use.

Appendix 6

The Ruler

Those people who will not be governed
by God will be ruled by tyrants.
- *William Penn, 1644-1718, early USA administrator*

In Revelation chapter 6, when Jesus opened the first seal we are introduced to the rider on the white horse. He looked like Christ, but obviously he is not Christ. He is a conqueror instead of a saviour. The same person is described in chapter 13 as '*the beast coming from the sea*'.

He is typically named the 'Antichrist', with *anti-* meaning 'pseudo' rather than 'against'. Although the word 'antichrist' does appear in the Bible, it is never used as a title for a person. It is always a description of a person's personality or activities.

Who is this person? He will be a major leader that will arise after the Rapture in the future. But what else does the Bible say about him?

One of the controversies surrounding the end times study is whether this person is a worldwide leader, or will he be a major regional leader in Europe or the Middle East. Either way, he is going to be a major influence in the future.

But does the world need a single leader? Fifty years ago, there were two 'superpowers' with large economies, nuclear weapons, and the ability to influence world politics. These were USSR and

USA. They and their allies kept the world in a state of balance.

Today, both these countries are much weaker politically, militarily, and economically. Other blocs of countries have equal or almost equal strength, such as European Union, Arabic nations, China, and India. Neither USSR nor USA are the superpower they once were.

Problems such as the proliferation of nuclear ability, climate change, trans-border economies, and now global pandemics means international agreements are becoming more important. The United Nations is continually being given more power to control international events.

The Roman Catholic Church has advocated for a single global power for centuries. The popes were both the political and 'spiritual' leaders during the Holy Roman Empire (800-1806),[1] and the church has recently tried to gain global recognition.

Pope Benedict XVI said, 'There is an urgent need for a true world political authority, to manage the global economy with God-centred ethics ... to end the current worldwide financial crisis.'[2]

Paul-Henri Spaak was the prime minister of Belgium in the 1930s and 40s. He is reported to have said, 'The truth is that the method of international committees has failed. What we need is a person, someone of the highest order or great experience, of great authority, of wide influence, of great energy. Either a civilian or a military man, no matter what his nationality, who will cut all the red tape, shove out ... all the committees, wake up all the people and galvanise all governments into action.'[3]

It makes sense that if the trends continue, the United Nations or another recognised body will be the final arbitrator in inter-

---

1. en.wikipedia.org/wiki/Holy_Roman_Empire
2. Quoted in *2017: 500 Years After Luther*, p 7.
3. Quoted in *Agents of the Apocalypse*, p 141.

national disputes. The recent rise of international terrorism and climate change are two reasons given as a need for a global government system.

A National Intelligence Council report in September 2010 listed three reasons for increasing global governance.[4] These are:

1. Local threats that may have a global impact. Examples may be ethnic conflicts, infectious diseases, climate change, food and water scarcity, and migration flows.
2. Power of non-state actors, for example Facebook, Google, etc. Illegal activities, such as drug smuggling, organised crime, triads, etc.
3. Civil wars or internal conflicts, especially protracted ones with seemingly no solutions. Examples cited are Nigeria, Afghanistan, Iraq.

Hence the potential for a gifted political leader to rise to a position where he has the major role in international affairs.

Satan must always have someone who he is grooming to fulfil this role, because he does not know when the trigger point will be. We can look back in history and see people like Napoleon Bonaparte, Adolf Hitler and Josef Stalin who caused a lot of death and destruction, and we think that they may have been candidates for this role.

What about the 'good' leaders at different times, such as Winston Churchill or Ronald Reagan? They may have been candidates as far as Satan is concerned because of their influence. There will be people alive today who Satan will be influencing to be a future ruler if the chance arises.

What does the Bible say about the future ruler? We are given

---

4. files.ethz.ch/isn/121625/Global_Governance_2025.pdf

detailed descriptions about his personality and some details about his political career. We are not given enough detail to attempt to predict who this person might be from the people alive today.

His personality

He will be a great and persuasive orator (Daniel 7:20, Revelation 13:5). But he will be arrogant and boastful (Daniel 7:8, 11, 20, 8:25, 11:36). He will be so proud that he will blaspheme against God (Daniel 7:25, 11:36; Revelation 13:6).

He will be an intellectual genius (Daniel 7:20, 8:23).

He will be a masterful politician (Daniel 7:24, 11:21). But a lot of his power will be by crushing any rebellion quickly and effectively.

He will be a commercial expert (Daniel 8:25, Revelation 13:17).

He will become a powerful military leader (Daniel 8:24, Revelation 6:2, 13:4). He will adore military strength (Daniel 11:38). He will use military force to expand his realm of influence. He will disperse political favours to people who honour him, and he will allow bribery for political control (Daniel 11:39).

He will become an influential government leader (Revelation 13:1-2, 17:17).

He will have no respect for any religion, but he will exalt himself above them all (Daniel 11:36-37, 2 Thessalonians 2:4). He will become a religious leader (Revelation 13:3, 14-15). He will exalt himself '*over everything that is called God*'.

This includes Allah of the Muslim faith, but he is somehow

accepted by the Muslims. It seems that he will want to take over all religions, such as the eastern and Sharman beliefs.

He will be able to perform miracles with Satan's help. Paul describes the '*coming of the lawless one*' that will be accompanied '*with all kinds of counterfeit miracles, signs, and wonders*' (2 Thessalonians 2:9).

He will be so antagonistic against any belief in God that he oppresses the saints, or believers (Daniel 7:25). These believers are largely Jews (Revelation 7), but they would include Christians. He wages war against believers and defeats them (Daniel 7:21, 27).

He will want to be worshipped as above every other god worshipped and will speak against the God of gods, Yahweh (Daniel 7:25, 11:36). This fulfils 1 John 2:22 where the antichrist spirit denies that Jesus is the Christ. In fact, he will claim to be God and perform miracles to prove his claim (2 Thessalonians 2:4, 9).

Probably the most often mentioned trait is that he will be deceitful (Daniel 8:23, 25, 11:21-23).

He will decide that he is independent of all power, including those who allowed him into his current position (will do as he pleases, Daniel 11:36).

He will ignore women's rights and aspirations (Daniel 11:37).

His political career

He will uproot or take over three nations or leaders to establish his power (Daniel 7:24). Remember horns are symbolic of authority or leadership. Obviously, this person has insignificant beginnings, but rises to subdue or take over three former leaders, probably by subterfuge. His insignificant beginnings will initially hide his identity.[5]

His rule will last forty-two months (Revelation 13:5).

His initial rule will be over a ten-nation federation or grouping (Revelation 13:1). Will this be the area of the original Roman Empire or Ottoman Empire? Or the current Muslim nations in the greater Middle East? The Bible does not say, so any explanation could be feasible.[6]

He will be an adversary of Israel and will subdue Israel to his authority (Daniel 8:24-25).

At some point there is an assassination attempt that causes a fatal wound (Revelation 13:3). He miraculously survives, but it will leave him with a damaged right arm and is blind in one eye (Zechariah 11:16-17). His revival from these injuries will be used as the basis for a personality cult that will make the North Korean system look like child's play (Revelation 13:4).

The ruler will '*confirm a covenant with many nations*' for a seven-year period (Daniel 9:27). Notice that word '*confirm*'. It implies an agreement has already been in force, and this ruler confirms it or extends it.

This is likely to be a multinational peace agreement. We have the beginnings of a similar covenant in the agreements between

---

5. *Agents of The Apocalypse*, pp 147-148.
6. This topic is discussed in more detail in Appendix 5.

Israel, Bahrain, Egypt and Saudi Arabia signed in November 2020 that were negotiated by President Trump.

But he will break the agreement in the middle of the seven-year period (after three and a half years). He will put an end to the sacrifices and offerings (Daniel 9:27). This shows the temple in Jerusalem will be rebuilt prior to this time and the sacrificial system reinstituted.

He will erect an '*abomination that causes desolation*' in a wing of the temple (Daniel 9:27). Jesus refers to this in Matthew 24:15. He says it will be placed in the Holy Place, where the ark of covenant sits, and the presence of God resides.

This is likely to be a statute of himself as he wants the world to worship him (2 Thessalonians 2:4, Revelation 13:8). This will cause Israel to rebel against him and set off a conflict that eventually leads to his demise.

He will combine forces with a second leader (the second beast or false prophet) to establish a religious and economic system that will give him global influence. He will produce an image that speaks. He will put something in the temple to defile it. Is that item the statue? His religion will be authenticated by miraculous signs and wonders (2 Thessalonians 2:9).

As part of his religious system, he will persecute anyone who believes a different religion. This will be especially harsh against Jews and Christians for three and a half years (Daniel 7:25, 8:24; Revelation 13:7). He will be involved in the murder of the two witnesses (Revelation 11:7).

The global economic system will be tied to their religion. Everyone opting into the cashless system is marked, and that is required to be able to engage in any financial transaction (Revelation 13:16-17).

He will try to change the set times and the laws (Daniel 7:25). This most probably refers to religious holidays or festivals and associated rules. But see Appendix 8 for a discussion on what else this could mean.

His influence will extend to be worldwide (Daniel 7:23). If the leader is based in either Europe or the Middle East, his influence will still be immense in a similar way to how both European and Middle Eastern politics influences the world today. Middle East politics is having an increasing influence, especially as alliances are being established.

He will eventually have splits from various groups of countries that result in a three-way war (Daniel 11:40-45). Is this because of the adverse effects of his rule? (Daniel 8:24)

He will succeed in somehow agreeing to combine his forces with the three coalitions coming against him so they can fight a common enemy. This enemy is God himself. He will be arrogant enough to wage a military war against God and think that he can win (Daniel 8:25, Revelation 19:19). He will bring the armies toward Jerusalem, but they will be defeated by the God he is fighting against (Zechariah 12:2-9, 14:2-3).

His ultimate destiny is that he and the second beast are captured by God and are the first people put into the Lake of Fire (Daniel 7:9-11, 26, 8:25, 2 Thessalonians 2:8, Revelation 19:19-20).

Could he have a Muslim background?

This person is obviously empowered by Satan (Revelation 13:4). But what type of religious background does he have? There are indications that he may arise from a Muslim country.

The ruler will have no respect for any religious heritage, including his own, but will exalt himself above them all (Daniel 11:36-37). Islam fits this description because it demands that all religions submit to their beliefs. The word Islam means 'submission'.[7] But this may indicate that he is not a Muslim because devout Muslims will not put themselves above Allah.

Islam predicts that a future Muslim will rule the world and force everyone to submit to Islam. This person is called the Mahdi, and he will be the twelfth Caliph.[8] If he thinks that he is the Mahdi, he may try to establish himself as Allah returned to earth.

He will ignore women's desires or aspirations (Daniel 11:37). Islam looks on women as second-class people and gives them very few rights. The Quran allows Muslim men to have as many wives as they can afford, and it allows them to beat their wives for any misdemeanour. Women are not allowed to get an education, have no influence on who they can marry, and have the same status as a slave in many cases.

He will adore military strength (Daniel 11:38). He will honour a god unknown to his fathers. This may be Satan as he has not been honoured by that name. '*A god of fortresses*' is '*a god of war*'. Islam honours a god of war. Islam is a militant religion, whereas Christianity and Judaism are religions of love.

Islam is also militant against disagreeing branches of Islam, for

---

7. en.wikipedia.org/wiki/Islam
8. *Understanding Islamic Theology*, pp 282-283.

example, Sunni against Shiite. There are very few Islamic countries today that do not have a conflict of some kind happening.

He will break a covenant made with many nations after three and a half years (Daniel 9:27). The Quran allows lies to be told if it furthers the spread of Islam. This is called *taqiyya.*[9] To most Muslims, promises made to non-Muslim are non-binding. In other words, you cannot trust a Muslim.

Hudna is an Islamic term referring to making a treaty with non-Muslims with no intention of keeping to it. They will keep the treaty until they have gained enough political and military strength to break it.[10] A good example is the 1993 Oslo Peace Accord, which is known in the Middle East as the Oslo Hudna Accord.

Comparison of Christian and Islamic Description of the Ruler

It will surprise many people that both the Christian and Muslim descriptions of end time events have a lot in common. Anyone who knows the history of Mohammed will be aware that early in his life he had contact with both Jews and Christians.

The ruler described in the Bible is given many different names, but he is commonly called the 'Antichrist' by most commentators (but not in the Bible). The future ruler in the Quran is called the Mahdi (essentially a reincarnation of Mohammed).[11] We know these are the same person because of common descriptions in the Bible and Quran.

Both deny the Trinity. Quran 5:73; *They blaspheme who say that Allah is the third of the three.*

Both deny Jesus is God's Son. Quran 5:17; *In blasphemy indeed*

---

9. *Understanding Islamic Theology*, p 428.
10. *God's War on Terror*, p 71.
11. *God's War on Terror*, p 53.

are those who say that God is Christ the son of a Mary. Quran 9:30; *The Christians call Christ the son of Allah. That is a saying from their mouth; in this they but imitate what the unbelievers of old used to say. Allah's curse be on them; how they are deluded away from the Truth.*

Both are blasphemous. Islam teaches that Jesus is just another prophet with Mohammed being the last and most truthful prophet.

Both are called Deceiver. 2 Thessalonians 2:9-10; *The coming of the lawless one will be in accordance with the work of Satan displayed in all kinds of counterfeit miracles, signs and wonders, and in every sort of evil that deceives those who are perishing.*

Allah calls himself Khayrul-Makireen, which means 'The Greatest of All Deceivers' (Quran 3:54). Remember Jesus' warning about being deceived in Matthew 24:24.

Both will work false miracles. Islamic tradition says *Allah will give him power over the wind and the rain, and the earth will bring forth its foliage. He will give away wealth profusely, and flocks will be in abundance.*[12]

Both try to change the law (Daniel 7:25 as quoted above). Muslims around the world are trying to change every country to the Sharia legal system.

Both will rule for seven years. Daniel 9:27. Abu Dawud, Book 36, No 4272: *The prophet said: The Mahdi will be of my stock and will have a broad forehead and a prominent nose. He will fill the earth with equity and justice as it was with oppression and tyranny, and he will rule for seven years.*

Both deny women's rights. Daniel 11:37 states the ruler will '*not regard ... the desire of women.*' Women are denied many rights taken for granted in most non-Muslim countries, such as, the right to drive a car, get an education, wear western-style clothing, etc. According to Islamic law, a woman inherits only a half of what a

12. *God's War on Terror*, p 83.

male inherits. In court, the testimony of two women is equivalent to the testimony of one man.

Mohammed said that women have half the mental capacity of a man.[13] Islam decrees death to a Muslim woman who marries outside their faith, but a Muslim man can marry non-Muslim women. The Quran tells men to beat their wives into submission (Quran 4:34).

Both will rule over ten other countries. Revelation 17:12-13. In 2002 a plan to re-establish the Caliphate was written with a ten-member council to assist the Caliph in his rule. In 2007 Al Qaeda set up a ten-member cabinet to control their land.[14]

13. *God's War on Terror*, p 88.
14. *God's War on Terror*, p 91.

Appendix 7

Similarities Between Joshua and Revelation

There are interesting parallels between the books of Revelation and Joshua.[1,2] The name Joshua is Hebrew; the Greek equivalent is '*Jesus*'. Both words mean 'salvation'.

Joshua's mission was to dispossess the usurpers from the land of Israel (or Canaan as it was called then). Revelation shows Jesus' mission to dispossess planet Earth of the usurpers.

Joshua yielded control for the battle of Jericho to '*the Captain of the army of the Lord*' (Joshua 5:13-6:5). Because he commanded worship, we know this is Jesus. Similarly, Jesus leads the victors at the battles of Armageddon.

Joshua sent two spies into Jericho. But the only thing they accomplished was to save a single family. Revelation chapter 11 has an account of two special witnesses who are a prominent element of the book. They may result in numerous believers.

When Joshua attacked Jericho, many laws were broken. The Levites were exempt from military duty, but they led the procession. Israelites were not supposed to do any work on the Sabbath, but they marched around Jericho seven days in a row. Revelation shows the world in a lawless state.

---

1. *Cosmic Codes*, pp 272-273. See also Appendix 6.
2. From Jonathan Cahn, *The Mystery of the Seven Trumpets*. www.youtube.com/watch?=ntr_NCFoLr8

Joshua uses trumpets to begin the destruction on Jericho. In Revelation God uses trumpets to bring judgement on the earth. The trumpets are linked to destruction in both cases.

Seven priests blow the trumpets in Joshua; seven angels blow the trumpets in Revelation. Both priests and angels are ministers of God. The seven priests stand before the presence of God at Jericho; seven angels stand before the presence of God in Revelation.

The trumpets reach their peak on the seventh day at Jericho; the trumpets reach their peak at the seventh trumpet in Revelation. The breakthrough happens at the final trumpet in both cases.

The Israelites had to keep silent until the final blast. Revelation introduces the seven trumpets after a strange silence in heaven.

Joshua encounters an alliance of nations under a leader, Adoni-Zedek (Lord of Righteousness). They are defeated with signs in the sun and moon, and the kings hide in caves. Similar things happen with the sun and moon in Revelation.

Joshua finishes with the Israelites settling into a new land. Revelation finishes with a New Jerusalem where the redeemed people live. Both Joshua and Revelation describe the end of one age and the entrance into the promised land of God. People move from temporary dwellings to their permanent dwellings.

Appendix 8

Historical Calendar Changes

Ethics and equity and the principles of justice
do not change with the calendar.
- D.H. Lawrence, 1885-1930, author

The future ruler will try to change '*the set times and the laws*' (Daniel 7:25). What does this mean? Will he try to change religious observances? Or does he try to change global laws? Or does he set up a new calendar system?

Most commentaries think this refers to religious observances. But could there be more to this simple statement than religion?

What are the set times? As far as the Bible is concerned, they are the days that God has set apart for specific purposes. These include the weekly Sabbath (Exodus 20:8-11, 34:21), and the seven Feasts (Leviticus 23). The Sabbath was instituted to give mankind and domestic animals a day of rest from the daily grind of work.

The aim was to allow man to spend some time reflecting on God's goodness. We need to do the same to prevent burn-out or mental illness. The Feasts have a dual purpose of commemorating certain events and they foretell other events associated with the Messiah.

There have been occasions in history when people have tried to change both Biblical set times and the calendar system.

Antiochus IV Epiphanes tried to stop the Jews observing their religious rites and sacrifices in 168 BC. He attacked and burned Jerusalem, killed thousands, and made it illegal for the Jews to speak Hebrew and to observe the sacrifices, Sabbaths and annual festivals.

Altars to idols were set up in Jerusalem, and on 16 December 167 BC, pig meat was offered on the altar and a statute of Zeus erected in the Holy Place. This was the '*abomination that causes desolation*' that Jesus spoke about in Matthew 24:15.

This event triggered the Maccabean Revolt which lasted about two years. The temple was finally cleansed and restored in 163 BC by Judas Maccabeus 1,150 days later, which is celebrated in the Jewish festival of Hannakh.

The laws that God gave to Moses requires people to worship Him on the Sabbath or Saturday (Exodus 20:8-11; Deuteronomy 5:12-15). The Roman emperor Constantine legislated Sunday as a day of rest on 7 March 321 AD.

This was enforced by the Roman Catholic Church at various conferences, starting with the eastern regional meeting at Laodicea in 364 AD.[1] It was reinforced at the Third Synod of Aureliani in 538 AD. It continues in most Christian churches today.

The Muslim day of worship is Friday. One of the aims of radical Islam is to rid the world of anyone who uses either Saturday or Sunday as their day of worship.[2]

The early Roman Catholic Church also changed the day that Passover is observed and changed its name to Easter. This was done to separate the church from the original Jewish festivals as detailed in the Old Testament.

At the Council of Nicaea in AD 325, it was officially decided that Christians should not celebrate the Lord's death and resur-

---

1. www.catholic.com/tract/sabbath-or-sunday
2. www.israelnationalnews.com/Articles/Article.aspx/24141

rection in conjunction with Passover and the Feast of First Fruits. The council arranged it so that Easter would never be celebrated on Passover. It unanimously ruled that the Easter festival should be celebrated throughout the Christian world on the first Sunday after the first full moon following the vernal equinox.

What's more, if the full moon should occur on a Sunday and thereby coincide with the Passover festival, Easter should be commemorated on the following Sunday. They sought to deliberately worship on a day other than what was ordained in the Bible.[3]

In 1928, the British Parliament enacted a measure allowing the Church of England to commemorate Easter on the first Sunday after the second Saturday in April. Thus, Easter is still considered a 'moveable' feast day. New Zealand has not followed with a similar law and observes Easter in late March or early April following the Council of Nicaea ruling.

Will the structure of the week be changed to remove the Biblical association with the six days of creation? This has been tried but failed every time.

During the French Revolution, the revolutionaries decreed the first year of the revolution as year 1, and they made the week 10 days long. This calendar endured for more than a decade, lasting until Napoleon crowned himself emperor.[4]

The Russians tried to introduce a continuous calendar after the 1917 Revolution. They tried a five-day week whereby everyone had one day off each week. Your day off work was dictated by the government so that one-fifth of the workers were absent on each day. But this experiment was abandoned in 1940 after eleven years.[5]

---

3. www.khouse.org/articles/2019/1353/
4. www.slate.com/blogs/the_eye/2015/04/11/history_s_failed_attempts_to_redesign_the_calendar_from_99_percent_invisible.html
5. www.history.com/news/soviet-union-stalin-weekend-labor-policy

Muslims believe the Mahdi will change the calendar and introduce Sharia Law. The Muslim calendar begins at the year that Mohammed conquered Medina in 622 AD. Muslims refer to this as the year of Hijra. Islamic years are shown as AD for 'after Hijra'. The year 2000 was 1421 in the Hijra calendar. Could another change in year numbers occur again under a Muslim leader?

> The default calendar recognised in almost all countries is based around the birth of Jesus Christ. It is called the Gregorian calendar, after Pope Gregory XIII who instituted it in 1582. It used the year 1 AD as the birth year of Jesus. This was calculated in the 6th century. But the data now shows that Jesus was most likely born in 2 BC.
>
> The Hebrew calendar is supposed to date back to the creation of the world. The year 2000 in the Gregorian calendar was 5760 in the Hebrew calendar.

Appendix 9

Armageddon

Don't wake me for the end of the world
unless it has very good special effects.
- *Roger Zelazny, 1937-1995, author.*

We are introduced to the War of Armageddon in Revelation 16:12-16. This event is covered here in a few verses.

But this war is mentioned elsewhere in the Bible in more detail. This is the final part of '*the Day of the Lord*' when Jesus Christ intervenes in human history in a way that has never happened before.

Armageddon has become a synonym for any doomsday scenario and large-scale devastation. There is a particularly good reason for that. When we read the predictions in the Bible, we see that there is much destruction of life and property. By the time it is finished, little of our civilisation may survive, especially in the Middle East.

Armageddon is located in the valley of Jezreel below Mount Megiddo, 100 km north of Jerusalem. The valley is sometimes called the Plain of Esdraelon. Jezreel means '*God will sow*'.[1] Megiddo means '*place of troops*'.[2]

Both names are prophetic (as are all names in the Bible).

1. *Analytical Concordance to the Bible*, p 545; *Compact Bible Dictionary*, p 284.
2. *Compact Bible Dictionary*, p 355.

Opposite the valley from Mount Megiddo is a small hill that has the village of Nazareth. Jesus lived here for most of his life.

This valley is ideally suited for warfare. The valley allows room for armies to manoeuvre while the hills allow the battle to be controlled by the generals, and it provides good sites for heavy artillery.

Mount Carmel is at the sea end of the ranges along the southern side of the plain. The ancient trade route from Persia to Egypt came through here on a road linking Gaza with Damascus, so it has always had a strategic significance.

This valley has a long history of war. Wars recorded in the Bible in this area are:

- Joshua defeated the king of Megiddo (Joshua 12:7, 21).
- Barak and Deborah defeated Sisera and Jabin's army of nine hundred chariots (Judges 4). The Kishon River goes through the plain of Megiddo.
- Gideon's army of three hundred defeated a combined army of Moabites and Amalekites (Judges 7).
- Samson triumphed over the Philistines (Judges 15).
- King Saul and many of his family were killed by the Philistines (1 Samuel 31). Mount Gilboa is located at the south-east end of the range that borders the plain.
- King Ahaziah was killed by arrows from Jehu's army (2 Kings 9:27).
- Pharaoh Neco killed King Josiah (2 Kings 23:29) in a battle that Josiah should not have been involved in.

Other historical armies to be in this area are the Saracens and Christian crusaders, Egyptians, Persians, Druses, Turks, Arabs, and Napoleon on his disastrous march from Egypt to Syria.[3] The earli-

3. *Prophecy 20/20*, p 86.

est battle for which there is good historical evidence is the Battle of Megiddo in 1457 BC between the Egyptians and Canaanites, fought at Kadesh.[4]

The British army led a campaign against the Ottoman Turks in World War 1. Among the divisions was the ANZAC Mounted Division, consisting of the Australian Light Horsemen and the New Zealand Mounted Rifle Brigade.

After the Allied defeat at Gallipoli, Turkey tried to take the Suez Canal from Britain. The ANZACs fought from the Suez Canal into the Sinai desert, then north to Jerusalem.

Among the battles in this war, probably the most famous was the desperate New Zealand cavalry charge on Beersheba on 31 October 1917 which turned the war to the allies' favour. The ANZACs entered Jerusalem on 11 December 1917, 400 years to the day from the start of the occupation by the Ottoman Empire. Many soldiers reported seeing angels prior to reaching Jerusalem.[5]

A final drive began with the Battle of Megiddo in September 1918 which resulted in the destruction of three Ottoman field armies and the capture of 76,000 prisoners.[6] The ANZACs captured Damascus on 1 October 1918 before being disbanded in 1919.[7]

This was one in a series of battles that brought about the demise of the Ottoman Empire and the eventual establishment of Israel and Jordan (and their neighbouring countries) as independent countries. It is a shame this series of engagements is largely ignored in both New Zealand history and ANZAC commemorations.

The other place referred to in the war of Armageddon is the valley of Jehoshaphat. Jehoshaphat means '*God is judge*'.[8] This val-

---

4. www.youtube.com/watch?v=bf-SUOCqbrI
5. *New Zealand's Christian Heritage*, pp 140-147.
6. nzhistory.govt.nz/war/palestine-campaign
7. en.wikipedia.org/wiki/ANZAC_Mounted_Division
8. *Compact Bible Dictionary*, p 268.

ley is located between Jerusalem and the Mount of Olives, and is also known as the Kidron Valley. Joel refers to this as the '*valley of decision*' (Joel 3:14).

Let's quickly review Daniel 11:36-39 because it describes the final world ruler who will have a major global influence for a period of at least seven years. He will be the instigator of the War of Armageddon.

1. He will be answerable to no one (verse 36). He will be a dictator.
2. He will be proud (verses 36 and 37). He will exalt himself above every god, including Almighty God and Allah. He will disregard all gods of all religions, and will set himself up as the supreme God to be worshipped (Revelation 13:8, 12-15).
3. He will honour a god of war (verse 38) and rely on military strength to enforce his rule (Daniel 8:24).
4. He will be a persuasive orator (Daniel 7:20, 8:23, 25).
5. He will be a master of deceit (Daniel 8:25, Matthew 24:24).

Although he will be the global ruler, there will be geographical divisions to facilitate the government of the world. Various political groupings are still in existence at the time. These will most probably be continued from previous alliances, such as NATO, various free trade agreements, etc. Four of these are named in this text.

A quick comment on some of the current ideas being touted. Canada, USA and Mexico signed an updated trade and investment agreement (CUSMA) on 1 July 2020.[9] A New Zealand and Australia merger is raised every few years, but quickly dies because of the economic disparities between the two countries.

---

9. www.international.gc.ca/trade-commerce/trade-agreements-accords-commerciaux/agr-acc/cusma-aceum/index.aspx?lang=eng

The European Union is continually expanding, but it may splinter into smaller groupings due to political and economic differences. For example, Britain left the EU on 1 January 2021, and this may be the start of this disintegration process. Turkey has tried to join the EU for many years but is continually rebuffed.

The ruler is described in this chapter as a descendant of the king of the North. This was originally part of the Seleucid Greek Empire. At this point he is leading a confederation that is either the revived Roman or Ottoman Empire (Daniel 2:40-43, 7:7-8, 24). Turkey is directly north of Israel. Is the leader of Turkey the person?

What political groupings are described in Daniel 11?

The '*king of the North*' in the earlier part of Daniel 11 refers to the Seleucid ruler who was based in Persia, or modern-day Iran and Iraq. In the last few verses, it could still refer to an Islamic coalition led by someone based in Turkey or Iran.

It could refer to a Russian grouping since Russia is to the north of Israel. Russia is developing close ties with Iran, and it is trading nuclear technology for oil. It has also developed good ties with Syria so that it can have a port that does not freeze over in the winter.

Many commentators say the Bible refers to Russia as Meshech and Magog (Genesis 10:2). It has been suggested that Meshech eventually became the word used to derive Moscow, the current capital of Russia (based solely on the similar sounds). The reality is that Meshech refers to a region of Turkey.[10]

The '*king of the South*' implies an African or Arab alliance. The king of the South earlier in this chapter refers to the Ptolemy ruler based in Egypt, but it included Libya and down the Nile River into Sudan and Ethiopia.

This could be an alliance of Arab nations based on their com-

---

10. *God's War on Terror*, pp 256-260.

mon religion, or it could include some African countries. So, the *'king of the South'* could be the ruler of Egypt at the time?

The *'kings from the East'* probably refers to Asian nations. Revelation 16:12 tells us the Euphrates River will be dried up to allow the kings of the east easy access to the Middle East.

China and India are the two major Asian military powers, but Pakistan and both Koreas also have large militaries. These five countries have a combined military force of 21.7 million.[11]

This is a four-way confrontation involving most countries of the world in the groupings somewhere. Let's follow the story as it develops. Be aware no time frames are given in the scriptures relating to this confrontation.

These predicted events may take anywhere from a few weeks to some years to fully unfold. They may involve the entire seven-year Tribulation period, or they may have begun prior to the beginning of the Tribulation. We are not given any clues.

Revelation 16:13-14 tells us that the rulers of the world countries are enticed to gather for a war. No other details are given. No one knows exactly how the events will play out. Almost every writer has a different theory. What I present here are some ideas from various writers to try to tie these events together.

Daniel 11:40. The southern group has a disagreement with the ruler and engages him in battle. We are not told why this happens, but some suggestions can be made.

1. It could be related to the image of the beast in the temple. Jerusalem is now the third most holy site for Muslims, even though it is not mentioned in the Quran. That is a political ploy to prevent the Jews building on the Temple Mount. But

11. worldpopulationreview.com/country-rankings/military-size-by-country

the Muslims may see this image as a desolation of what they consider is a holy site, and they may decide to fight it.

2. Daniel 9:27 says the Antichrist breaks a covenant in the middle of the seven-year period, and ushers in the Great Tribulation Period. Maybe this is a military action to enforce the treaty because they feel betrayed in some way.

3. The conditions during the Great Tribulation period are so bad that these countries may decide to take military action against the ruler and hope to get rid of him. Maybe he has double-crossed them. He is predicted to be a master of deception.

4. Is this a battle over resources (for example, oil or water)? Oil basins have been discovered in Israel.[12]

The northern group joins the war (Daniel 11:40). Ezekiel 38:1-6 lists countries that join an alliance at some time, but is it this alliance? Gog is called '*the chief prince of Meshech and Tubal*'. He is obviously a demonic power behind the nations.[13]

Meshech = Turkey, Georgia
Tubal = Turkey
Persia = Iran
Cush = Sudan, Somalia
Put = Libya
Gomer = Central Turkey (Cappadocia)
Beth Togarmah = Eastern Turkey
Magog = Scythians, Black Sea region, Kurds

12. www.jewishvirtuallibrary.org/oil-and-natural-gas-in-israel
13. Described in *God's War on Terror*, pp 254-266.

Why are these names unfamiliar? Because the people migrated over the centuries, and the initial languages changed. But ancient historians (e.g., Hesiod and Herodotus) tell us where these countries were.

Some commentators associate Meshech with Moscow and Tubal with Tobolsk, both of which are cities in Russia. This idea seems to have originated from the *Scofield Study Bible*, and it was based on the similar sounds of the words.[14]

Maybe this is another political move by the northern alliance in the hope to regain some military, political, or economic advantage. The northern group brings chariots (tanks? APV? trucks?), cavalry (tanks? rocket launchers? maybe include aircraft?) and a great fleet of ships (navy).

But the ruler and his armies will '*invade many countries and sweep through like a flood*'. There are only a few countries with a significant military force in the Middle East, so many will be easily over-run. Isaiah 17 predicts the total destruction of Damascus and other cities in that region. Does this happen during this time? Does Psalm 83 happen now?

Daniel 11:41. The site of the initial engagement is not given, but the Valley of Jezreel is the staging area. At some point the Antichrist invades Israel (called '*the Beautiful Land*' by Daniel). Is this when two-thirds of the population is killed (Zechariah 13:8)? Is this when half of Jerusalem is taken into slavery (Zechariah 14:1-2)?

Many countries fall to the invaders, but Edom, Moab and Ammon will not be captured. There seems to be some supernatural protection on these countries. The wording is that these countries '*will be delivered from his hand.*' This sounds like he may try to attack them, but he will be prevented. Why? Because the believing Jews will be hiding from the Antichrist there?

---

14. *God's War on Terror*, p 257.

Daniel 11:42. The ruler will extend his power over many countries. Egypt is specifically mentioned. Why? Does Egypt initiate the southern rebellion against the ruler that starts all this? Or is Egypt a rebellious state that leads an Arab rebellion against the ruler?

Isaiah 19:4 predicts Egypt being handed over to a cruel master and fierce king. Later verses in the chapter talk about the environment changing and the Nile River drying up. Ezekiel 29:6-16 predicts that Egypt will be invaded and completely devastated.

No one will live there for forty years, and then be restored but will remain a minor country. Does the devastation happen at this time? If not, when?

Daniel 11:43. Egypt is stripped of its economic resources, and therefore its political and military power. The Libyans and Nubians (Sudan, Ethiopia) are in submission to the ruler. There is probably a peace treaty signed between these countries. Are these the three horns that are uprooted in Daniel 7:8?

It seems that the southern group is defeated or decides to make peace before being totally destroyed.

Daniel 11:44. News reports from the north and east alarm the ruler. What news? The fact that armies from these regions are advancing on him? (Revelation 16:12) Have they made a military agreement to unite against a common enemy? The eastern armies will have easy access because the Euphrates River will be dried up (Isaiah 11:15, Revelation 16:12).

China is currently building the 'Silk Road' from China to eastern Europe under the Belt and Road initiative to facilitate trade.[15] This road can also be used to transport troops. The ruler will set out in a rage to stamp his mark on the world by trying to destroy and annihilate many people.

If this coincides with the sixth trumpet (Revelation 9:13-16),

15. en.wikipedia.org/wiki/Belt_and_Road_Initiative

one third of the population will be killed (two billion people). How can so many people be killed? Nuclear weapons? Famine? Plagues?

From here, there is a difference of opinion as to what will happen. Three possible scenarios are given.

Scenario 1

Verse 45. The ruler sets up his base between the seas at the holy mountain. What seas? The main sea is the Mediterranean Sea. The other could be either the Dead Sea or the Sea of Galilee. If the verse means Galilee, then they will be at Megiddo. If the Dead Sea is meant, the '*beautiful holy mountain*' would be Mount Zion. This is a term applied to the range on which Jerusalem is located, and Mount Zion is considered holy by the Jews. Jerusalem will be his next target.

Christ shows up personally to lead an army against the assembled armies who agree to combine to fight against Christ (Isaiah 34:1-3, 63:1-6, 66:15-16, Revelation 19:11-15, 19-21). Is this the Valley of Jehoshaphat battle (Joel 3:2, 12)? Is this the winepress in Revelation 14:19-20? Revelation 16:14 calls this the '*battle on the great day of God Almighty*'.

This seems to be the point at which Israel realises who their Messiah is. They repent of their rejection and confess their sin. Is there a three-day battle (Hosea 6:1-2)? They petition the Messiah to return and intervene in their country (Hosea 6:1-3; Zechariah 12:10-13:9). Do they pray Isaiah 64? God responds by sending the Holy Spirit upon the nation to cleanse it of idolatry (Joel 2:28-32; Zechariah 13:1-2; Romans 11:25-27).

But God pours out his judgement on all the armies and destroys them all completely (Joel 3:1-16, Revelation 16:16). How many people are killed at this stage? We know the army from the east will have 200 million people (Revelation 9:16). What will the total death toll be? (Revelation 14:19-20) Will it be greater than the earlier battle at Jerusalem?

You may remember that Jesus spoke in the synagogue at Nazareth. In Luke 4:16-21 we read that Jesus read from Isaiah 61:1-2, and He said that He fulfilled these scriptures. But when we read Isaiah, we find out that Jesus did not read the last part of verse 2; '*the day of vengeance of our God*'. The day of vengeance is this time. Interestingly, the view from that synagogue at Nazareth is across the valley of Jezreel to Mount Megiddo.

If God does not intervene at this point, there is a risk that the entire population would be killed (Matthew 24:22). Is that because of the risk of a nuclear war getting out of control? Or are plagues out of control? But God's intervention is totally unexpected (Revelation 16:15).

Scenario 2

Another scenario for the final phases is that the ruler goes to Armageddon to confront the other armies, and he persuades them to agree to a multi-lateral force against a common enemy, God (Daniel 8:25). The combined forces try to flush out the Jews in Edom, but they are prevented from achieving their goal. Does God intervene in Edom (Isaiah 34:5-6)? They advance on Jerusalem, but Christ returns and fights for Jerusalem.

Scenario 3

The southern coalition moves against the ruler and his armies (Daniel 11:40). The southern coalition is joined by the northern group who attacks the ruler with a great land and sea force (Daniel 11:40). The eastern armies arrive to help the coalitions. Jerusalem is destroyed (Zechariah 12:2).

In time to prevent the destruction of Jerusalem, Christ appears to defeat the armies of the ruler and the coalitions. This causes Israel to acknowledge Christ as their Messiah.

Which is the correct scenario? We cannot tell because each scenario fails to account for some aspect of the prophecy somewhere. Revelation 17 and 18 describe the destruction of Babylon, and it is also predicted in the Old Testament. But when does it fit into these scenarios?

But the major predictions are common to all scenarios:

- There will be a gathering of the armies of the world in Israel.
- Jerusalem will be largely destroyed.
- It will be delivered by the physical appearance of Jesus Christ. If you think the Rapture will occur immediately prior to Jesus' return, this is time of that event.
- The Jews will recognise Christ as their Messiah and deliverer, and usher in a new era.

After the victory of Jesus Christ, the ruler and the false prophet are captured and are thrown directly into the Lake of Fire (Daniel 8:25, Revelation 19:20-21). They are the only people there for 1,000 years, until they are joined by Satan (Revelation 20:10).

This ends the time that mankind rules the world. From now on Christ will reign for 1,000 years. There are a few things to happen before He takes His throne. Finally, the Lord's prayer will be answered: '*Your kingdom come. Your will be done on earth as it is in heaven*' (Matthew 6:10).

Notice that no scripture says that there will be a battle at Armageddon. It states the armies will meet and prepare themselves there. The main battle will be at Jerusalem.

There are two other wars predicted in the Bible that have not happened yet. Where do these wars fit into the timeline of the end times? Do they happen prior to the Rapture? Before or after the world leader takes power? Are they part of why the leader reaches his place of importance? Are they part of the reason for Armageddon? Do they both describe different aspects of Armageddon?

War 1: Psalm 83

This Psalm indicates that a confederation of nations will combine to fight Israel. It starts with the writer asking God to hear the threats being made against Israel (verses 1-4). They want to erase Israel from the list of nations.

Many people have tried, but none has been successful. But the chant continues throughout the world, and particularly in the Middle East. The Iranians and Palestinians are probably the most vocal today.

In verses 5 to 8 a group of nations will conspire to fight against Israel. The nations are listed:

- Edom, Ishmael, Ammon and Moab are nations that lived in what is now Jordan.
- Hagar was an Egyptian, and she returned to Egypt when she left Abraham.
- Gebal, Amalek and Philistia occupied the land now known as Palestine (The West Bank and Gaza).
- Tyre is in Lebanon.
- Assyria was based in Nineveh, which is in Iran.

Note that these nations are all immediate neighbours of Israel apart from Iran.

Both Egypt and Jordan have peace treaties with Israel, while there is an unspoken truce between Lebanon and Israel not to invade each other's country. Something obviously happens that will cause these nations to invade Israel. Iran is the financial and military supplier of Hezbollah[16] and Hamas[17] which are based in Lebanon, Syria and Palestine.

The writer asks God to deal with them in a similar way to earlier invasions in verses 9 to 18:

- Gideon defeated the Midianites (Judges 7).
- Jabin was a king in Canaan, and Sisera was his army commander. Jabin was killed in battle, and Sisera was killed while hiding from the Israelites (Judges 4).
- Oreb and Zeeb were commanders of the Midianite army defeated by Gideon (Judges 7:25).
- Zeeb and Zalmunna were kings of the Midianites (Judges 8:5).

These battles virtually eliminated these nations, and the writer asks God to again eliminate their enemies. The ultimate purpose is to show that God alone is the God of the earth, and that Allah is ineffective against Israel.

War 2: Ezekiel 38 and 39

This war may describe Armageddon, but there are a few differences. One such difference is that the immediate neighbours to Israel are not mentioned. The names are identified earlier in this Appendix.

Another option is that this war will occur during the first half of the seven-year peace agreement. Israel will be unprepared

16. en.wikipedia.org/wiki/Hezbollah
17. en.wikipedia.org/wiki/Hamas

because of the covenant.[18] This attack is led by a northern alliance and it appears to be a challenge to the ruler on how he can enforce the covenant.

Notice verse 8:

- God leads this military alliance to a land that has been restored from violence. Is the Psalm 83 battle above the preceding war prior to this one?

- The land is described as having been *'formerly a continual waste'*. The Romans removed almost all trees after 70 AD to make the country unattractive for the Jews to try to resettle there. It has been since Israel became a country in 1948 that the land has again become productive. Israel is the only country to end the 20th century with more trees than it had at the beginning. It is agriculturally the most productive part of the Middle East.

- The population is described as having come from other nations. This is particularly true of Israel. Jews have returned from every country (with the possible exception of North Korea).

- The population is living securely. The country is at peace, probably as the result of a peace treaty, or from defeating their previous enemies. Verse 11 says the population has no defences.

Verse 13 says some countries question the motives of the attacking armies. Sheba is the southern part of the Arabian

18. *Major Bible Themes*, pp 316-317.

Peninsula (Yemen and Sudan). Dedan is now largely known as Saudi Arabia. Tarsus is the major city in a region called Cilicia in southern Turkey.[19] But the invasion will continue despite international protests.

Verse 15 mentions God summoning a nation from '*the far north*'. This must apply to Russia because it is the country that is the most northern of Israel. Russia has long had plans to expand into the Middle East to secure a long-term oil supply.

They supplied arms to many countries in the 1960s hoping that they would eliminate Israel, but the pre-emptive strike by Israel that started the 1967 Six Day War dashed those hopes. Israel was helped by President Ronald Reagan taking a strong pro-Israel stance.[20] There is no reason why Russia may not try this strategy again.[21]

God's response is swift and spectacular. There is a massive earthquake that causes worldwide damage and geographical changes (verse 19-20). The coalition armies will begin to fight each other instead of Israel (verse 21).

The armies will die from a combination of disease (caused by unhygienic conditions? Or caused by God?) and in-fighting (verse 22). This will be combined with flooding, hail, fire, and brimstones. God has used all these as judgement in the past, but not in the total combination seen here.

Chapter 39 continues the description. Verse 6 says that Magog (Turkey?) will be burned with fire. Judgement falls on people living on islands (does this include New Zealand?) even though no island nation is listed in the list of allies.

---

19. *God's War on Terror*, pp 282-285. The apostle Paul was from Tarsus in Cilicia (Acts 9:11, 22:3).
20. *Epicenter*, pp 139-142.
21. *Epicenter*, pp 159-170.

As a result of this judgement, all nations will know the God of Israel is the Lord. Israel benefits economically from the military equipment left behind from the invaders. A special burial site will be set up by the Dead Sea. So many people will be killed that it will take seven months to clean up. Most importantly, Israel will have a spiritual revival.

Because Israel has been peaceful for a long time, the timing of this war is a problem. It could occur toward the middle of the seven-year peace covenant that Israel agrees to. This would lead into the '*great tribulation*' that much of Revelation seems to describe as the Eastern and Western world vie for political leadership.

There are similarities with the Armageddon scenarios, which leads many people to think it is describing Armageddon.

Another option is that this war is the uprising after Satan is released after one thousand years imprisoned in the bottomless pit (Revelation 20:7-9). This war involves all nations, Gog and Magog are specifically mentioned, the armies are extremely large, Jerusalem will be the site of the war, and fire from heaven will destroy them.

The one item that negates this theory is the clean-up described in Ezekiel that takes over seven months (Ezekiel 39:12-16). The next happening after Satan's final defiance is the re-creation of a new heaven and earth (Revelation 21).

Islamic End-times Teachings

The Quran has end-times teachings that Iran and ISIS use to recruit adherents to their beliefs. They are almost always the direct opposite to what the Bible teaches:

Christian teaching	**Islamic teaching**
The time before the return of Jesus is called the 'Tribulation'.	The upheavals of the apocalyptic last days are called 'Tribulations'.
The return of Jesus ends the Tribulation, culminating the end of days.	The return of Jesus (Isa) heralds the last days.
Jesus returns to Jerusalem to defeat the Antichrist.	Jesus returns to Damascus to defeat Dajjal (the Antichrist figure in Islam).
Jesus delivers the Jewish people.	Jesus leads Muslims to fight the Jews; He also shatters the crucifix and kills the pigs.
Jesus establishes a global kingdom of peace and prosperity on earth.	The result of the return of Jesus and the Mahdi is a global Islamic caliphate.

But there are similarities between Biblical and Islamic eschatology:

- Gog and Magog are mentioned in the Surahs, are both involved in the final battle, and are vanquished by Jesus. Gog and Magog seem to be identified as lawless tribes which will cover the earth and cause trouble for Muslims.[22]

- A beast will arise and will be able to identify who is a believer and who is an infidel.[23]

22. *Understanding Islamic Theology*, p 266.
23. *Understanding Islamic Theology*, pp 267-268.

- Mohammad gives a description of the Antichrist (called ad-Dajjal). He will have the word *kafir* (infidel) written on his forehead. He will be blind in the right eye.[24]

- Jesus will return to earth to be seen by all. But Islam teaches he will return to earth at Damascus and will kill the Antichrist. But after that he and his followers will be chased by Gog and Magog before being rescued by Allah.[25]

---

24. *Understanding Islamic Theology*, pp 251–252.
25. *Understanding Islamic Theology*, pp 257-258.

Appendix 10

Babylon

A hugely complicated, centrally planned,
social and economic system can only be kept
on the rails for as long as people believe in it.
- *Paul Kriwaczek, 1937-2011, historian*

Revelation 17 introduced an adulterous woman called '*Babylon the Great*'. We find in chapter 17 that this woman is a political, economic and religious system that is set up in the end times. The woman rides a beast with seven heads and ten horns. The beast represents the world rulers, and the system is based on their rule (verse 12). But the ten kings will ultimately try to destroy the woman (verse 16). Verse 18 tells us that the woman is a great city that rules over the earth.

So, what do we know about Babylon? What is its history? Does the Bible have any predictions for it?

Genesis 10:8-12 is the first mention of Babylon, and the first mention of cities. The first time anything is mentioned in the Bible is important. It sets the stage for all future mentions of that topic or person. It often has importance in terms of the meaning of any symbolism.

Babylon means 'gate of the gods',[1] it is where the tower of

1. en.wikipedia.org/wiki/Babylon

Babel was erected. Babel is the Hebrew and Babylon is the Greek. Babel sounds similar to the Hebrew word for 'confused' (*ballal*).[2] Genesis 10:25 tells us that the languages (or earth?) were divided in the lifetime of Peleg, who was the fourth generation after the flood (100 years). So, what is important about Babylon?

Religious History of Babylon

First, its establishment was contrary to God's command to spread over the earth (Genesis 9:1). Cities were an attempt to prevent people spreading out, but to keep them confined and to control people.

Cities are important in today's political environment because it makes controlling the population much easier. Propaganda is easier to spread through a city than in a dispersed rural environment. The economy can be more easily manipulated to control people. People become more dependent on the government than people living a self-directed life in villages.

Second, its founder is Nimrod. This name sounds like the Hebrew verb 'to revolt' (*marad*).[3] The Hebrew text is unclear, but it can easily be translated as '*he was a mighty hunter in opposition to the Lord*'. There is an indication that the main thing he hunted were people to build his empire. One Hebrew writer says the meaning is 'trapper of men by strategy and force.'

Nimrod built both Babylon and Nineveh. Both these cities were centres of world empires at different times. Both cities were involved with taking the Israelites captive at different times (Jeremiah 50:17). Neither of these empires allowed any Israelites to return to their country.

A 19th century book (now discredited) claimed that Nimrod

2. *Bible Knowledge Commentary: Old Testament*, p 44.
3. *Bible Knowledge Commentary: Old Testament*, p 43.

had a wife called Semiramis, and that she was responsible for developing secret religious rites that have been passed down to this day and age.[4]

Some of these include recognition of the mother and child as God, creating an order of virgins who became religious prostitutes, and many of the traditions associated with Christmas, Easter, and Halloween. For example, December 25 dates to this religion as the end of the winter solstice. Easter is a celebration associated with spring.

Babylon is mentioned in Genesis 10. Here the people are making a tower to reach the heavens for two reasons. One was to make a name for themselves, and the second reason was to prevent themselves being scattered over the earth (Genesis 11:4).

The first reason was pride, and the second reason was to deliberately disobey God. Both reasons are in defiance to God. We see this in the history of Babylon. Josephus gives the reason for the tower as a way to escape any future worldwide flood,[5] obviously ignoring God's promise to never again flood the world.

Babylon is the source of many heathen and pagan religions. Many of these have opposed the faith of Israel and the faith of the church.[6] Many of the ancient myths and legends have similar story lines, and these can often be traced to a common source, which is most likely to be the original Babylon before God confused the languages (Genesis 11:5-9).

There are about 3,000 references to Babylon in the Bible. The majority refer to the physical city because of its political importance during that time. But some verses refer to Babylon as a satanic religious program opposing the true worship of God.

---

4. en.wikipedia.org/wiki/Semiramis
5. Josephus, *Jewish Antiquities*, chapter 4, paragraph 4.
6. *Bible Knowledge Commentary: New Testament*, pp 969-970.

In Daniel 4 Nebuchadnezzar's pride caused him to have a mental breakdown for seven years (Daniel 4:28-33). His pride in himself and his accomplishments in expanding Babylon were despite God warning him in a dream what would happen.

He knew what would happen, but defied God and continued with a proud attitude. What was the trigger for Nebuchadnezzar's recovery? It was his recognition that God is more powerful than he was (Daniel 4:34-37).

After the Persians took over Babylon in 539 BC, they discouraged the mystery religions of Babylon in favour of their own religion. Subsequently the Babylonian cultists moved to Pergamum.

Crowns in the shape of a fish head were worn by the chief priests of the Babylonian cult to honour the fish god (Dagon in the Old Testament). The crowns bore the words 'Keeper of the Bridge' (between man and Satan). This title was adopted by the Roman Emperors who used the Latin title *Pontifex Maximus* and it was later used by the bishop of Rome and later popes.[7]

Political History of Babylon

The earliest known historical mention of Babylon is on a clay tablet from the Akkadian Empire. It dates to around 2300 BC. The Amorite king Hammurabi (1728-1686 BC) built Babylon into a major city in the 18th century BC. It became the region's most important religious city. (Are Hammurabi and Nimrod the same person?)

Babylon later declined to a minor city until Nabopolassar destroyed the Assyrian Empire between 612 and 605 BC. He made Babylon the capital of the Babylonian Empire.

His son Nebuchadnezzar (605-562 BC) embarked on a rebuilding program. He is credited with the construction of the Hanging

7. *Bible Knowledge Commentary: New Testament*, p 970.

Gardens of Babylon, said to be one of the seven wonders of the ancient world. But there is doubt whether they existed.

Babylon was captured by the Persians without any bloodshed in 539 BC (Daniel 5) after the Battle of Opis. Belshazzar was executed as a means of stopping any rebellion against the Persians.

The city was made the capital of the Persian Empire for the first few kings, but it was still an important city in the later part of the empire after the capital moved to Susa.

Alexander the Great used Babylon as a base while conquering the Middle East. He captured it in 331 BC, and it again flourished as a centre of learning and commerce. Alexander died there while on his way back to Greece in 323 BC.

After Alexander's death, the Greek empire was divided into four regions, and constant war meant the people left the region for safer areas to live in. By 141 BC when the Parthian Empire was established, Babylon was a decaying town.

In the mid-7th century AD, it was described as a town in ruins and was used as a source of bricks.

What does the Bible predict for Babylon?

There are three sets of chapters that deal with Babylon: Isaiah 13 and 14, Jeremiah 50 and 51, and Revelation 17 and 18.

Isaiah 13 talks about the Day of the Lord, the time of God's final judgement on earth (Isaiah 13:6, 9).

Verse 19 tells us that Babylon will be overthrown like Sodom and Gomorrah. How was that done? By divine intervention, by fire from heaven, by total destruction, and in a few hours. That has not happened. Babylon was abandoned and decayed over a few hundred years.

Babylon will never be lived in after that event, neither will animals be farmed there (verse 20).

Babylon will be a place for desert animals (verse 21). Isaiah 14:23 predicts Babylon will become a swamp.

Jeremiah chapter 50 gives a fuller description about its predicted destruction.

Verse 3 says that Babylon will be destroyed by armies from a northern nation.[8] (Russia?) The devastation will be total so that men and animals do not go back there. This has not yet happened. The Persians came from the east, but they did not destroy the city, and the Greeks came from the west and continued to use it.

Verse 9. The attack from the north will be by an alliance of nations.

The reference to arrows is interesting. The Hebrew word (*chets*) can mean an arrow, dart, a javelin, or any missile fired from a machine of war. The Hebrews says the skill (or intelligence) is built into the arrows, and it is not related to the men firing the arrows.

The Hebrew says, '*the arrows will not miss their mark but will do the killing of men*'. Every arrow will hit its target and result in death. Does this refer to guided missiles or smart bombs?

Verse 13 predicts that Babylon will be completely destroyed and be uninhabited. It will become a place of scoffing. Verses 39 to 40 say the desert animals and owls will be the only things living in Babylon after its destruction.

Verse 41 tells us that a group of armies from the north will attack Babylon. They will be supported by rulers from other parts of the world.

Jeremiah 51 continues the theme.

Verse 7 sounds similar to Revelation 17 and 18. In Revelation 17:4 the woman holds a gold cup in her hand. In Revelation 18:3 the nations got drunk with the woman.

---

8. www.khouse.org/articles/2008/773

Verse 8 talks about the sudden destruction of Babylon. Revelation 18:8 says the destruction will occur in a single day. Verse 17 says it will take one hour (is this literal, or figurative for a very short time?).

Verse 13 refers to rich people living by many waters being punished. Revelation 18:17-19 gives the reactions of the sea captains and traders.

Verse 26. None of Babylon will be reused for building materials. Is this the result of nuclear weapons? Verse 29 repeats the fact that no one will live there again.

As you read these four chapters, you realise Babylon was not destroyed as predicted here. Ancient Babylon was slowly abandoned as the centre of power moved away after Alexander the Great died. It was not totally destroyed by an invading army. This still has to occur.

The logical conclusion is that Babylon will be rebuilt as a centre of commerce. Saddam Hussein had started to rebuild Babylon, but this has stopped since the American invasion in 2003.

The United Nations has discussed the possibility of relocating its headquarters from New York for various reasons.[9] One possibility being discussed is to rebuild Babylon specifically to house the UN headquarters. This may be a part of the plan to bring peace to the region.

The Shiites in Iraq see Babylon as their historic capital. Another possibility is that Babylon is rebuilt as part of a Middle East stability programme, and it becomes the regional commercial centre.

---

9. www.laetusinpraesens.org/musings/moveunje.php

Appendix 11

The Millennial Kingdom

Joy to the world! The Lord has come.
Let earth receive her king.
- Isaac Watts, 1674-1748, minister and hymn writer

Revelation 19 predicts Jesus Christ with a heavenly army returning to earth to judge the world, to deal with the rulers, and to fight for Israel.

Revelation 20 predicts that Satan and his demons are imprisoned for a period of one thousand years, and Jesus Christ rules the world during that time. This Appendix looks at what the world will be like during that time.

Revelation 20 passes over this event very quickly. Verses 2-3 tell us that Satan is captured and bound in The Abyss for one thousand years. Verse 4 tells us that the believers who were beheaded during the Tribulation are resurrected and will reign with Christ. Verse 7 jumps to the end of the thousand years.

For some reason, many church leaders regard the kingdom as a metaphor, and not as a future reality. There are at least 1,845 references to Christ's physical rule on earth. Seventeen Old Testament books mention it, sometimes in extensive and precise terms.

There are 216 chapters in the New Testament, but 318 references to the second coming. It is mentioned in 23 of the 27 books in the New Testament. For every prediction relating to Jesus' first coming, there are at least seven related to his return.[1] I think we should take it as a literal event.

There are a few views about whether the millennial kingdom is a literal event or a metaphor for something else:[2]

- *Postmillennialism* takes the view that the thousand years represent the triumph of the gospel in the period leading up to Christ's second coming. Christ will reign spiritually on earth (in the hearts of people) through the work of the church, and He will return to earth to rapture the believers at the end of the 1,000 years. People will go into the new heaven and earth immediately after Christ's return.

  This view has been largely discarded because of the rise of many anti-Christian movements, and because the world generally has not progressed spiritually. If anything, the world is becoming more pagan over time. But this view is still held by many denominations.

- *Amillennialism* denies there is a literal millennial kingdom or reign of Christ on earth. Instead, Christ reigns in the hearts of believers. This idea infers that we are already living in the metaphorical millennial kingdom. Because Christ does not physically return to earth, there is no rapture of believers.

  It is thought Augustine was the first person to advocate this idea, and it was adapted by the early Roman Catholic Church so that the millennial kingdom would not cause a political clash with the Roman emperors.

  Augustine was a religious eclectic. He merged several different and pagan beliefs into the formal church. He rede-

1. *Prophecy 20/20*, p 91; *Major Bible Themes*, p 352.
2. *Bible Knowledge Commentary: New Testament*, pp 977-978.

fined salvation as conformity to the rule of the church, not as relationship with God through Christ.[3] Many Protestant denominations also take this point of view.

- *Premillennialism* takes the view that the 1,000-year reign of Christ will be an actual event. It will be after the physical return of Christ (hence the prefix *pre-*). This was the view of the early church. There are many passages in the Bible that speak of Christ coming to earth and a subsequent reign of righteousness on earth.[4]

This book takes the pre-millennial view. It is the most literal interpretation of the scriptures. But please do your own research to determine what you will believe.

Christ's return ushers in not only a new physical and political regime, but a new spiritual regime. This is the time when the request in the Lord's prayer, '*Your kingdom come, your will be done on earth as it is in heaven*' (Matthew 6:10) is fully answered. God's kingdom will come. God's will definitely will be done.

One of the first decisions will be to determine who will populate the new millennial kingdom. Jesus will judge the nations and individuals to determine who is worthy to live under His rule.[5]

Matthew 25:31-36 describes the process. '*All the nations will be gathered before Him, and He will separate the people one from another as a shepherd divides his sheep from the goats. He will put the sheep on his right and the goats on his left*'. What is the criteria for entry into the Kingdom? Compassion for the poor and needy.

---

3. prophecywatchers.com/the-death-of-the-church/
4. *The Bible Knowledge Commentary* reference above lists 23 passages.
5. 'Life During the Millennium', Larry Ollison, in *The Prophecy Watcher*, Nov 2020, pp 26-27, 32-34.

Jesus mentions similar separations of good from bad in other Kingdom parables. He talked about separating tares (weeds) from wheat (Matthew 13:24-30) and separating good and bad fish (Matthew 13:47-50). This separation of good from bad must be prior to the Kingdom rule of Christ.[6]

Jesus Christ will be the King of Kings during the one thousand years. What we think is a Christmas verse is actually a three-part prediction. It will finally be fully fulfilled. Isaiah 9:6 predicts Jesus Christ:

- '*For to us a child is born*' talks about his birth at Bethlehem.
- '*To us a son is given*' talks about his sacrifice at Calvary.
- '*And the government will be on his shoulder*' refers to this period when Christ rules the world.

After King David was settled in Jerusalem, God sent a prophecy through Nathan in 2 Samuel 7. Verse 16 promises that David's throne will endure forever. Psalm 89:29 says David's throne will last as long as heaven endures. God reinforced part of the covenant with David in Jeremiah 33:19-21. The only time it can be revoked is when the day and night do not come at their appointed times. When does that happen? It will happen at some point.

Jesus Christ will be king over all other rulers:

- When the angel Gabriel announced Jesus' birth to Mary, he said that Jesus would be a king on David's throne (Luke 1:32-33). That did not exist when Jesus was born.

- The Jews rejected him as their king in front of Pontus Pilate (Mark 15:12-14).

6. *Major Bible Themes*, p 355.

- When Jesus was crucified, He was crucified as the King of the Jews (Matthew 27:37, Mark 15:26, Luke 23:38, John 19:19). Pilate wrote (or dictated) the indictment. Did he know something that the Jewish leaders did not know?[7]

- When Christ returns to the earth, He will have the title '*King of Kings and Lord of Lords*' (Revelation 19:16).

Many Old Testament passages predict that Jesus Christ will be the King on David's throne:

- Isaiah 9:6-7. The names attributed to the ruler can apply only to God. His government will be a time of peace, justice, and righteousness.

- Isaiah 11:1-5. The ruler will be a descendent of Jesse (father of King David). He will be full of the Holy Spirit. He will see the motives, and not only the outward actions. This can apply only to Jesus. He will rule with perfect righteousness.

- Isaiah 24:23 states categorically that the Lord Almighty will reign in Jerusalem.

- Isaiah 40:10 says the Sovereign Lord will come in power. But verse 11 tells us that He will rule with compassion.

- Daniel 2:44 tells us that God will set up a kingdom that will never be destroyed.

---

7. He wrote an acrostic that in Hebrew spelt YHWH. See *Learn the Bible in 24 Hours*, p 190.

- Micah 4:2 tells us the God of Jacob will be the ruler.

- Micah 5:2 says the ruler will come from Bethlehem, but His origins are from ancient times.

- Zechariah 9:9 says the king will ride a donkey's colt into Jerusalem. This was fulfilled four days before the crucifixion, but will it happen again? Revelation 19 talks about Jesus riding a horse into battle, but it does not mention what he will ride into Jerusalem.

What will be the features of Christ's government?

Political Leadership

1. *Jesus Christ will rule over the entire earth*

Daniel mentions Christ reigning over all nations, languages, and peoples in many places:

- Daniel 2:44 – Christ's kingdom will overtake all existing kingdoms on earth and bring them to an end.
- Daniel 7:14 – the Ancient of Days will be given authority over all peoples, nations, and men of every language, who will all worship Him.
- Daniel 7:27 – when the last beast has his power taken away, his kingdoms are given to the saints of the Most High.

Other verses saying that Christ will reign over all the earth are Psalm 72:8, Jeremiah 33:19-21, Micah 4:3, and Zechariah 9:10.

2. *Jesus Christ will rule with absolute authority and power*

Christ will rule '*with a rod of iron*' (KJV) or '*with an iron sceptre*' (NIV) (Psalm 2:9, Revelation 2:27, 12:5, 19:15). This means absolute authority – iron rods do not bend easily. Man is still sinful and will need strong ruling.

Christ will punish any who oppose Him. They will be punished by destruction (Psalm 2:9, 72:9-11, Isaiah 11:4). Open sin will be punished, and no one will be allowed to rebel.

Any nation that does not help Israel will be punished (Isaiah 60:12).

3. *Jesus Christ will rule with righteousness and peace*

God's kingdom will be characterised by justice and righteousness (Isaiah 9:7, 60:21). Isaiah 11:1-5 specifically mentions righteousness and justice, especially for the poor and needy (see also Ezekiel 34:17-19). Notice the clothing that is mentioned here and compare it with the believer's armour in Ephesians 6:13-18. Psalm 72:2 mentions judging with righteousness and justice.

Examples of the peaceful environment are:

- Christ will judge between nations and settle disputes for people (Isaiah 2:4).
- Weapons of war will be converted into agricultural tools and military studies will not exist as a course of study (Isaiah 2:4).
- Armies will be disbanded (Isaiah 2:4).
- Garments used by warriors will be burnt (Isaiah 9:5).

This can happen only because Christ has already judged sin,

judged the nations, and bound Satan in The Abyss. The only source of evil will be the sin nature in people. The reign begins with all adults acknowledging Christ is the Messiah. Anyone who dies early will be because of sin (Isaiah 65:20).

4a. *King David will be resurrected to rule Israel*

One thing that is overlooked is the role that King David will have during this time:

- Jeremiah 30:9 tells us that David will once again be a king. This was written 400 years after King David's death. This verse therefore refers to the resurrected David.
- Jeremiah 33:17 tells us that a man (not God) will sit on the throne of Israel. That man could be Jesus, but the rest of the Bible says the man is David.
- Ezekiel 34:20-24 says David will be the ruler over Israel. He will be a prince under God.
- Ezekiel 37:24-25 repeats that David will rule over Israel.
- Hosea 3:5 tells us Israel will seek the Lord their God and David their king.

David will be resurrected before this event, and he will again be the king over Israel. This is another reason the church is not a replacement for Israel like some people believe. David does not rule in the church, and never will. But he will rule Israel again in the future.

4b. *Resurrected people will co-rule with God*

Revelation 20:4-6 describes the administrative system God will employ. Judgement is committed to the resurrected people. Note that only believers and righteous people had been resurrected at this stage.

One special group is mentioned here. These are the people '*who had been beheaded for their witness, who had not worshipped the beast or his image, and had not received his mark on their forehead or hand.*' This group will be priests of God and will reign for a thousand years.

The twelve apostles will have a role of helping King David judge Israel (Matthew 19:28). Other people will have different roles (1 Corinthians 6:2).

5a. *Israel will be a Prominent Nation in the Kingdom*

Israel will enjoy a special place of privilege and special blessing during this time. They will be special objects of God's favour. It will be a time when Israel is regathered, re-established as a nation, and David's kingdom is renewed. Israel will finally possess the land promised to it from God as far back as Abraham (Genesis 15:18-21).

Israel will be larger than at any time in its history, and it will be more productive (Isaiah 26:15). Foreign workers will be involved in rebuilding the country and in agriculture (Isaiah 60:10-12, 61:5-6). Jews from around the world will be regathered to Israel (Isaiah 43:5-6).

Jews will be recognised as having a special status because of their relationship with Jesus. They will be sought out to explain God's way to Gentiles (Zechariah 8:23).

5b. *Israel will be regathered and restored.*

Numerous passages refer to Israel being restored to their land after centuries of being distributed among the various nations. Examples are Jeremiah 30:3, 31:8-9, Ezekiel 34:11-16, 39:27, and Amos 9:11-12, 15.

Jews will be reclaimed from around the Middle East (Isaiah

11:11-12), from around the Mediterranean (Isaiah 66:18-21) and from other areas (Jeremiah 23:3, Ezekiel 36:24). Many returning Jews will bring their wealth with them (Isaiah 60:4-9). Does verse 8 refer to aircraft?

This has been partially fulfilled during the twentieth century, but the total fulfilment is still future. Current data shows only 30 percent of Jews currently live in Israel with the rest scattered predominately in Western countries.[8]

The nation of Israel will be united both physically and socially (Isaiah 11:13). Ephraim was part of the northern kingdom that eventually became known as Samaria after the Assyrians brought in other races (2 Kings 17:2-6, 24).

The geographical borders of Israel were originally given to Moses in Numbers 34. Historically, Israel never fully occupied those borders. The revised borders in Ezekiel 47 are similar.

5c. *Israel will be united, and David's kingdom restored.*

The split kingdoms of Israel and Judah will be united again (Isaiah 11:13, Jeremiah 3:18, 33:14, Ezekiel 37:20-23, Hosea 1:11).

This destroys the myth of 'the ten lost tribes'. They were never lost. When the nation was split into Israel and Judea, there was a migration of people from their tribal regions into the country that best suited their spiritual beliefs.

God knows who their descendants are, and they will be returned to Israel.

5d. *Jerusalem will be recognised as the centre of the world.*

Jerusalem will become the political and spiritual centre of the

8. en.wikipedia.org/wiki/Jewish_population_by_country

world (Jeremiah 3:17). Instead of Jerusalem being a city of political turmoil, it will become a city of peace (Isaiah 66:12-13).

Jesus is predicted to return to Jerusalem, and this will cause the surrounding towns to be very prosperous (Zechariah 1:16-17).

Jerusalem will be a city where multitudes will visit for various reasons:

- People will come to Jerusalem to learn God's requirements (Isaiah 2:3, Jeremiah 3:17).

- National representatives will be required to make annual pilgrimage to Jerusalem for the Feast of Tabernacles (Zechariah 14:16-20). Any nation that does not worship at Jerusalem will be punished (Isaiah 60:11-12).

- International disputes will be settled in Jerusalem (Isaiah 2:4).

- Israel will be the financial centre of the world (Isaiah 60:5-7, 11). They will have a disproportionate share of the world wealth (Isaiah 60:17, 61:6, 66:12). Some of this may be the result of the War of Armageddon (Zechariah 14:14).

Spiritual Leadership

Isaiah 24:21-22 describes changes in the spiritual realm. Spiritual evil forces will be imprisoned along with evil earthly rulers. This will allow God to reign without interference.

1. *Jesus Christ will be the centre of worship*

Everyone on the earth will know the Lord. Isaiah 11:9 says, '*the earth will be full of the knowledge of the Lord'*. People will know what Christ's requirements are. The Holy Spirit will put Christ's requirements in people's hearts or consciousness. It will be an intuitive knowledge that everyone will have (Jeremiah 31:33-34).

2. *Israel will have a special spiritual relationship with Jesus Christ*

The relationship between Israel and Christ will be changed. Isaiah 26 may be one of the songs sung to glorify God. God will establish peace for Israel (verse 12). God will rule over the country (verse 13). God will expand the country beyond its previous boundaries (verse 15). Jews will be resurrected (verse 19).

Isaiah 10:20-23 talks about a small number of the original Jews relying on the Lord. They will turn to the Mighty God. Idolatry will be unknown in Israel (Isaiah 27:9). They will travel to worship in Jerusalem (Isaiah 27:12-13). They will be in awe of God and willing to learn Godly principles (Isaiah 29:23-24).

God will restore his relationship with Israel and will pour his love on the people (Isaiah 54:4-10). Ezekiel 39:27-29 says that God will pour out his spirit on the house of Israel.

Prayers will be answered before they are said (Isaiah 65:24).

Hosea 2:16-17, 19-20. The relationship between Israel and God will resemble that of husband and wife instead of master and servant. The names of foreign gods will no longer be heard as they follow their Messiah. God will enter an eternal contract with Israel.

Israel's sins will be forgiven (Jeremiah 50:20).

Zechariah 12:10-14 talks about the time when Israel recognises their Messiah and the results it brings. It will initially be a time of national mourning. It will be the result of the Holy Spirit working in the nation, and especially in Jerusalem.

As a result of all the changes, Israel will be filled with joy (Isaiah 9:3, 12:3, 25:9, 35:10, 61:10).

3. *The New Temple*

A new temple will be built in Jerusalem, and a new set of regulations will be instituted (Ezekiel 40-47). The sacrifices described are different from those prescribed by Moses. They seem to be commemorative and look back to the cross. Morning sacrifices are still performed (Ezekiel 46:13-15), but no evening sacrifices are mentioned. The only feasts to be continued will be the Passover (Ezekiel 45:21-24) and the Feast of Tabernacles (Ezekiel 45:25). The inner court will be open only on Saturdays and the day of the new moon (Ezekiel 46:1).

The nations will make an annual pilgrimage to Jerusalem to worship the Lord and celebrate the Feast of Tabernacles (Zechariah 14:16-19). Nations that do not make the annual pilgrimage will be punished with drought and more plagues.

This feast was originally instituted as a commemoration of God protecting and feeding the Israelites on their journey through the wilderness from Egypt to Canaan. It will now commemorate God restoring the kingdom and preserving the Jews during the times of the Gentiles (Isaiah 32:18).

The Feast of Tabernacles required the Israelites to live in tents for a week. It commemorated the journey from Egypt to Israel at the time of Moses. This action symbolises the world at peace and not needing to have any fortifications or protection.

Any nation refusing to worship at Jerusalem will be punished with no rain (Zechariah 14:17-18). Egypt is specifically mentioned twice as a warning. Is this a prediction that they will not go to Jerusalem as required?

Ezekiel 29 is a prediction of Egypt's devastation. The result is a forty-year period when Egypt becomes completely desolate with its population being dispersed into the other nations of the world.

At the end of the forty years, the Lord brings the citizens of

Egypt home (Ezekiel 29:8-16). Does that happen during God's reign, or at a previous time? There is nothing here saying this is because of a failure to worship at Jerusalem, but neither does it rule out that possibility.

> Why is Jerusalem so important to God?
>
> Rabbinic literature says that Adam was created from soil at Jerusalem.[9] Therefore, Jerusalem is the centre of God's work with mankind.
>
> The first recorded King of Salem was Melchizedek, and he is said to be both a king and a priest of God Most High (Genesis 14:18). Thus, the earliest mention of what eventually became Jerusalem is associated with God. This continues with Joshua defeating Adoni-Zedek (*king of righteousness*), the king of Jerusalem (Joshua 10:1). David captured Jerusalem from the Jebusites and made it his capital (2 Samuel 5:6-7, 9). The temple was later built in Jerusalem (2 Chronicles 3:1-2).
>
> Psalm 48 states that Jerusalem is God's city – the one place on earth where he can be associated. Verse 2 states that Jerusalem is '*the city of the Great King*'. Psalm 132:13-14 states that '*the Lord has chosen Zion*' and is enthroned there.

4. *The Role of the Holy Spirit*

The Holy Spirit will be evident in people's lives:

- The Holy Spirit will guide people, and especially turn them from idolatry (Isaiah 29:22-24, 31:6-7).

9. en.wikipedia.org/wiki/Adam_in_rabbinic_literature

- Isaiah 32:15 talks about the Holy Spirit being poured out.
- Isaiah 44:3-4 uses the metaphor of pouring out water to describe the way the Holy Spirit is '*poured out*' on people.
- Ezekiel 39:29 again uses the term '*pour out my Spirit*'.

Probably the most famous reference to the spiritual conditions during this time is Joel 2:28-29. Peter quoted this passage in Acts 2 when the Holy Spirit came upon the apostles.

But at this time, the Holy Spirit will cause effects that did not happen in Acts. Young and old people will operate in prophetic speaking and having visions. It seems like this time will show greater spiritual blessings than any other previous time.

Environmental Changes

Because sin has been judged and removed, the physical environment will be changed. Romans 8:19-22 tells us that the creation (environment) is groaning and waits to be liberated from decay. It seems that planet Earth will return to its pre-flood conditions.

1. *Geological Changes*

Revelation 16:17-20 tells us what happens when God pours out the seventh bowl onto the earth. One of the results is the biggest earthquake the earth has ever had. Verse 20 says that every island will disappear, and all the mountains will be flattened. See Isaiah 24:1, 3, 5-6, 18-20 and Haggai 2:6-7.

Zechariah 14:4 tells of another earthquake when the Lord stands on the Mount of Olives to fight against the armies of the Antichrist. The Mount of Olives will split in two from east to west and form a new valley.

Jerusalem will continue to be on a high hill (Isaiah 2:2-3). Will this be the highest hill in the new look earth? If the mountains cannot be found (Revelation 16:20), Jerusalem probably will be on the highest point on earth at this time. It could be like the original creation where the Garden of Eden was on a high hill that had four rivers flowing from it (Genesis 2:10-14).

Ezekiel 47:1-12 describes a river coming from near the altar in the new temple. It flows out the south side of the temple and flows into the Dead Sea (see Zechariah 14:8). The Dead Sea will become a place where there will be plenty of fish, while the banks of the river will grow all kinds of fruit trees which will be harvested every month.

Are the earth and sky completely recreated to like before Noah's flood? Isaiah 65:17-18 talks about new heavens and earth. '*Former things will not be remembered.*' Does that mean that everything from our current earth is destroyed so that there is nothing to remind us?

The same thing happened during Noah's flood. Nothing from the pre-flood era was left. No building ruins, no animal skeletons or fossils, only the memories of those saved from the flood. Will the same situation exist after God establishes his kingdom? Or do these events refer to the new Jerusalem described in Revelation 21?

2. *Biological Changes*

The relationship between animals will change. All animals will become herbivores, and animals that were poisonous to people will lose their ability to hurt. Does that mean that parasites will be eliminated, and bacteria and viruses will no longer adversely affect people?

Isaiah 11:6-9 describes examples of how the animal world will be changed. Predators will no longer hunt other animals, but they will become grass eaters. Children will be able to play with what are currently dangerous animals. See Isaiah 51:3, 65:25. Is this also a return to conditions in the Garden of Eden?

Isaiah 30:23-26 describes changes in agriculture. Regular rain will produce an abundance of food. Sunlight will be seven times brighter than now, and the moon will be brighter. Both Isaiah 35:1-2 talk about wilderness areas blooming with plant life, while verse 7 predicts more water springs to water what is currently parched land.

Isaiah 41:18-19 describes deserts being watered and producing food. God cursed the earth after Adam and Eve's sin in Genesis 3:17-19. The curse is removed during the millennium and productivity is increased. Israel is predicted to be particularly productive (Ezekiel 36:29-32).

Hosea 2:18 mentions God making a covenant with animals of the field, birds of the air, and crawling animals. It does not mention what the covenant entails.

The earth will be more productive of crops. Hosea 2:21-22 says that the sky and earth will be changed to cause the production of large quantities of grain, wine, and oil. Israel in particular seems to be a beneficiary of this (Isaiah 27:6, Ezekiel 34:25-31, 36:24)

Joel 3:18-21 talks about wine and milk production. New sources of water are described.

Zechariah 8 shows that the climate will be ideal for food production. Verse 12 predicts the vine will give good yields, the ground will produce crops and the sky will deliver dew (not rain). Does that mean the air pressure will increase?

There is a lot of fossil evidence showing that both the air pressure and the oxygen content were significantly higher before Noah's flood.[10] Air pressure may have been double what we experience today.

Israel will produce so much food they can export it to the rest of the world. Genesis 2:6 says the early earth was watered by mist

---

10. www.icr.org/article/hyperbaric-research-and-the-pre-flood-atmosphere; genesisapologetics.com/faqs/pre-flood-world-what-was-it-like/

or dew. Rain is not mentioned until Genesis 7:4 when God gives seven days warning.

3. *Human Changes*

Lifetimes will be extended to close to those mentioned in Genesis. All infants will survive to become adults; a person dying at 100 years old will be considered a youth; and anyone failing to reach 100 years will be considered cursed (Isaiah 65:20). God will kill wicked people (Jeremiah 31:30).

People will be healed of physical ailments. Deaf and blind people will not exist (Isaiah 29:18, 35:5). Mental issues will be healed (Isaiah 32:3-4).

Zephaniah 3:9 implies Israel will be given a purified language, one that is better suited for worshipping God.

Will only unbelievers die during God's kingdom? There is no reference in the Bible to a resurrection of millennial believers.[11] God will make a new covenant with Israel where He will write the law on their arms.

As a result, there may be no Jewish unbelievers in the kingdom (Jeremiah 31:31-34). All Jews born during the millennium will accept the Messiah before their 100th year (Isaiah 65:20). Unbelief would thus be among the Gentiles only, and therefore, death would exist only among the Gentiles.

Revelation 20:8 tells us that at the end of the millennium there will be a rebellion against God. The number of people involved is not given, but the description is that the number '*is like the sand on the seashore.*'[12]

---

11. www.khouse.org/articles/2002/395/
12. The population at the time of Noah's flood may have been around 10 billion people. The calculated range is 5 to 17 billion. See www.

This shows us the birth rate must be high to produce that type of population growth. It indicates that the earth must be productive to be able to support that population.

4. *Specific Country Changes*

Two countries (Egypt and Edom) are specifically stated to be desolate as a punishment for the violence done against Israel.

4.1 *Egypt*

Isaiah 19 has a few predictions about Egypt. Do these happen during the millennium, or earlier?

- There will be a civil war within the country (verse 2).
- The people will consult idols, spirits of the dead, mediums, and spiritists (verse 3). Ancient Egypt revered the dead and worshipped the gods associated with death.
- They will be controlled by a cruel master and a fierce king (verse 4). Is this the first beast or the Antichrist? The previous two points suggest this will happen prior to the start of the millennium.
- The River Nile will dry up causing drought and economic hardship (verses 5-10). Does this mean the Aswan dam will

---

ldolphin.org/pickett.html for the calculations. The time period was 1,600 years. See also www.ldolphin.org/popul.html for another article that deals with more recent population history.

be destroyed so that there is no control of the water flow?[13] Or does the Great Ethiopian Renaissance Dam (GERD) reduce the water supply to Egypt?[14] This will cause the economy to disintegrate and people to leave the country for a time.

- Israel will take over part of the country (verses 18-19).

- As a result, Egypt will turn to God and be restored (verses 20-25). There will be a highway from Egypt to Assyria (Iraq).

- After forty years, the people will return to Upper Egypt to resettle the land (Ezekiel 29:12-15).

4.2 *Edom*

Edom (Jordan) is predicted to become a land of burning oil (pitch) making the land uninhabited by humans. Birds and desert animals will be the only life in the region (Isaiah 34:5-15, Jeremiah 49:17-18). This is because Edom did not help defend Judea when the Babylonians attacked (Ezekiel 25:12-14).

13. prophecywatchers.com/the-tower-of-syene-a-prophetic-wonder/
14. en.wikipedia.org/wiki/Grand_Ethiopian_Renaissance_Dam

Bibliography

Of making many books there is no end,
and much study wearies the body.
- *Ecclesiastes 12:12*

Alberino, Timothy. *Birthright. The coming posthuman apocalypse and the usurpation of Adam's dominion.* Alberino Publishing, 2020

Ames, Richard F. *Armageddon and Beyond.* Living Church of God, 2007.

Bryant, T. Alton (Ed.). *The New Compact Bible Dictionary*, Zondervan Publishing House, 1967.

Carey, Nessa. *The Epigenetics Revolution*, Icon, 2011.

Chafer, Lewis Sperry, rev Walvoord, John F. *Major Bible Themes.* Zondervan Publishing House, 1977

Crone, Billy. *Hybrids Super Soldiers and the Coming Genetic Apocalypse.* Get A Life Ministries Inc, 2020. Volumes 1 and 2.

Hunt, Dave. *A Woman Rides the Beast.* Harvest House Publishers, 1994.

Jeremiah, David. *Agents of the Apocalypse.* Tyndale House, 2014.

Josephus. *The New Complete Works of Josephus.* Translated by William Whiston, Kregel Publications, 1999.

Missler, Chuck. *Cosmic Codes: Hidden Messages from the Edge of Eternity.* Koinonia House, 2004.

Missler, Chuck. *Daniel's 70 Weeks.* Koinonia House Inc, 2015 (also available as an e-book download from *khouse.org*).

Missler, Chuck. *Learn the Bible in 24 Hours.* Thomas Nelson Publishers, 2002

Missler, Chuck. *Prophecy 20/20: Profiling the Future Through the Lens of Scripture.* Nelson Books, 2006

Missler, Chuck. *The Rapture*, Koinonia House Inc, 2014 (also available as an e-book download)

Missler, Chuck and Nancy. *The Kingdom, Power and Glory: The Overcomer's Handbook.* King's Highway Ministries, 2007.

Ogwyn, John H. *The United States and Great Britain in Prophecy.* Living Church of God, 2008. (This is a booklet based on a book *The United States and British Commonwealth in Prophecy*, written by Herbert W Armstrong.)

Putman, Chris and Thomas Horn. *Exo-Vaticana*, Defender, 2013.

Rosenberg, Joel C. *Epicenter*, Tyndale, 2008.

Shoebat, Walid. *God's War on Terror: Islam, Prophecy and the Bible*, Top Executive Media, 2010.

Sookhdeo, Patrick. *Understanding Islamic Theology*, Isaac Publishing, 2013.

Spencer, Robert. *The Truth about Muhammad.* Regnery Publishing, 2006.

Stringer, Col. *New Zealand's Christian Heritage*, Col Stringer Ministries Inc, 2001.

Struksnes, Abel and Bente. *2017: 500 Years After Luther*, booklet available from Autumn Leaves NZ Ltd.

W.E. Vine, Merrill F. Unger, William White (ed), *Vine's Complete Expository Dictionary of Old and New Testament Words,* Thomas Nelson Publishers, 1884. (Note that this book has two page numbering systems; one for the Hebrew words and one for the Greek words.)

Walvoord, John F. & Roy B. Zuck (ed), *The Bible Knowledge Commentary: New Testament*, Victor Books, 1983

Walvoord, John F. & Roy B. Zuck (ed), *The Bible Knowledge Commentary: Old Testament*, Victor Books, 1985

Young, Robert. *Analytical Concordance to the Bible*, Religious Tract Society, 1865?

About the Author

Graham Missen is a student of the Bible who began his spiritual journey at the Cambridge Gospel Hall (now known as Raleigh Street Christian Centre). Shortly after marrying Jen, they moved from Cambridge and have lived in various places around the North Island. They were both part of the leadership team at Napier Oasis Church (now called Napier Elim) for about ten years. They have both led small groups in different towns. They have also participated in and led short-term mission trips to south-east Asian countries.

Graham graduated Waikato University with a degree in chemistry (most of which has been forgotten) and learned biochemistry and quantum physics at level 2. This was followed by various roles in various dairy and food companies, sales, volunteer ambulance, relief teaching, and fibre optic installing. The engineering side of these jobs allowed Graham to keep up to date with emerging technologies such as robotics, genetic engineering, trans-humanism, and related issues.

Graham is married to Jen and has two children, three grandchildren (one in heaven), and one great-grandchild. Graham and Jen now live in Tauranga and are active members of Freedom Centre Tauranga.

You can contact Graham via gdmissen@gmail.com

www.ingramcontent.com/pod-product-compliance
Lightning Source LLC
Chambersburg PA
CBHW051416290426
44109CB00016B/1325
9780473643973